Praise for *Na*.

MW01004690

"The best single book on annexation."
—*The Nation*

"This book raises important and still unresolved issues about the annexation of Hawai'i by the United States, explaining that the U.S. Senate would not approve the proposed treaty of annexation, that virtually all Native Hawaiians opposed annexation, and that the ultimate procedure used—a joint resolution passed by a simple majority of both chambers of Congress—was controversial at the time and was questioned by constitutional scholars in the decades that followed. *Nation Within* is much livelier than the usual history book, but also much more detailed, carefully researched, and thoughtful than most journalism."
—Jon M. Van Dyke, Professor of Constitutional Law, University of Hawai'i, author of *Who Owns the Crown Lands of Hawai'i?*

"No one has taken the time to explicitly search out the relationships between and among Americans who stole our independence with as much tenaciousness and perspicacity as *Nation Within*. Even better is [Tom Coffman's] exemplary analysis of how the Japanese threat to the Islands was essentially created by confused and greed-inspired policies in the republic and outright deception at the U.S. State Department level. . . . But what I found most valuable about this work was his portrayal of the republic as an opportunistic masquerade of democratic ideals that swindled an entire nation of its inheritance. In no other history that I've seen is the cynical and manipulative nature of annexation so clearly displayed. His ironic recounting of how voting under the republic was to be constructed in such a way as to adopt all of the finest traditions of the Jim Crow South tells us all we need to know about the nature of the government that surrendered that nation of Hawai'i to the United States. . . . [Coffman's] analysis of Lili'uokalani's leadership is sensitive and perceptive. . . .

To this date I have not seen a more believable analysis of the queen's leadership, nor a more compelling analysis of the failure of President Cleveland's leadership in the end."
—Jon Kamakawiwoʻole Osorio, author of *Dismembering Lahui: A History of the Hawaiian Nation to 1887*, Professor of Hawaiian Studies, University of Hawaiʻi at Manoa, from *The Hawaiian Journal of History*

"Written with power and clarity, *Nation Within* narrates a history of dispossession but also of complicity and resistance. It correctly situates Hawaiʻi's annexation within the global context of U.S. imperialism; it insightfully points out that the nation was never completely extinguished because Hawaiʻi continues to stir within the hearts of the Hawaiian people."
—Gary Y. Okihiro, author of *Island World: A History of Hawaiʻi and the United States*

"As a historian, Tom [Coffman] has done a tremendous job in revealing the events and circumstances that led to the illegal overthrow of the Hawaiian Kingdom government in 1893. More important, however, he unveils how the queen and Hawaiian subjects were politically and legally astute and were able to organize themselves, in the aftermath of the overthrow, into a formidable political force that prevented the annexation of the country by treaty. While they succeeded in preventing the U.S. Senate from ratifying two attempts to annex the country by treaty, they were unable to prevent the U.S. Congress from unilaterally enacting a joint resolution of annexation (in the heat of the Spanish-American War) that served as the basis to illegally seize and occupy the nation of Hawaiʻi for military purposes—an occupation that is now over a century long."
—Keanu Sai, political scientist

"A far-reaching treasure hunt for long-buried facts, revealing for the first time the full array of events and shifting international forces that led to the overthrow and annexation of the Kingdom of Hawaii. . . . [N]ot to be missed."
—Herb Kawainui Kane, artist/historian, author of *Ancient Hawaii*

"A page-turner—and an eye-opener."
—*Honolulu Weekly*

"*Nation Within* is the most original and best researched account I know on the U.S. annexation of Hawaii—and the Hawaiians' opposition, then and now, to that annexation. The story is compelling for many reasons, not least the Hawaiians' trust that the American democratic process would protect their independence and their lands."
—Walter LaFeber, Cornell University, author of *The New Empire: An Interpretation of American Expansion, 1860–1898*

"All Americans who wish to understand how and why the United States annexed Hawai'i in 1898 should read this book. Tom Coffman has forever dispelled the commonly held belief that annexation was a benign and inevitable process of self-determination. Readers of *Nation Within* also will come to understand why Native Hawaiians today seek justice and reconciliation from an American government that usurped and destroyed their national sovereignty a century ago."
—Edward P. Crapol, Professor of History, College of William and Mary

"*Nation Within* explores those 'strange five years' from 1893–1898 during which a cabal of 'missionary boys' hijacked a sovereign nation, deposed its monarch, prostituted the words 'republic' and 'democracy' as badly as any Third World Communist dictator ever has, and handed over an unwilling native people to the care and keeping of the breast-beating, muscle-flexing expansionist United States. (And if you think I overwrite, then I challenge you to read the book.) . . . weep, grow angry . . ."
—Dan Boylan, Professor of History, University of Hawaii, *MidWeek*

NATION WITHIN

The History of the
American Occupation
of Hawai'i

REVISED EDITION

Tom Coffman

Foreword by Manulani Aluli Meyer

DUKE UNIVERSITY PRESS

LONDON AND DURHAM

2016

Library of Congress Cataloging-in-Publication Data
Names: Coffman, Tom, author.
Title: Nation within : the history of the American occupation of Hawai'i /
Tom Coffman. Description: Revised edition. | Durham : Duke University
Press, 2016. | Includes bibliographical references and index.
Identifiers: LCCN 2016005264 (print) | LCCN 2016007871 (ebook)
ISBN 9780822361978 (pbk. : alk. paper)
ISBN 9780822373988 (e-book)
Subjects: LCSH: Hawaii—Annexation to the United States. |
Hawaii—Politics and government—1893–1900. | Hawaii—Foreign
relations—United States. | United States—Foreign relations—Hawaii.
| United States—Territorial expansion—History—20th century.
Classification: LCC DU627.4 .C64 2016 (print) | LCC DU627.4 (ebook) |
DDC 996.9/03—dc23
LC record available at http://lccn.loc.gov/2016005264

Cover art: Photo: U.S. Marines at the Hawaiian annexation ceremonies,
August 12, 1898, Hawaii State Archives, Call Number PP-35-8-015.
Background: Page from 1897 Petition Against the Annexation of Hawaii,
National Archives.

Contents

Foreword
MANULANI ALULI MEYER

Truth is the highest goal,
and aloha is the greatest truth of all.
—HALEMAKUA

Nation Within is a truth telling embedded within a Hawaiian cultural context, yet relevant to the world. History told from a different interpretation changes *everything*. Author Tom Coffman speaks of Hawaiian people as a "separate society that calls out across time to be understood in its own terms." (page 10) What a relief to read such ideas! As if the drought ended and water returned to fields, crops and our own disposition. Finally, there is a reckoning in our collective consciousness that *Hawaii is an independent country illegally occupied by the United States of America.*

I remember receiving a phone call from my sister Maile in 1996, while I was studying abroad, about Noenoe Silva finding the 1898 Anti-Annexation Petition in the National Archives in Washington, D.C. It was a document signed by 38,000+ Hawaiians and other loyalists declaring their unwavering *aloha* for their Hawaiian Nation and beloved Queen Lili'uokalani. They were asking for the return of their Hawaiian government, illegally overthrown by missionary-descended, business elite five years earlier. My grandfather, Noa Webster Aluli, was seventeen years old when he signed this piece of living history. The petition holds the names of all my aunties, uncles, cousins, grandparents, and great-grandparents. I recall sobbing when

I finally got to see my *kupuna* signatures shaped in beautiful flowing cursive strokes. It changed us all because *we didn't know*. By 1900, the petition was hidden in the propaganda of post-overthrown Hawaii and never mentioned in history texts or tourist summaries.

We were taught that Hawaiians wanted and asked for annexation, but, as Tom Coffman explains, "Their petitions said the native people had not been consulted on the proposed dissolution of their nation. Nor was the Republic of Hawaii a republic, but rather a tyranny of the many by the few, bolstered by the nearly continuous presence of U.S. warships." (page 2) Almost every Hawaiian alive during that time put their signature to paper to tell the American people and government they *did not* want annexation. My great-grandmother's sister, Aima Nawahi, was the wife of Joseph Nawahi. Both worked in their respective chapters of *Hui Aloha Aina* to facilitate the Anti-Annexation Petition throughout the islands—by canoe, by mule, by horse, by foot, by word of mouth. Reading about their involvement, their passion, their commitment to the love of land and people has strengthened our family.

This *new* knowledge in *Nation Within* that you are about to read is unknown to most of America and still not taught at mainstream schools in Hawaii. A good historian tells a story in a cultural *context*, and, when this occurs, our *seeing* of the *content* has the opportunity to mature. Here is a rare chance for growth!

The truth then becomes evident: Hawaiians have survived, and the essence of our knowing has taught me many things, including that there *is* a Hawaiian nation-within and we thrive beyond a tourist and military economy. We have reestablished the role of *aloha* in the development of *intelligence* and thus our sustainability with people and land. *Change is here.* The new edition of this book is proof. *Nation Within* is a piece of the larger puzzle situated within an even larger movement that encourages self-reflection and understanding so we can get along better. It is summarized best by *kumu hula* Olana Kaipo Ai: *Aloha is the intelligence with which we meet life.*

I could not turn back the time for the political change, but there is still time to save our heritage. You must remember never cease to act because you fear you may fail. The way to lose any earthly kingdom is to be too inflexible, intolerant, and prejudicial. Another way is to be too flexible, tolerant of too many wrongs, and without judgment at all. It is a razor's edge. It is the width of a blade of pili grass. To gain the kingdom of heaven is to hear what is not said, to see what cannot be seen, and to know the unknowable—that is Aloha. (QUEEN LILI'UOKALANI)

If *aloha* is our intelligence, what does an intelligence of compassion look like? And what of truth? As a Native Hawaiian, I have come to understand there is relative truth and absolute truth. The contents of this book are indeed relative, but the energy that brought them forth is absolute. The ideas contained within this mosaic of stories and events are of high impact. They bring wisdom and animating purpose that helps me write from a place of forgiveness and compassion. Authors such as Tom Coffman affirm the *kuleana* of my family. The story of Hawaii's annexation is now being offered to a wider audience, who may be ready to learn about a place and people shaped by *aloha*. It is no coincidence that the current president, Barack Obama, came from this place. The role of *aloha* is clear and instructive when he said to the world: *Our differences define us, they do not divide us.*

Liberating truth telling will always help humanity evolve.

Mau ke aloha no Hawaii.
Love always for Hawaii.

Dr. Manulani Aluli Meyer
Alaelama, Hilo One
Moku O Keawe
February 20, 2009

Introduction

When an understanding of history is trampled in the street, its best chance for survival may be in the shelter of odd doorways. Places like the Tusitala Book Store in Kailua, O'ahu, become important, because Tusitala tries to keep the dust level down, and it deals in old and out-of-print books. *The Transformation of Hawaii* survived on the shelf of the Tusitala Store, not to quickly set the record straight—which would be too simple—but to give clues about the distortion of the history of Hawai'i.

The first paragraph gets directly to the book's work. The Hawaiian Islands were annexed to the United States "not by purchase, nor by conquest…(but) *by the vote of the Hawaiian people, who offered them to us as a gift.*" The writer's name is Belle M. Brain, who, according to the book's spine, wrote *Stories of Missions.* The copyright date is startling, because the U.S. Congress voted to annex Hawai'i in July 1898 and *Transformation* came out in September, at a time when typesetting was slow and distance mattered.

And now Belle's book comes back around after a century, and its pages open to suggest why so little is known about the past. For example (I will be brief), the period during which 90 percent of the Hawaiian people died is a period of remarkable progress, while in their pre-Western condition it would be "hard to conceive of a more depraved race of beings." Problems of "corruption and misrule" by the Hawaiian monarchs led to the overthrow of the native government. Bumps lay in the road, but when annexation occurred, the enthusiasm of the Hawaiians "knew no bounds."

There is a certain isolation that results from going back to the Tusitala Book Store for a second time, the second day warmer than the first, in the dust, struggling to decide whether Belle's small volume is now worth forty-five dollars. But for the Hawaiians there was a certain isolation in having their country taken, and then being told it was a lovely gift.

WHEN I ARRIVED IN HAWAI'I in 1965, the effective definition of history had been reduced to a few years. December 7, 1941, was practically the beginning of time, and anything that might have happened before that was prehistory. Hawai'i had finally been accepted as a state in 1959, and justice had been done. From the stylebook of the morning newspaper, disconcertingly named *The Honolulu Advertiser*, where I had my first reporting job, I learned that the word statehood was always to be capitalized. The year 1965 was the sixth year of Statehood. I am acutely aware only now that I began writing a book in 1970 by saying (paragraph one) that the year 1970 was the eleventh year of Statehood, and Hawai'i "was still young."

Many years passed before I realized that for Native Hawaiians to survive as a people, they needed a definition of time that spanned something more than eleven years. The demand for a changed understanding of time was always implicit in what became known as the Hawaiian Movement or the Hawaiian Renaissance, because Hawaiians so systematically turned to the past whenever the subject of Hawaiian life was glimpsed. Indeed they were often critiqued for looking back, which in the self-confident vocabulary of America in the 1960s was akin to being backward-looking.

While this past to which a certain minority of Hawaiians looked may have lacked definition, it inescapably had something to do with the events that Belle M. Brain had helped cover up. Slowly, through many experiences in dusty places, we have been compelled as a society to deal with the essential question of Hawai'i's past, which is the question of what happened to the Hawaiian people. What really happened? Like good journalism, good history is supposed to be balanced and tell both sides of the story. But what if history is mute, and the essence of the story is hidden? What if there is a past, but there is no satisfactory definition of history?

THROUGH THE WIDELY SCATTERED activities of a relatively small number of individuals, I witnessed fragments of the resurgence of Hawaiian life. One of these individuals particularly excelled—both in his writing and in his brilliant conversation—at making the issue of time and history explicit. His name was John Dominis Holt. John Holt was both charming and brainy, and the doors of American society were open to him at many levels, but he chose to embrace his fellow Hawaiians and the Hawaiian past. He dared to grieve aloud. He paid tribute to the queen, raged, and laughed darkly. He went back and back. He studied the archives of Belle Brain's primary informants, the descendants of the missionaries, and he despised them for their sanctimony, and for their assault on the dignity of the Hawaiians.

Dreading the tragedy he would find, he turned to the even more distant past—to the Hawaiians' first contact with the West. He then began to look through the window of contact at the people and events of pre-Western Hawai'i. He memorized the names and genealogies of chiefs and priests, and their ties to migrations, districts of islands, and wars of conquest. He conjured visions of their beings, of their faces, and even of their deaths. Through a process of torment, he became unashamed to be Hawaiian.

"He Hawai'i Au"—I first heard those words from John, which I now see on the T-shirts of Hawaiian nationalists. "I am Hawaiian."

John Holt's quest continued over many years, when he could have more easily come to rest, when people from around the country and around the Pacific Ocean approached him in his house on the hillside as a savant. Yet he was never content to be comfortable. He insisted that we free ourselves from the hodgepodge of seeing events in isolation. He posed as an alternative the development of chronologies and the development of cultural context. He believed that when Hawaiians came to be understood within the progression of time, they would be treated as a real people again.

AS WITH THE HAWAIIANS, so it is with Hawai'i's story. Where the American definition of Hawai'i is of a pleasant and quaint place, an exploration of Hawai'i as a suppressed nation is disturbing but epic. Where people in the twentieth century persistently have written little tales of the Islands, the story of Hawai'i as a nation is a turbulent mo'olelo.

Those people, John in particular, who went against convention and generated an alternative viewpoint, also generated a new set of possibilities. These new possibilities begin with taking the Hawaiian nation seriously, and they lead to a serious reexamination of America's history in the Pacific.

Tom Coffman
Kāneʻohe, Hawaiʻi, 1998

A NOTE ON THE SECOND EDITION

I am as pleased as any writer with a second edition and grateful to my new publisher, Arnold Kotler, for his commitment and interest.

I am compelled to add that the continued relevance of this book reflects a far-reaching political, moral and intellectual failure of the United States to recognize and deal with its takeover of Hawaiʻi.
In the book's subtitle, the word *Annexation* has been replaced by the word *Occupation*, referring to America's occupation of Hawaiʻi. Where annexation connotes legality by mutual agreement, the act was not mutual and therefore not legal. Since by definition of international law there was no annexation, we are left then with the word *occupation*.

In making this change, I have embraced the logical conclusion of my research into the events of 1893 to 1898 in Honolulu and Washington, D.C. I am prompted to take this step by a growing body of historical work by a new generation of Native Hawaiian scholars. Dr. Keanu Sai writes, "The challenge for ... the fields of political science, history, and law is to distinguish between the rule of law and the politics of power." In the history of Hawaiʻi, the might of the United States does not make it right.

In the years between the 1993 Apology Resolution (by the U.S. Congress to the Hawaiian people) and 2000, the Democratic Party fumbled away its opportunity to set in motion a process of negotiation between the United States government and the submerged nation of Hawaiʻi. Thereafter, the more nakedly imperial Republicans succeeded in quashing the debate. The administration of a President who led the United States to occupy Iraq also, by some of the same impulses, led the United States away from examining its past as it pertains to the status of Hawai'i.

Dear President Obama of Hawai'i, let us go back and start over. With truth might come some form of reconciliation. And with it, the once bright promise of Hawai'i would be renewed.

Tom Coffman
Hawai'i, 2009

This book is dedicated to the person who sat up late and took the risks, Lois Lee, a sensational mate and a font of provocative ideas and informed opinions. All of that and laughter too.

Nation Within

CHAPTER ONE

A False Spring

Having survived the brutal cold of Washington's winter, the Hawaiian delegation welcomed spring. Having survived yet another campaign to annex their homeland to America, they took a brief moment to remark cheerfully on the survival of Hawai'i as an independent nation. Perhaps the moment for America to take over Hawai'i had come and gone, and perhaps the Hawaiians could now get their country back.

The queen of Hawai'i had been living in a hotel in Washington during most of 1897, and the delegates of the native political societies had arrived toward the end of the year, in the dead of winter, to support her with the most ambitious of their many petitions. The delegation had come from mass rallies in Hawai'i against annexation that had been attended by thousands of Hawaiians, who now were nearly one quarter of the earth's surface away. At one of the rallies against annexation, a speaker had likened the Kingdom of Hawai'i to a house, which had been built by the great king, Kamehameha. A handful of foreigners had taken over the house, and they had given the Hawaiians a *lei* stand in return, where the Hawaiians were expected to reside and sell flowers.

Would the Hawaiians live in the *lei* stand? '*A'ole*, the crowd had shouted back. No, never.[1]

When the delegates to Washington closed their eyes they could remember the faces, the families, and the petitions passing from hand to hand for people to sign their names. As a result of the petition drive, the Hawaiian delegation had arrived in Washington with thirty-eight thousand signatures protesting America's proposed annexation of their country, and they were eager to call the petitions to the attention of influential Americans. Considering that only forty thousand or so Hawaiians survived, it was surely true, as their opponents said, that some of the signatures were duplicates, and some were the names of children, and perhaps some were names of the dead. But the petitions nonetheless were a virtual census of the Hawaiian nation, as Hawaiians still called themselves, and the petitions said eloquently that in spite of everything that had happened, they wanted to be what they had been, a nation in the world system of nations.[2]

Culturally it was very Hawaiian to recite stories of the past, and their desire to survive led them to recite the story of the preceding five years over and over. Americans seemed to have short memories, and so the Hawaiian delegates had to constantly remind people that their government had been taken over by a handful of *haole* men, many of them descended from American missionaries. The disloyal acts of this Committee of Annexation had been prompted by the United States minister to Hawai'i, and the committee had thereafter been shielded by the might of the United States navy. At many points along the twisting five-year path, the Hawaiians had challenged the committee's resulting Provisional Government—and challenged America—to open the question of annexation to a democratic vote, but their appeal had always been refused.

As their petitions said, the native people had not been consulted on the proposed dissolution of their nation. Nor was the Republic of Hawaii a republic, but rather a tyranny of the many by the few, bolstered by the nearly continuous presence of U.S. warships. Now, through the draft treaty of annexation, this small group of *haole* was trying to turn the land, sovereignty, and prospective naval bases of the nation of Hawai'i over to the United States. There was a name for such a transaction, former President Grover Cleveland had said, but he never wrote down what it was.

To describe the situation in words that Americans might understand, the queen of Hawai'i was to write that America surely would not want to become "a colonizer and a land-grabber." If the American government was to follow the British, French, and Germans into colonialism, was this agreeable to the American people? While no doubt Americans could rival the Europeans in the sad business of conquest, was this how an idealistic nation wanted to be known in the world? Would a nation that originated from an anticolonial revolution now want to be known for its colonization of others?

Although the queen was one of many Hawaiians who steadfastly resisted annexation, naturally it was she whose name would be remembered, Lili'uokalani. In the years following the overthrow, Lili'uokalani had gone from exalted sovereign to prisoner to parolee. When she left Hawai'i, she told the president of the white government that she was going to visit a sick relative, but after circulating among acquaintances in Boston long enough to dignify her story, she had taken a night train to Washington, D.C., and there she had tried to regain the sovereignty of her nation. In a short time she had reached a remarkable number of people, many of them highly placed in the world, just as she was. Given the racial stereotypes that sometimes confronted her in the press, and given that much of the globe had descended into the organized violence of colonial takeovers, there was a kind of mad civility to the events that engaged her.

Masons were among the many groups of people who came to see her. One day a hundred Masons from Philadelphia came calling. They sang her song, *Aloha 'Oe*, which spoke of one fond embrace before departing. Lili'uokalani played the piano superbly, and when Masons wanted to sing their national anthem, she obliged them by playing the accompaniment, *O Say Can You See?* She wrote in her diary that all were filled with good tidings for her. Grover Cleveland, the twenty-fourth president of the United States, had welcomed her warmly, and Mrs. Cleveland had honored her with a reception at the White House. Now, she wondered, with America in a more nationalistic mood, would the twenty-fifth president of the United States likewise entertain her, and entertain her thoughts as well?

Among the Hawaiian delegation who joined her, the two most prominent figures were James K. Kaulia and David Kalauokalani. James Kaulia was the leader of Hui Aloha 'Āina, which translates loosely as the Hawaiian Patriotic League and more literally as the gathering of people who love the land. Hui Aloha 'Āina was a mass protest organization that had sprung up to support traditional rule against "a handful of foreign adventurers," as one of their earlier petitions had phrased it. David Kalauokalani was president of Hui Kālai'āina, which had started as something closer to a conventional political party, organized to reassert native influence in the Kingdom of Hawai'i.

They had arrived in Washington fearing the U.S. Senate's imminent approval of the annexation treaty. They had been confronted by wild claims that the Japanese were incrementally invading Hawai'i, so they had to work particularly hard to remind people that the problem was not the Japanese, but the small handful of white annexationists who had taken over their government. By spring, they sensed they had been effective. If the battle was far from over, it was encouraging that the treaty of annexation as drafted had been stalled again—perhaps indefinitely. News traveled back and forth to Hawai'i by letter, and the letters of the delegates made their way into the native language press. They made the point that even though foreigners sat in their house of government, Hawai'i was still an independent country. It seemed as if Hawaiians might gain time, and what they had most needed from the moment of the first Western contact was time to adapt to the sweeping changes imposed by the outside world. With time, they might cope with the onslaught and regain control of their house.

A FEW BLOCKS AWAY, the annexation commissioners of the Republic were variously ignoring, sidestepping, or dashing off to counter the protests of the Hawaiians, in the interest of focusing their own influential American friends on a larger picture. The best-known of the small group, Lorrin Thurston, was still thought of by some Americans in connection with the phrase "stolen kingdom," which had become widely used in the debate over annexation during 1893. Thurston was inclined to be argumentative when such accusations arose, but his colleagues told him not to dwell on what had happened five years ago, and to talk instead about what could happen now, in 1898, and the exciting role that Hawai'i could play in a world that seemed to be changing at a dazzling pace.

To gain support for annexation, Thurston and his colleagues had initially attempted to elicit America's traditional antagonism for the British, but the British had proven to be insufficiently antagonistic.

They were, in fact, busy cultivating an alliance with the Americans. Thereafter the little white group had turned to the Japanese. In response, the U.S. secretary of state had confessed that problems with Japan were unknown to him, but he had listened intently. With nurturing, the phobia of Japan had gone a long way toward diverting America's attention from the Hawaiians, but even the supposed menace of Japan had not resulted in an "aye" vote on annexation.

Now, in the springtime of what would be a momentous year, the question of Hawai'i was being pushed aside, as Americans turned to the brutality of the Spanish colonialists in Cuba. The phrase, "our Cuban brothers," circulated through the ever-changing American vocabulary. The ambassador of the *haole* government of Hawai'i wrote gloomily to Honolulu that annexation was nowhere in sight.

TO EXPLORE HAWAI'I'S STORY more deeply, it is useful to begin with the fact that there had been a movement of long standing in Honolulu to bind Hawai'i and America together, and a movement of long standing in Washington with a comparable goal. The members of the little group in Honolulu wanted to gain stability and ease their own fears, while those in Washington wanted to capitalize on instability and strike fear in others. The goals of the American annexationists had to do with the United States evolving into a great power, stretching across oceanic frontiers, and by the spring of 1898 they had come to know precisely what they wanted to do. They had described their plans in great detail, but in the heat of the moment they talked most vociferously about their indignation with the behavior of the Spanish in Cuba, and even about their indignation with the growing number of immigrant Japanese field workers in Hawai'i. As this small circle of men moved America ever closer toward the eating of foreign lands, euphemisms were devised that described distant islands not as nations but as fruit. Misleading semantics are an important part of delusion. Hawai'i was no longer a country in their recitations, but variously a pear, a peach, or an apple, ripe for the plucking.

Many historians, including both admirers and detractors, have described this circle of aggressive expansionists as conspirators, or as members of a cabal. Objectively, they were men with a plan, of which Hawai'i was the most preliminary part. How Hawai'i was to be taken was a detail to be worked out, but the existence of a plan would prove to be pivotal, even if it was not widely held, because the plan would serve as a guide to action in an atmosphere of chaos.

The gist of the plan had evolved from the events of the preceding quarter-century. The specifics of the plan were devised at the Metropolitan Club in downtown Washington, D.C. Among the members of the circle who met at the Metropolitan Club in the early months of 1898, one stood out for his tenacity, daring, and high spirits. And much to the point of the story, no one in Hawai'i was ever to grasp his role, and very few people outside Hawai'i were ever to care about what he was doing at the Metropolitan Club.

Americans know a great deal about Theodore Roosevelt in his subsequent capacity as a progressive president, an enemy of corruption, and a savior of forests. They know about his childhood asthma, and about his setting the bullies of his boyhood straight. But virtually nothing is known about the governmental position Theodore Roosevelt held in 1898, why he had secured it, and what happened to Hawai'i in the process.

While Queen Lili'uokalani was writing her final appeal to the conscience of America's people, Roosevelt was struggling with the tantalizing possibility of a little war. "I should welcome any war," he said, "for I think this country needs one." He was frustrated by the failure of the annexation treaty, complaining that his fellow Americans had a "queer lack of imperial instinct." But while others polarized over little issues, Roosevelt remained focused on big issues and, in his mind's eye, something changed. He announced to the president that if war should come he would be obligated to resign his desk job and go off with the troops. His superior, Secretary of the Navy John D. Long, said Roosevelt was acting like a fool. Then he paused, as if he could hear his words rattling through the corridor. He remarked how absurd he would sound if, by some turn of fortune, his tiresome underling should "strike a very high mark."

CHAPTER TWO

Retrieving History

An excruciating process of retrieving pertinent fragments of its history occurred in Hawai'i during the years leading up to January 1993, which was observed as the hundredth anniversary of the overthrow of the Hawaiian monarchy. The concept of native government was discussed seriously by a broad spectrum of the community, probably for the first time in the twentieth century. In this discussion, the kings and queens of Hawai'i became something more than conversation pieces, and 'Iolani Palace, which is at the center of Honolulu, was something more than an oddity—"the only royal palace in America," as visitors are told.

By wrestling with the cultural definition of time, the thought began to occur to a widening circle of people that the culture imposed by the West had come to be mistaken for timeless reality. In this new (or retrieved) mode of thinking, people began to see that the monarchy (which had been so dutifully "overthrown") had originated from ancient Hawai'i, and that it was the institution through which Native Hawaiians had attempted to maintain control of their homeland. It further dawned on a certain number of people that the colonizing culture had defined most of the written, as opposed to oral, history of Hawai'i, and that this history typically reduced Hawai'i's total human history to a relatively few years, the focus of which was narrow and parochial. A crushing process of Westernization, and a concomitant devaluing of the indigenous experience, had thereby defined the shape and weight of Hawai'i's story, until America's takeover of "the Islands" was transformed into a set of local tales. And confined by this small, languid paradise, where breezes blow and palm trees sway, where the natives may be heard playing music far into the night, writers have turned again and again to the actions of a handful of willful people, within several square blocks of Honolulu, during the four days culminating on January 17, 1893.

QUEEN LILI'UOKALANI WAS FIFTY-FOUR years old. She had traveled the world. She dressed on occasion in the finest gowns of Europe, spoke three languages, and wrote prolifically. She said it was as natural for her to compose music as to breathe. She was a devout practitioner of Christianity, which had been the state religion of the Kingdom of Hawai'i since 1824. She was in her second year as queen. She was a widow. Her brother was dead. Her young siblings from childhood were long since dead, and all the Kamehameha monarchs with whom she had attended the Chief's Children's School were dead. Her adoptive sister, Bernice Pauahi, was dead.

Nonetheless Lili'uokalani was a person of considerable energy who refused to be overwhelmed by the tragedies she had experienced. She was besieged by petitions from the native people seeking a new constitution to strengthen indigenous rule through her, the queen, as their traditional ruler, and through a reassertion of influence in the Kingdom's Legislature proportionate to their numbers. The queen's desire to proclaim a new constitution in response to the native petitions became known, and the white annexationists in the port town of Honolulu set out to crush her. The cabal of annexationists in Hawai'i had been to Washington to secure the blessing of the American annexationists, and the American ambassador in Hawai'i was implacably hostile toward the continuation of a Hawaiian government. A ship filled with American marines was in the harbor, armed with revolvers, rifles, machine guns, and enough cannon to level the little city. The once-great armies of the Hawaiians, from the time of Lili'uokalani's great-great-grandfather, no longer existed. Although a few Hawaiians were armed and prepared to fight, they were hopelessly outgunned and outnumbered. Largely as a result of introduced disease, the Hawaiian population was one-tenth of what it had been, perhaps even a twentieth.

The American ambassador called the marines from the ship even before the leaders of the revolt were ready to announce their coup, forcing the hand of the missionary descendants. The marines streamed off the ship under the pretext of restoring order and protecting American lives. Above the harbor they found people strolling in the streets. Parties were starting. The troops were mistaken by passersby for another foreign contingent taking exercise, but the queen knew the ominous meaning of their arrival. She looked from the balcony of her palace and tried to decide what to do.

LILI'UOKALANI WAS THE EIGHTH MONARCH of the Kingdom of Hawai'i, all of whom had traced their ancestry to the powerful chiefs of Hawai'i Island. In a recounting of generational time, the historian Samuel Kamakau had written that for the first twenty-eight generations "no man was made chief over another," and that only when people became more numerous was government by chiefs established. In these early steps of forming governments, the chief was known for working alongside the people and sharing their fate.

As the island population grew, a second and more fierce tradition of chiefly power was imported by Tahitian voyagers, who propounded the necessity of fierce chiefs who ruled from above. Within a few generations a chief emerged from Hawai'i Island who personified this idea. His name was Kalaunui'ōhua, and he succeeded in organizing all the district chiefs of Hawai'i Island into a war party. As they were ready to sail he encountered a strange, gray-haired woman. He asked her to prophesy, "What lies ahead?" She gave a simple answer, "*Maika'i ka ho'omaka 'ana 'ino ka pau 'ana*. Good in the beginning, bad in the end."

Kalaunui sailed nonetheless. He invaded the islands of Maui, Moloka'i, and O'ahu, only to flounder on the shores of Kaua'i, where he was held captive for a long while, until the Kauaians deemed it fit to send him home. Although things had gone "bad in the end," Kalaunui had demonstrated the power of the fast-moving invader who strikes from the sea. He had shown that invading armies could move more quickly in their fleets of canoes than defending armies could move on land. The invaders could nearly always make a landing, protect their line of retreat, and, if things did not go well in battle, make a run for their canoes.

As the chiefs became more powerful, they moved from district to district and island to island, and on their journeys they encountered worlds within worlds. Each bay, stream, valley, ridge, and peak was perceived as different and special, and each had a story. Winds of a particular valley, a certain mammoth stone in a wall, rains, tides, and waves, all were the subjects of infinitely varied stories. A goddess had been here and cast a spell and made love with a certain person. A great chief had shown compassion to a certain person. A beautiful girl had died here but was brought back to life by an owl, which watched over her. A man lived on the point of land by the sea, and at sundown he would dive into the water and swim to the reef, until one evening a boy saw in the dimming light that the man was actually half-shark.

THANKS PARTLY TO PHOTOGRAPHY, Lili'uokalani's image is of a monarch seated on a throne, but she was also a chief who followed ancient tradition by traveling from district to district. When she traveled among the Hawaiian people she was greeted with *aloha nui*, but Westerners were always critiquing her. A writer of history, Albertine Loomis, said that while Lili'uokalani had been blessed with the acquaintance of Britain's Queen Victoria, she did not seem to understand that in England the question of governmental authority had been settled in Parliament's favor. Implicit in this writer's thinking was the separation of a native figure from the land that gave her life meaning. Likewise implicit was the reduction of an epic world to a quaint little place on the map of the West.

While Lili'uokalani appeared to begin her memoir in good Western fashion with a chapter entitled *A Sketch of My Childhood*, she actually launched a Polynesian discussion of her genealogy. She dwelled on her great-great-grandfather, Keaweaheulu, who connected her across generations to the origins of the Hawaiian nation. While this sort of recitation may cause the minds of today's readers to shut down, the genealogies of the Hawaiians provide a glimpse of a highly complex, separate society that calls out across time to be understood in its own terms.

Lili'uokalani knew as a Hawaiian what scientific investigation lately has confirmed, that her ancestors played an extraordinary role in the exploration and settlement of the planet. They departed from

Southeast Asia perhaps as early as six thousand years ago,[1] migrating slowly across the southern and far western regions of the Pacific, then pausing in several groups of islands—Fiji, Tonga, and Sāmoa—that formed a triangle. Here they developed a distinctive language and culture. They became Polynesian. Where metal was fundamental to the development of continental people (the Bronze Age, the Iron Age, etc.), the island environment contained no metal. Accordingly, the islanders of Polynesia were severely limited in their potential to devise machines, develop precision instruments, cut, drill, and carve holes. Nonetheless they mastered the design, construction, sailing, and navigating of great double-hulled craft, which they sailed across unimaginably long distances to colonize the widely separated islands of the largest body of water on earth.

From Western Polynesia, they voyaged into the prevailing trade winds until they reached Tahiti, Bora Bora, Raiatea, the Marquesas, and the Tuamotos, which today are known as Eastern Polynesia. From there they voyaged east to Rapa Nui (Easter Island, as it was renamed by the explorer James Cook); southwest all the way back to Aotearoa (New Zealand); and north—across immense spans of open ocean, with no other islands in sight—to a grouping of fabulous islands that lay in an irregular line running from northwest to southeast, like an oceanic net designed to attract the navigator's searching eye.

The vast amount that is known today about the evolution of the Hawaiian settlements is an overlapping combination of archaeology and oral history. The coastal areas were rich in fish and shellfish. The wet valleys readily grew taro. Where the first round of archaeology in Hawai'i suggested a settlement that was about a thousand years old, this finding was contradicted by chants written down in Lili'uokalani's time describing a hundred generations of human experience, suggesting a settlement of Hawai'i that was nearly two thousand years old. As the digging and analysis have continued, the scientific view has gone to ever-earlier dates, so scientists now typically assign the time of settlement to around A.D. 300. Some dates, while disputed, are from the time of Christ.

The initial population grew slowly during the first eight hundred or so years of settlement. Then, around A.D. 1100, the population began to climb steeply upward. People moved from the coastal lowlands into the uplands. They migrated from the wet windward sides of the islands to the drier leeward sides. The hydrology systems of the taro fields became increasingly complex, extending further and further up the valleys and further away from the streams and rivers. Enormous offshore ponds were built for the culture of fish, to complement the protein supplies from the streams, the reefs, and the open ocean. According to Kamakau, the construction of a large fishpond required the labor of ten thousand men.

Family shrines, and the religious shrines of fishermen and farmers, now functioned within a system of ever-larger temples. Like the fishponds, the building of the temples required the work of large numbers of people, the stockpiling of food to feed them, and powerful chiefs to rule over them. People today can readily study this ancient society, and imagine what life might have been like, because all of these structures—the walls of the agricultural system, the fishponds, the platforms of the temples, and the places of refuge—were made of stone. The connections of the past were secure, and everywhere Lili'uokalani was reminded of the stream of humanity that had gone before her in the days of old.

By the time Lili'uokalani reached adulthood, the landscape was changing rapidly as a result of the spread of sugar plantations. Many of the agricultural and aquacultural systems had fallen into disuse, and the indigenous population had shrunk to what it had been roughly eight centuries previously, before its period of phenomenal growth. Lili'uokalani herself knew all too well about the cataclysmic spread of disease. When she was ten, three of the children from the royal families had died of measles in quick succession. The last was her little sister, Kaiminaauao. "This sad event made a great impression upon my younger days," she wrote, "for these relatives and companions of my youth died and were buried on the same day, the coffin of the last-named resting on that of the others."

Lili'uokalani was sensitive to the accusation that the chiefs were well off at the expense of their retainers. She said anyone who had seen Hawai'i even fifty years earlier would know she spoke the truth, citing her biological father Kapa'akea as a shining example. "... my father was surrounded by hundreds of his own people," she was to write, "all of whom looked to him, and never in vain, for sustenance."

Although the population was greatly reduced, enough people were left for her to describe her reception in the countryside as hearty and enthusiastic. Since the time of James Cook, Hawai'i had survived and adapted. It was the object of enormous fascination, particularly in Europe and also in East Asia and North America. It had been accepted by the most powerful nations on Earth as a modern nation, and that alone was reason for optimism about its future.

Lili'uokalani was one among intricate circles of learned Hawaiians who were determined that their history and culture would survive. Accordingly, they committed enormous quantities of information from the collective memory of their oral culture to paper. Lili'uokalani herself was to translate the creation chant known as the *Kumulipo*, perhaps the most seminal of all Hawaiian stories. Her brother, Kalākaua, directed the writing of a long volume of "myths and legends." While the name contributes to the sense that the past is only vaguely defined, the stories themselves were told with great specificity. Around the same time, a Swedish immigrant, Abraham Fornander, wrote a voluminous summary titled *An Account of the Polynesian Race*. Fornander was married to a Hawaiian woman and learned how to speak, write, and read Hawaiian. His principal informants were a circle of young Hawaiian scholars trained at Lahainaluna School on Maui. Among them, Samuel Kamakau was the most brilliant and wrote the most prolifically and incisively about the traditions of the Polynesian chiefdom as it developed in the competing kingdoms that formed the net that originally snagged the navigators—Kaua'i far to the west, O'ahu and Maui in the inner cluster, and giant Hawai'i to the southeast.

To the uninitiated, this Hawaiian epic may have sounded unreal, particularly when it was separated from the artistry and conviction of the storyteller, but in fact it reflected a brilliant culture that differed fundamentally from the Western culture that came to envelope it. As archaeology has progressed, and as Polynesian voyaging has been replicated in the present day, scholars of all types the world over have come to accept that there was, indeed, a period of intense voyaging across the north-south barriers of wind and equatorial calm, at a time when Western man hovered near his shore. People from not only the Marquesas and Tahiti, but a wide variety of islands participated. The heroes of the voyages founded the lines of the Hawaiian chiefs. Kalākaua wrote of "the old Ulu and Nanaulu line" of Windward O'ahu, from whom infinitely storied generations of chiefs descended. Fornander wrote down the genealogical trees of the original settlers, stretching from generation to generation across millennia, to the times in which he lived. As a result of such genealogies, there are people in Hawai'i today who can trace their family trees back as far as two thousand years.

TO IMAGINE A HAWAIIAN CHIEF who traveled the districts is one thing, but to think about Theodore Roosevelt in connection with the Hawaiian Islands is another. It requires thinking about the histories of America and Hawai'i as interrelated. It further requires understanding Theodore Roosevelt not as a caricatured figure riding up a distant hill, but as a political leader of enormous importance whose most far-reaching achievements were not about forests or parks, but about projecting American power into distant seas. His achievements, which define America to this day, had to do with making the United States a first-rate naval power, an aggressively expansionist power, and finally a global power. In extraordinary ways, he summarized his age. On the surface, he was the boisterous American politician, but underneath he was no less cunning or autocratic than a Hawaiian chief in the days of epic warfare.

He was the seventh generation of Roosevelts born within the same few square blocks of Manhattan Island, which made him an islander of a sort. By the time he wrote his autobiography, he would recite his genealogy—describing a stream of Dutch immigrants who intermarried with English, Irish, Scotch, and German immigrants. His Roosevelt grandfather, who continued to speak Dutch at the family table, achieved considerable success as a merchant, and the Roosevelts were well on their way to becoming prominent New Yorkers, if not yet prominent Americans.

Theodore's father was an expansive variation on the Roosevelts of Manhattan. In 1850, he heard a story about a plantation in Georgia called Bulloch Hall. He went south, where he met a girl named Mittie, then fifteen years old. When the historian David McCullough dug into Mittie's story, he began to think she was Margaret

Mitchell's inspiration for the character Scarlett O'Hara in *Gone with the Wind*. Mittie was full of talk and full of life, a seemingly stereotypical belle of the Old South. At eighteen she married Theodore Sr. and moved to Manhattan, then moved her mother with her. With a Southerner wife, Theodore Sr. was aghast at the prospect of war between the North and South. He spoke at street rallies in hope of forestalling the war. When it came, he resorted to a common practice of the wealthy, employing a man to fight in his place, determined that his hands not personally be touched with the blood of Mittie's kinsmen.

Theodore Jr. was born in 1858, three years before the war began. As a child of seven, he looked out from the second floor of the family's New York brownstone house at a horse-drawn coffin passing in the crowded street. Lincoln was dead. A photograph of the funeral procession survives that was taken from street level. It shows the tiny figure of Theodore at the window with his brother Elliott, who would grow up to have a daughter named Eleanor Roosevelt.

Theodore was fixated on the powerful personalities of his parents. Even though his father had not fought in the war, he was, in young Theodore's eyes, a combination of strength and gentleness, courage and tenderness. The senior Roosevelt carried Teddy through the terror of nights when he struggled to survive his asthma attacks. "I could breathe," he would write, "I could sleep, when he held me in his arms." The senior Roosevelt was more interested in charity than business. He helped found an orthopedic hospital and a charitable society for needy children. He was active in the Young Men's Christian Association. He was alarmed by the poverty resulting from the Civil War. He developed a plan through which soldiers could voluntarily allot part of their pay to their families back home. He went to Washington, talked with Lincoln, lobbied the legislation through Congress, then rode from camp to camp urging men to make the allotments.

He was a kindly face in an austere family. Teddy's sister remarked how difficult her Southern mother's life must have been. "... I should hate to have married into them at that time unless I had been one with them in thought. They think they are just, but they are hard in a way." Writers consistently reach for theories of psychology to

Kamehameha at Kailua-Kona with Russians. (Drawing by Louis Choris.)

describe the young Theodore who gasps for breath and dreams of great things. On one side the child is confronted by stories of gallant Southern relatives on horseback, on the other by a saintly father who declined to fight in the war of his time.

The image of the plantation lived on within the Roosevelt brownstone in Manhattan, long after it ceased to be the centerpiece of Southern society. The author McCullough wrote, "Guns, violence, savage death, episodes that seemed more like the stuff of fable or fantasy, were all part of the world Mittie spun." Mittie's half brother, in a rage, turned on the black slave boy who was his "little shadow." He shot and killed him. Mittie's half-brother—Theodore's uncle— was so upset (apparently with himself) that he went away for a year. On his return to the plantation, he engaged a white boy in a rifle duel and shot him dead as well.

Teddy said he grew up on tales of every nook and corner of the plantation, the ghosts included, and "queer goings-on in the slave quarter." While Theodore's father was away in the camps of the Northern army, his mother and grandmother wrapped packages of clothing and money for the doomed riders of the South. When Roosevelt's mother died, he inherited the paternal relationship with former slaves who, he said, refused to be emancipated from the family plantation. Once a year they appealed to him to send money for a new, overpriced mule, because the old mule kept running away. The names of slaves survived in Roosevelt's autobiography—a "very old darky" named Bear Bob, half-scalped by the swipe of a lethal paw, and a coachman named Daddy Luke.

If the issue for Hawai'i is how Roosevelt extended America's power into the Pacific, the issue for his biographers is typically how he made sense of his diverse background—how he was to combine the Puritanical certitudes of Manhattan with the chaos and violence of the men on horseback. As an enormously prolific writer whose work is still in print, Roosevelt is always close at hand to help with the task, having labored mightily not only to understand himself but to convey this understanding to the world. Perhaps he was an original in the practice of narcissism in American politics. If there is anything you may want to know, he conveniently directs your eye to a rich mythology, in which you need only search out the details.

David McCullough writes that Theodore's boyhood asthma was worse around the weekends, close to church time. Paul R. Cutright argues that he had more asthma attacks on weekdays. Theodore does indeed ride off to the countryside on a stagecoach for fresh country air, and it is on this ride that Teddy is pounced upon by bully boys, and here Teddy vows to remake himself into a man's man.

Despite the huge autobiography, the numerous biographies, and the thirty-eight published books, Roosevelt's connection to Hawai'i has remained obscure. Nonetheless, the historic persona who resides in the archives is as impatient to dominate America's course of action in Hawai'i as Roosevelt was to dominate all other aspects of life in the late nineteenth century. While it is true that he was far from alone in his desire to expand the horizons of the American nation, in his uncanny capacity for translating ideas into action, he was alone—in this story he waits alone—above the now-forgotten crowd.

WHEN LILI'UOKALANI embarked on her tour of the Island districts, she wrote of her future subjects: "They showed to us their love. They welcomed me as Hawaiians always have the ruling chief." She stopped in the district that lay around Kāne'ohe Bay in Windward O'ahu, which visitors observe today from the Pali lookout. The ancient stories often speak of Kāne'ohe because it provided the Polynesian settlers a wide reef for harvesting marine protein and a broad plain for farming. Rain fell abundantly on the mountaintop, as the updraft of warm moist air, blown in by the trade winds, hit the cold air along the cliffs. The streams ran full.

From Kāne'ohe the princess traveled to the northern tip of the bay, a dramatic point of land called Kualoa, which was renowned as a landing place of the early voyagers. A navigator named Kaha'i had transported a breadfruit tree across thousands of ocean miles and planted it at Kualoa. This point of land lies at the intersection of two districts, and on each side there is a protecting ridge that runs nearly down to the sea. Kualoa was a place of refuge, a safe haven. Infants born to chiefly lines were brought there for training in how to conduct themselves as chiefs.

From Kualoa, Lili'uokalani continued through two more district chiefdoms on the windward side of the island, then looped back through three districts on the leeward side. These six districts of O'ahu, Hawaiians knew, had maneuvered, fought, coalesced, formed councils, negotiated marriages, made peace, and fought again, over many centuries. And so it went on Lili'uokalani's journey. Even as a new era of Western imperialism began to rage out of Europe and around the globe, she continued her travels of affirmation, through a world in which each small niche was infused with meaning.

Within this intimate view, the politics of weaving together a series of valleys into a district chiefdom can be appreciated as a considerable feat. The weaving together of district chiefdoms—and then chiefdoms that governed whole islands—became the stuff of stories that Kalākaua and Lili'uokalani knew as part of their beings. Their ancestral Hawai'i was a compendium of stories of chiefs from the vast regions of Hilo, Puna, Ka'ū, Hāmākua, and Kohala. But the most famous of all stories were of places chosen by nature, such as the Waipi'o Valley in Kohala. Waipi'o is a deep, wide valley that traps the windward rains. It grew—and still grows—huge quantities of taro, and it became a center for the royalty of Hawai'i Island. A high-born chief of Waipi'o, Līloa, made love with a beautiful commoner he encountered in the countryside. Līloa gave the woman a royal pendant that was made of whale's tooth and strung on braids of human hair. A young man presented the pendant to him in his old age as proof of their father-son relationship. This legendary commoner-son was 'Umi, and through him the six districts of the island of Hawai'i were united into a single kingdom.

The island of Maui is so visibly made up of a great mountain in the east and a range of mountains in the west. Initially there were two separate settlements in East Maui, two in West Maui. Then the districts of West Maui united, and the districts of East Maui united. Just as Hawai'i islanders were sensitive to the line of 'Umi, Maui islanders thought of the ali'i Pi'ilani, who arose from the dry leeward side of West Maui in the 1400s to unite the entire island. A trail was built by his son, Kihaapi'ilani, that encircled the island. An enormous temple was built called Ka Hale Pi'ilani. The domain of Pi'ilani incorporated the small, surrounding islands, including Lāna'i and Kaho'olawe, forming the first interisland kingdom, which was known as Nā Hono a Pi'ilani, the bays of Pi'ilani.

The queen probably thought of O'ahu as not only the capital of the modern kingdom, but as the source of the earliest chiefly lines. Lili'uokalani's contemporary, Samuel Kamakau, wrote that O'ahu was the place "where the first man was made." Science agrees, at least for the moment. The oldest archaeological datings are found on O'ahu, around the hospitable windward bays. Late in the expansion period, a council of O'ahu chiefs held the first recorded election in Hawai'i, elevating a chief from the dry 'Ewa district to the status of supreme chief of the entire island. This man, Mā'ilikūkahi, moved the seat of government to Waikīkī, which continued as O'ahu's governing center for most of the following four hundred years.

On the island of Kaua'i, the heart of the northeastern district was the Wailua River. On the south end of Kaua'i, a second district was formed around the Waimea River. In times of war, the Waimea district and its allies typically were pitted against the Wailua district and its allies. When the island was united, the court of the Kaua'i kingdom held forth in the cooler north during the summer, and in the more protected south during winter.

During the 1600s and 1700s, these four kingdoms—Hawai'i, Maui, O'ahu and Kaua'i—amounted to four nations in the making. Each was a complex, highly developed chiefdom. Each had a supreme chief, district chiefs, and chiefs who directly oversaw the land. The antagonism among these nations-in-the-making was considerable, but so were their inter-connections. The genealogies of the chiefs were intertwined. They were united by marriages and offspring. They traced their ancestries to Sky Father and Earth Mother. They shared gods and religious practices, as well as culture, performance, and art.

In succession, each of the four kingdoms bid for supreme power, with the inner kingdoms making the first moves. O'ahu abandoned its peaceful ways, annexing Kaua'i to the west and Moloka'i to the east. As a result of O'ahu's rising power, the Maui kingdom was threatened on both sides—by O'ahu on the west, and by the island of Hawai'i on the east. The fierce, storied chiefs who descended from 'Umi mounted raids on Maui again and again. They took over the fertile Hāna district of Maui for generations, establishing yet a third interisland kingdom. By the late eighteenth century, as Americans were contemplating the possibilities of nationhood, the major island chiefdoms were contemplating nationhood in their own way. They were competing furiously for dominance of the entire group, but the geography of the Islands did not readily allow for an all-powerful victor. The channels were wide and turbulent, particularly the channel that separated Kaua'i. The coastlines were intricate, allowing a diversity of people to come and go. The terrain was mountainous, providing refuge for the vanquished. It was in the middle of war that a totally unfamiliar sight appeared—the tall, square-masted ships of the British explorers.

CHAPTER THREE

Coping with Great Powers

How Lili'uokalani was to respond when the American marines marched through her streets in 1893 was conditioned by the more than century-long struggle of the Hawaiian chiefs to cope with the appearance of the naval powers of the West, beginning with Captain James Cook. Cook had departed England on July 14, 1776, not knowing that the thirteen American colonies had declared their independence from the Crown ten days previously.

Cook's exploration of the Pacific followed the Spaniard's Portuguese navigator, Magellan, by two and a half centuries. By Cook's time, Spain nominally was still the largest colonial power on Earth, controlling the western and southern parts of North America, Central America, most of South America, the Caribbean, the Philippine Islands, and other islands in the western Pacific. Spain's success as a plunderer was testimony to its brutality and its one-time superiority of sea power. Spanish galleons sailed back and forth between the ports of Acapulco in Mexico and Manila in the Philippines on a route that ran far to the south of Hawai'i. While there is considerable reason to believe that a Spanish galleon had visited Hawai'i prior to Cook, the Spanish made no enduring, repeated contact.[1]

On Cook's first and second voyages, he had discovered and mapped so much of the Pacific, including Australia and New Zealand, that the British Admiralty insisted he undertake a third voyage. In the nineteenth month of his third voyage, in early 1778, Cook for the first time saw the westernmost of the major islands of the archipelago, Kaua'i, rising dreamlike from the sea.

Cook's job was to explore, not conquer. He was the great navigator of his age. He kept an extensive diary, as did at least six other persons on his ship. He mapped. He was a mathematician. He could locate himself in a time-space relationship between the clock that ticked on his ship and the clock that ticked in Greenwich, England. He had a superb artist, James Webber. A surgeon's mate, William Ellis, also drew well. Cook collected material culture, as well as samples of plants. His contact was richly recorded and soon to be repeated. In Western terms, it was the beginning of Hawai'i's history, and it is typically treated as such to this day—the first fundamental clue to the Western process of devaluing an indigenous people.

Trading for metal commenced at a feverish pace. The people of Kaua'i already possessed small artifacts of metal, which presumably had washed up in the wreckage of ships, so they knew how useful it could be. Otherwise, their isolation was such that they had no experience, either genetic or immediate, to prepare them for what lay ahead. The memory of their Polynesian origins survived in their oral traditions, but this memory had to do with oceanic people like themselves—vigorous, healthy people who were remarkably free of disease, people whose idea of warfare was hand-to-hand combat, people attuned to the natural elements who saw themselves as part of a continuum of island and ocean. The practice of long-distance voyaging had ceased several hundred years earlier, and they were well along in the process of creating a united government in the long archipelago that stretched across the central part of the northern Pacific. They had become a world unto themselves.

In the meeting with the chief of Kaua'i, the British unwittingly touched the top of the chief's head. An important taboo had been broken with impunity. Cook's men, despite his injunction against sexual contact, infected the people of Kaua'i with syphilis. When Kauaians crowded around one of Cook's water-gathering parties to continue the trading, the British "were obliged to fire, by which one man was killed." Almost casually, the first life of a native of Hawai'i was taken by means of gunfire—by a controlled explosion of powder that caused a lead projectile to fly forward at a phenomenal speed and considerable accuracy.

Cook sailed north, then returned for the winter to the opposite, easternmost, and largest of the Islands, Hawai'i. He arrived in the aftermath of a battle between the forces of Hawai'i and Maui. At sea, he met the supreme chief of Maui, Kahekili. He then happened upon the fleet of the supreme chief of Hawai'i, Kalani'ōpu'u, and in Kalani'ōpu'u's entourage he met a young war chief named Kamehameha. Kamehameha was six and one half feet tall, and he was renowned for his bravery. He boarded Cook's ship, studied it, and stayed the night. He was aware of the guns that had taken the life of the man on Kaua'i, but this was his first direct exposure to Western technology.

Cook spent six weeks circling the island of Hawai'i. Then he sailed into an astonishing gathering in progress at Kealakekua Bay—the annual celebration of the land's abundance, the *makahiki*, a time for paying tribute to the chiefs, when war ceased and everyday work ceased as well.

Cook's diary suggests how many people there were, and how well they were doing. He described canoes arriving "from all parts so ... there were not fewer than a thousand about the two ships, most of them crowded with people and well laden with hogs and other productions of the islands. All the shore was covered with spectators. Many hundreds were swimming round the ships like shoals of fish." Webber recorded this scene in sketches and a line-drawing. The artist-historian Herb Kawainui Kane has reconstructed the scene in an enormous painting, and of it he says: "The arrival of Cook at Kealakekua Bay was probably the most exciting event of all of Cook's travels. What he encountered was a society in full flower—a healthy, affluent society." Cook's lieutenant described the taro fields as plantations divided by regular ditches. "It appeared hardly possible for the country to be cultivated to greater advantage," he wrote, "or to yield a larger supply of food." As to the quality of workmanship, "In everything manufactured by these people there appears to be an uncommon degree of neatness and ingenuity... a superiority of taste ... " As to the quality of human relationships, one diary said: "We did not hesitate to trust ourselves amongst them at all times and in all situations."

The extensive accounts of the Cook voyage form a window into the state of Hawaiian development in the eighteenth century.

Wherever the British went, they found both the coastal areas and the valleys to be densely populated. The plantations extended far upland. They were well-tended by settlers and governed by a centralized authority. The drawings at Kealakekua show hundreds of people wherever the artist looked. The people in the drawings were robust and athletic. They gave every indication of enjoying themselves immensely. They wore the most beautiful, refined bark cloth in the Pacific. Their chiefs were adorned with feathered capes that their visitors craved. The *makahiki* or festival season, which Cook observed, reflected an abundance that allowed everyone to stop their normal labors for weeks on end. The Hawaiians (and the people of Kaua'i before them) inundated the British with food—eighty hogs at one time, and great mounds of breadfruit, taro, yams, and bananas.

The dwellings of the Hawaiians were handsomely built and well-suited to the environment. Most impressive of all, the Hawaiians possessed thousands of canoes, many of them large, double-hulled canoes joined by platforms. The largest canoes rivaled the British ships in length, and they were faster and more maneuverable. The hulls were rounded to ride high in the water and clear the reefs. Everyone seemed also to have smaller, single-hulled canoes, which they paddled with ease. Otherwise people swam, with women carrying babies and staying for hours in the ocean. The British, who did not swim, were amazed.

Cook stayed for over a month. Finally he sailed, then broke a mast, which forced him to return to Kealakekua Bay. The *makahiki* season was over. In the cycle of gods it was now the time of Kū, god of combat. Relationships were fraying. A longboat was stolen from his ship and broken up for its metal. As Cook had done elsewhere on his voyages, he decided to take a hostage. With a contingent of armed British marines, he attempted to take Kalani'ōpu'u, the highest chief. Cook was threatened with a piece of metal that was mounted on a pole. He fired, causing his marines to also fire, expecting to frighten the Hawaiians away, but to Cook's surprise they stood their ground. Cook fell, along with four of the marines. It is symptomatic of written history that British casualties can be readily recited, while the many dozens of Hawaiian casualties cannot. In retaliation, the British killed and burned, until an uneasy and sad truce was struck.

The Hawaiians and British parted ways, knowing they would meet again. In his last diary entry, Cook had said that of all his discoveries, Hawai'i was the most important. He respected the Hawaiians for what they were, but in the wider world, the power of Britain was such that the Hawaiians would be known not so much in their own right but as the people who had killed the great Cook.

Within Hawaiian society, the havoc resulting from Western contact had been set in motion—the obsession with trading, the stockpiling of metal weapons, the distorting of traditional relationships between chief and commoner, and the bewildering spread of disease. Nonetheless, outward events followed the scenario that had been so long in the making—the pursuit of unifying all the Islands into a single group.

IN THE GENEALOGY THAT LILI'UOKALANI DESCRIBED, the Kona district chief Keaweaheulu was her most important link to the origins of the Hawaiian nation. At the time of Cook's arrival, Keaweaheulu lived on the northern point of Kealakekua Bay. When Cook sailed into Kealakekua, he sailed past Keaweaheulu's compound, and when Cook fell, he died near Keaweaheulu's house. He and three other Kona chiefs subsequently came to greater prominence, when they met to assess their future after the death of Kalani'ōpu'u. Kalani'ōpu'u had left most of his land claims to the son who had the finest genealogy, but he left the care of the war god to Kamehameha. This division of power recurred in Hawaiian society. On one side was the purity of genealogical tradition; on the other side was prowess in battle. The system bowed to genealogy-based tradition while challenging the status quo with new and potentially more vigorous leadership from lower-ranking chiefs. It facilitated the introduction of new blood and new energy. It also made for intrigue.

Keaweaheulu and the other chiefs of Kona, disgruntled by the division of land, enticed Kamehameha to join their cause. While his genealogy was not the highest, he was a phenomenon on the field of battle. In a society of great warriors, he was to be renowned as the greatest warrior. A long, uneven war ensued that was to become the basis of the Hawaiian nation. It began as a localized conflict on the island of Hawai'i over claims to the six districts. It evolved into a war to reunify the island as 'Umi originally had unified it, and it continued on as an interisland war of conquest. As one of the Kona chiefs, Keaweaheulu was a key member of Kamehameha's forces, and he played an integral part in winning the war.

Keaweaheulu and the other three Kona chiefs were called the Kona uncles. They were given choice tracts of land by Kamehameha on each of the islands they conquered. Keaweaheulu's lands included beautiful tracts on the windward side of O'ahu, at Ka'a'awa and also at Punalu'u near Kualoa, where the bones of high chiefs of ancient O'ahu were hidden. In making this grant of land, Kamehameha departed from tradition by assigning Keaweaheulu the right to pass his lands on to his children.[2] In the view of Dr. Lilikalā Kame'eleihiwa, the native nationalist scholar, "By doing so, he effectively shared his sovereign rights with these four Ali'i Nui ... "[3] Lili'uokalani, mindful of her family's claims, described Keaweaheulu as not only Kamehameha's chief counselor but "the founder of the dynasty."[4]

KAMEHAMEHA I HAD QUICKLY GRASPED the importance of Western technology. He had boarded Cook's ship and stayed the night. When the British retaliated, he had learned about the devastating power of guns. He had begun his career as a trader by dealing for spikes that made good knives. He quickly advanced to trading for muskets and cannon, which would forever alter the nature of indigenous warfare. Within his expanding domain, he reserved the right to control all trade with foreigners. He controlled the freshwater sources, the salt supply, and the surplus supply of food. His huge fields produced storehouses of taro, yams, bananas, fish, chickens, pigs, and goats.

He also became friends with Captain George Vancouver, who had sailed with Cook, and who returned after a fourteen-year absence to affirm Britain's interest in Hawai'i. Vancouver was keenly interested in the possibilities of the archipelago and visited each of the major islands on three occasions, in 1792, 1793, and 1794. By the time of Vancouver's 1792 visit, Kamehameha dominated Hawai'i Island. On the other end of the group, Kaua'i was under the control of an independent-minded young chief named Kaumuali'i. The islands in between, including O'ahu, were controlled by the aged but still-vigorous chief of Maui, Kahekili.

Vancouver went from one center of power to the next, attempting to make peace. As a result, he left behind a record of the geopolitical conflicts that were occurring within the island group, making observations that were distinctly more perceptive in political terms than Cook's. "Vancouver," Kamakau wrote, "was the friend of every chief and of every government."[5] When Kamehameha sought to trade for weapons, Vancouver is said to have replied, "It is not right to sell things for killing people." Since a major endeavor of the time was the transfer of lethal firepower from Western traders to the contending kingdoms, this was a lofty sentiment, but nonetheless one that Vancouver repeated with variation and apparent conviction.

At Kealakekua Bay, he observed the large number of chiefs who had pledged loyalty to Kamehameha, the size of their armies, and the depth of their assets—everything from the size of their fields to their canoe fleets and their growing arsenals of firearms. Thereafter, Vancouver attempted to tell Kahekili of Maui that Kamehameha had a following of many chiefs. In his broken Hawaiian, he referred to Kamehameha as *nuinui ali'i*, a great chief. Kahekili was contemptuous. "Kamehameha has come up from nothing," he announced. "I am a great chief."

On Kaua'i, Vancouver gave the name of the king of England, King George, to Kaumuali'i, but it was for Kamehameha that he reserved the most serious conversations. Vancouver's stories suggest a self-confidence on Kamehameha's part that was tempered by an appreciation for Britain's power.

Vancouver addressed Kamehameha's habit of worshipping his gods each morning and evening, arguing that Kamehameha's wooden images were not the true god. "The true God," Vancouver said, "is in heaven." He offered to ask King George to send missionaries to teach the lessons of the true God, but Kamehameha replied, "These are my gods, they are gods with *mana*; through them I gained control of the government and became supreme chief."[6] While Kamehameha was closed to outsiders meddling with his religion, he was agreeable to a treaty—proposed by Vancouver—to make his domain a protectorate of Great Britain. Kamehameha sent lavish presents to King George, including feather capes, royal standards, feather lei, and helmets. Long after, he believed in the existence of a special relationship with Great Britain, but in fact the Vancouver treaty was only a draft, and it was rejected by the British government.

When Vancouver had urged peace among the chiefs, Kamehameha made no reply. In fact, Kamehameha was engaged in elaborate preparations for a long interisland campaign. He had built up his plantations and stockpiled food. He had built up his armaments and his fleet, until it included a thousand canoes and the first of his many Western ships. He completed the Pu'ukoholā Heiau, which he dedicated to his war god. It is an elegant structure overlooking the Kona Coast of Hawai'i Island that has been restored to perfect condition.

In 1794, Kamehameha embarked on his great rampage. He defeated the armies of Maui not once but twice,[7] camped at length on Moloka'i, then sailed for O'ahu. His canoes covered the beaches from Wai'alae, around Diamond Head Crater, through Waikīkī. He fielded an army of sixteen thousand men, defeating an opposing force of nine thousand. With his victory, the last great battle of the war of unification was over.

Kamehameha I ruled the kingdom from 1795 until his death in 1819. His Kona uncle, Keaweaheulu, the grandfather of Lili'uokalani's grandfather, enjoyed the spoils of war for less time than he had warred. He died in the plague of 1804 at Ka'a'awa, his new place on the windward shore of O'ahu. After his death, his son, Nāihe, took on a prominent role. Lili'uokalani described Nāihe as the great orator of Kamehameha's reign. Certainly he was a favorite of the court until Kamehameha's passing. Nāihe died in 1831 at his father's compound at Ka'awaloa, where Cook had died. Nāihe's son, 'Aikanaka, was in charge of a garrison and gun battery at Punchbowl Crater overlooking Honolulu Harbor. These guns, Lili'uokalani made a point of saying, had been moved to O'ahu from Hawai'i Island—presumably as history pieces from the war of unification. 'Aikanaka's daughter, Keohokalole, was a counselor to the long-reigning Kamehameha III. With the onset of Western landownership, she was given many tracts of land. Her marriage to another chief, Kapa'akea, brought forth David Kalākaua and then, on September 2, 1838, Lydia Kamaka'eha, who was to become known as Lili'uokalani, Her Royal Highness, Queen of Hawai'i.

Immediately Lili'uokalani was wrapped in fine soft *kapa* cloth, as was appropriate to a person of rank. In the Hawaiian tradition, she was adopted by a granddaughter of Kamehameha.[8] At the age of four, she was carried by a servant to the Chief's Children's School, where she and her brother, David, were surrounded by offspring of the mighty Kamehameha clan. Altogether four of these students were to become kings, and Lili'uokalani was to become queen. The two families, then, were locked together—sometimes uncomfortably— first by the interisland war, second in distributions of land, third through participation in the early days of Western education, and finally by the challenge of trying to perpetuate the indigenous government of Hawai'i.

Theodore Roosevelt, Jr.

CHAPTER FOUR

Roosevelt's Frontier

The closest Teddy Roosevelt came to intimacy with the sea was rowing his boat at the family's summer house at Oyster Bay on Long Island, New York. Nonetheless, as a student at Harvard he reached back into the American experience and seized, almost prophetically, on an obscure war that was fought to a great extent at sea, the War of 1812. One of his biographers, Nathan Miller, wrote that Roosevelt was browsing in the Harvard library when he came upon a naval history written from a British point of view. Aroused by its "bombastic anti-Yankee tone," he resolved to write "an accurate and objective history of his own."[1] By graduation, he had written two chapters. While he was a law student at Columbia, he expanded his earlier work into a full-blown book, *The Naval War of 1812*. It was published when he was twenty-three and was the first of his thirty-eight books.

The War of 1812 was a lesson to America of what the Hawaiians had learned from bitter experience at Kealakekua—that the British did not suffer setbacks lightly. As they had sacked and burned at Kealakekua in 1779 after Cook's death, they sacked and burned Washington in 1812. "Had we been as roughly handled on water as we were on land during the first year of the war," wrote Roosevelt, "such a succession of disasters would have had a most demoralizing effect on the nation at large." By a rigorous analysis of naval battles, Roosevelt determined that the American navy, although small, had performed better against the celebrated British navy than had the navies of the continental European powers. He analyzed the sailing and fighting skills of the men aboard, their comparative training and marksmanship, the effect of different guns, the qualities of fighting ships, their maneuverability, and their durability under fire. The breezier passages celebrated the "American Jack" as the finest of all sailors. In a ranking of sailors by national origin, he reflected the Social Darwinism he had been taught at Columbia, describing the British as being nearly as good as the Americans, while Italians and Portuguese were lesser sailors and quick to draw knives in the event of a brawl.

Roosevelt's book was embraced as the definitive history of the naval aspects of the war. To this day, it is a basic text. Its essential point was that America needed to reverse the long-term deterioration of its navy and invest in first-rate ships. *The Naval War* played to a public that was engaged in transition. America was recovering from the Civil War and looking around for renewed challenges. Its ships were made of wood and propelled by sail, but the age of steel and steam had arrived. Within a few years, Navy Secretary B.F. Tracy would rate America's navy as being somewhere below the top ten in the world. America had a distinctly second-rate navy, but wanted to be first-rate in all the obvious ways. In 1881, a naval advisory board raised the alarm, pressing for the construction of steel ships, and Roosevelt's book was published the following year.

Harper's Magazine said *The Naval War* was not only accurate but intrepid. *The New York Times* proclaimed Roosevelt a promising young historian. The U.S. navy used the book as a text at the Naval War College and put copies on all its ships. As a result, Roosevelt gained a special niche in American public life at an amazingly young age. He had qualified himself to both credibly discuss and confidently create naval policy, and from this point on it was as if he were waiting for the country to catch up.

In the lag between his own discoveries and America's discovery of its inferior navy, he digressed in an uncanny way through the American continent. This story likewise begins during his days at Harvard. He fell wildly in love, and not long after graduation, he married. He dashed around New York society with his bride, wrote his naval history, and studied law at Columbia University, all at once. With his book in galley form, he stood for election to the New York assembly. On election day, he voted, then returned to his writing while his campaign workers turned out the vote. He won by a more than two to one margin, finished the book, and went off to the statehouse in Albany. There he quickly rose to the leadership of the Republican minority.

With his wife, Alice, four months' pregnant, he went off to hunt buffalo in the Dakota Territory. He was enthralled by the West and invested family money in a pair of ranches on the Little Missouri River. He returned home and was reelected easily. He was in Albany when news came of the birth of his daughter. This was immediately followed by word that Alice was experiencing kidney failure, and that his mother was dying. He rushed home and found his Alice in an upstairs bedroom, declining rapidly. His mother died in a downstairs bedroom, where his father had died. Roosevelt returned to Alice and held her, and on the next day, which was Valentine's Day, the fourth anniversary of their engagement, she died at the age of twenty-two. Roosevelt wrote in his diary, "The light has gone out of my life."

He returned to his ranches in what he described as "a land of vast silent spaces, of lonely rivers, and of plains where the wild game stared at the passing horseman." He wrote about working in the scorching sun and living a free and hardy life. He saw "men die violent deaths as they worked among the horses and cattle, or fought in evil feuds." As a boy he had been a precocious naturalist. Now he catalogued the animals he shot—buffalo, elk, antelope, deer, grouse, and ducks. At night he wrapped himself in buffalo hides and bear skins. He made friends. The cowpunchers were "lean, sinewy fellows, accustomed to riding half-broken horses, at any speed, over any country, by day or by night." He spoke warmly of "these old friends of the cattle ranches and the cow camps—the men with whom I had ridden the long circle." He made acquaintances among gunmen as well. Some enforced the law, while others lived on its edge. Among his friends he counted Pat Garrett, who was to shoot Billy the Kid. Roosevelt himself became a deputy sheriff. In his autobiography he gave a capsule inventory of his rough acquaintances, in whom he took such an obvious pride: "I made up my mind that the men were of just the kind whom it would be well to have with me if ever it became necessary to go to war."

In truth, Roosevelt's brief but well-publicized residence in Dakota Territory was as a denizen of a shrinking pocket of the frontier, but the persona of the cowboy, the rider, became an integral part of his identity. He talked romantically about the homesteaders breaking up the ranches. The sodbusters were to the good of the country, he said, but they damaged the interest of real ranchers such as himself.

"It was right and necessary that this life should pass," Roosevelt wrote, "for the safety of our country lies in its being made the country of the small homemaker." And so the West was "gone now, 'gone, gone with lost Atlantis, gone to the isle of ghosts and of strange dead memories.'"[2]

The timing of Roosevelt's search for solace enabled him to not only grasp, but to symbolize, the American sense of loss at the closing of the frontier. When he returned, rejuvenated, to the city, he was photographed in buckskin with a rifle that seemed longer than he was tall. He wrote a widely read series of books, *The Winning of the West*. As his *Naval War* was to become a companion to American treatises on sea power, his *Winning of the West* became a companion to the work of Frederick Jackson Turner, the dominant American historian of his age. Turner said Roosevelt depicted America's expansion "as probably no other man of his time could have done."[3] Turner was to talk about Roosevelt through his long and influential academic life, referring to him in his first major essay, *The Significance of the Frontier*,[4] as well as in his last major address. Turner understood that the energy Americans had poured into the frontier would be transferred to some wider sphere. "He would be a rash prophet," wrote Turner, "who should assert that the expansive character of American life has now entirely ceased. Movement has been its dominant fact, and, unless this training has no effect upon a people, the American energy will continually demand a wide field for its exercise."[5]

While Turner's theme of the frontier is remembered today, the racial content of Roosevelt's work—which stressed the nature of the white triumph over the Indian—is conveniently forgotten. "Success is for a mighty race," he wrote, "in its vigorous and masterful prime." He runs on: "If a race is weak, if it is lacking in the physical and moral traits which go to the makeup of a conquering people, it cannot succeed."[6] Even strong races usually fail to seize the moment of conquest, he argued, unless the right leader came along to fulfill their destiny. "Only the most farseeing and high-minded statesmen can grasp the real weight, from the race-standpoint, of the possibilities which to the men of their day seem so trivial."

Queen Lili'uokalani of Hawai'i

CHAPTER FIVE

The Queen's Dilemma

When American marines came off their ship in 1893, their nominal mission was to protect the American consulate and legation. Actually, only a few of the troops peeled off to cover those buildings. The rest set up across from 'Iolani Palace, which was the center of the government of Hawai'i. The American soldiers' camp was even closer to the second most important building, which was called Ali'iolani Hale, the house of the chiefs of heaven,[1] or what the *haole* would call the legislative building. Together these two structures symbolized the sovereignty of the Kingdom of Hawai'i. Knowing the American minister John Stevens's intense antagonism for the continuation of the Kingdom, Lili'uokalani easily could have assumed that the American troops would protect the American residents of Honolulu in whatever they did. What she did not know was that John Stevens had told Lorrin Thurston that he would recognize whoever occupied the government buildings as the legitimate government of Hawai'i.

The queen had two obvious choices and one not-so-obvious choice. One of her obvious choices was to ritually spill blood. She could start with a small royal guard. She also had over two hundred armed men under the command of her marshal, the Tahitian C.B. Wilson. The Hawaiian population, which was at an eight-hundred-year low, had several hundred arms scattered about the island, although many of their guns must have been muskets that dated to the time of Keaweaheulu. If everything worked, the flint fired the powder. The iron ball flew out of the unrifled barrel. Precise control of the explosion was uncertain, and the lack of spin on the projectile meant that it strayed in a short distance off the marksman's intended course.

The comparative superiority of *haole* armaments has never really been documented. Most elementally, it is important that the *haole* militia were armed with rifles, not muskets. They also had repeating machine guns capable of controlling an entire field of fire, and they possessed cannon as well. They were well-trained. In 1887 the *haole* militia had emerged as the strongest military force in Hawai'i, and to it had been added the American ship of war, the S.S. *Boston*, and its troops. One writer inventoried the firepower of the marines as follows: On board the *Boston*, a combination of eight-inch and twenty-six-inch cannon with 174 cannon shells; ashore, 162 armed men equipped with fourteen thousand rounds of rifle ammunition and twelve thousand rounds of pistol ammunition.[2]

Several times previously, the Hawaiians had faced the issue of fighting bands of Westerners, or the armed forces of Western nations. When Cook kidnapped their chief in 1779, to Cook's surprise they stood against the exploding guns and defended their chief. They took heavy losses, and their villages at Kealakekua were burned, but they killed Cook and several of his men and prevented the kidnapping of their chief. On a second occasion, an American trader heinously slaughtered over a hundred Hawaiians who had come out to trade off the coast of Maui. He then whipped a high chief of the island of Hawai'i with a rope. The chief, Kame'eiamoku, happened to be one of Kamehameha's famous four uncles. In retaliation, he jumped the next ship that came along, killing several sailors as well as the young captain, who by chance was the son of the offending trader. In the process, a British sailor, John Young, was detained from the murderous trader's ship. An American, Isaac Davis, was spared in the battle with the small crew of the son's ship. Young, Davis, a cannon, powder, and cannon balls were all taken to Kamehameha. The two *haole* became Kamehameha's enthusiastic military advisers. The ship, its supplies, and the expert gunners became the catalyst for Kamehameha's rampage. But in general Kamehameha pursued a strategy of avoiding armed conflict with foreigners. He provided them with safe ports and then engaged them in trade.

Ship captains sometimes complained that Kamehameha controlled everything and drove a hard bargain, but he was both predictable and trustworthy. In the aftermath of his interisland military victories, he was known as *Ka Napoleana*, the Napolean of the Pacific. He was an enormously powerful and athletic man, and he had confidence in both himself and his armies. The longer he traded, the more he acquired. He came to possess an entire fleet of Western ships, and he also developed a new double-hulled canoe design, equipped with swivel guns on the bow. These augmented his preexisting fleet of over one thousand large canoes. He also had a large collection of cannon and thousands of rifles and pistols.

He made selective use of forts, a fact that contradicts the romantic but erroneous contention that Hawaiians always engaged one another hand-to-hand in the open, with a minimum of bloodshed. If the image of ritual battle is picturesque, it also supposes that Hawaiians were unthinking, because forts can be an essential feature of maintaining control of a given terrain. It is true the geography of Hawai'i militated against making a huge investment in fortifications because, as Kalaunui had first demonstrated in the fourteenth century, the coastlines are long, irregular, and either difficult or impossible to protect against landings by armies in fast-moving canoes. However, there were instances in which geography combined with history, and forts played a significant part in interisland warfare. Kalākaua's book told the story of a noble chief of Moloka'i in the eleventh century who was irked by the incursion of voyaging Polynesian chiefs from islands to the south. He built a fort in a natural redoubt on the north shore of Moloka'i, which is the fifth largest island of the group and lies between O'ahu and Maui. He fortified one of the smaller valleys in such a way that several thousand warriors could be withdrawn to the fort. Their canoes could be snatched from the rough sea that breaks against Moloka'i's shore and hoisted safely inside the fort. Using his ingenious fort as a base, the Moloka'i chief raided the crass newcomers all the way from Hawai'i to Kaua'i.

The most famous fort in early Western time dominated the little half-moon Hāna Bay on the far end of Maui, across the channel from Hawai'i Island. The fort at Hāna was held by the Hawai'i islanders during their colonization of the Maui kingdom, and the warrior-king of Maui, Kahekili, paid a bloody price to regain control of it. Kamehameha, as a result of the Hawaiians' frequent wars with Maui, was keenly aware of this fortification.

When Cook's ship visited Hawai'i, the surgeon's mate, William Ellis, drew the wall of an ancient fort. An ancient temple downhill from Kamehameha's new temple at Kawaihae Bay likewise was transformed into a gun emplacement and armed with cannon.

These examples of fortifications are background to the issue the Hawaiian chiefs faced constantly. How were they to discourage the aggressive Westerners from taking over? The story of the recurring conflict between Kamehameha and the king of Kaua'i, Kaumuali'i, illuminates this issue, as well as the role forts played in it. By 1795, Kamehameha controlled the islands from Hawai'i to O'ahu, but the kingdom of Kaumuali'i lay beyond his grasp. He planned to correct this by invading Kaua'i. His fleet set out across the channel to Kaua'i, but was battered by a storm, took heavy losses, and turned back. On Kaua'i to this day, there is a story that Kamehameha actually landed on Kaua'i but was routed. A second invasion was organized. Edward Joesting, in his excellent book, *Kaua'i, A Separate Kingdom*, inventoried the size of Kamehameha's second force. It contained seven thousand Hawaiian men and fifty Europeans, almost all of them armed with muskets. They were also armed with eight cannon, forty swivel guns, and six mortars. The men and their weaponry were transported by twenty-one armed schooners in addition to a vast flotilla of canoes. This second invasion also was frustrated, this time by the deadly 1804 epidemic that took the life of Lili'uokalani's ancestor, Keaweaheulu.

Despite the frustration, Kamehameha was *Ka Napoleona*, the great conqueror, while Kaumuali'i was the king of a small domain to the leeward. The sense of Kaua'i not being as thoroughly "Hawaiian" survives in many ways on the Kaua'i of today. Some of the stonework on Kaua'i is distinctly different. Poi pounders have ringed handles. Images of gods are highly distinctive. Finally, the Kaua'i Museum celebrates not Kamehameha but Kaumuali'i. Unlike most of the chiefs from the time of early contact, Kaumuali'i was not sketched or painted. No image survives, but he is repeatedly described as a handsome gentleman and a fine dresser. He learned to read and write English and handled his own correspondence, examples of which survive. Western traders brought him news of Kamehameha, including the news that

Kamehameha's army had been laid low by epidemic. They also brought threatening messages to the effect that he had best subordinate himself to the Kingdom.

In 1810, in the fifteenth year of the Kingdom, Kaumuali'i ritually capitulated. He sailed to Honolulu and met the great king of Hawai'i in the harbor. "Here I am," Kaumuali'i said. "Is it face up or face down?" Was he to live? Kamehameha shrugged off the question. Kaumuali'i made a grand statement. "This is my gift at our meeting," he said, "the land of Kaua'i, its chiefs, its men great and small, from mountain to sea, all above and below, and myself to be yours."

Kamehameha replied: "I shall not accept your land, not the least portion of your domain. Return and rule over it." He asked only that if his son, Liholiho, visited Kaua'i, Kaumuali'i should receive him kindly—a fateful little request, as things were to turn out.

"We have met and I am now returning," Kaumuali'i said, suggesting an interest in an early departure. Kamehameha said he must come ashore. Kaumuali'i did so. While ashore, Kaumuali'i was warned by Kamehameha's *haole* lieutenant, Isaac Davis, to beware a plot of the chiefs—unnamed—to poison him. It is not recorded how well Kaumuali'i ate or drank after Davis' warning, but it is known that he was allowed to return to his island chiefdom. He was to live to old age, but within a few weeks Davis was dead, apparently poisoned.

After the nominal inclusion of Kaua'i in the Kingdom, Kamehameha wrote a letter to King George of England, saying that all ports of Hawai'i, from windward to leeward, were secure and open to the ships of his majesty.

Kaumuali'i, despite his statement of allegiance to the Kingdom of Hawai'i, began to look around for a countervailing alliance. Perhaps he was a compulsive maneuverer. Possibly he could not abide the idea of Kamehameha being above him. Perhaps he wanted to keep Kamehameha on the O'ahu side of the channel and prevent a real invasion and a redistribution of his lands. Kaumuali'i would have immediately discarded the British from his list of possible allies, because they were allied with Kamehameha. The American traders sailed the seas making deals without an apparent national strategy. But a third power, Russia, had consistently shown more than a passing interest in Hawai'i.

Russians were organized in the Pacific through the Russian American Company, which was chartered by the Russian government. The headquarters of the company was in Sitka, Alaska, where the Russians eagerly dealt in furs. They were creating a colonial ownership of Alaska, and in the early 1800s it occurred to the Russian American Company to also create a settlement in Hawai'i. The company's agents had made glowing reports of how much food could be grown in Hawai'i, and to this soon would be added the interconnection of the Pacific Northwest fur trade and the Hawaiian sandalwood trade.

The world was becoming increasingly complicated. Two years after Kaumuali'i met Kamehameha in Honolulu, the British undertook to thrash the Americans in the war that Theodore Roosevelt was to write about as a precocious young author. As a result of the War of 1812, American trading ships laid low in the Pacific to avoid British warships. With the British and Americans preoccupied by their conflict, Russians appeared in the Hawaiian Islands with increasing frequency. They began to think about Hawai'i as more than a stopover. In 1814, Kaumuali'i, four years after swearing allegiance to Kamehameha, provisioned Russian ships at Kaua'i in return for guns. In 1815, a Russian ship loaded with fur and other valuables was blown aground at the mouth of the Waimea River, the southern compound of the great chiefs of Kaua'i. Conveniently for Kaumuali'i, the ship practically rolled over into the entryway of his chiefly estate.

The head of the Russian American Company, Alexander Baranov, believed a problem was an opportunity. He thought the cargo might lead to Russia establishing its colony in the Hawaiian Islands. He sent a medical doctor, Georg Scheffer, to retrieve the goods. Scheffer's orders were to make friends with King Kamehameha, who was by then sixty-seven or so years old. He had been at war for roughly three decades. He had sustained injuries, probably many injuries, in combat. He had contracted but survived the virulent plague that had killed his Kona uncles in 1804. He was immensely famous and wealthy, and he was in the market for a new doctor.

Scheffer wrote a glowing report, saying he had treated Kamehameha for heart trouble, and that he had cured Kamehameha's wife, Ka'ahumanu, of yellow fever. In conversation with Scheffer,

Kamehameha asked, "Will the Russians come and fight?" Kamehameha had divined that the Russians had a recurring interest in colonizing Hawai'i. One of their agents had told the Russian American Company they could take the Islands. Baranov had written a letter to Kamehameha laying out his demands for return of the cargo on Kaua'i. If Kaumuali'i did not deliver the contents of the shipwreck, he said, "I shall be obliged to take measures myself in order to obtain just satisfaction and, with your permission, I shall treat him as an enemy." Baranov was walking an irregular line, alluding to Kaua'i as part of the Kingdom on the one hand, threatening violence against Kamehameha's nominal subordinate on the other.

Scheffer's job was to enlist Kamehameha in the cause of Russia. Kamehameha sidestepped. He gave Scheffer land on O'ahu, but refused to sail to Kaua'i. Scheffer sailed to Kaua'i himself. He was a schemer, and on Kaua'i he must have quickly concluded that he should have been talking with Kaumuali'i all along, because Kaumuali'i wanted to make a deal. In the Russians, Kaumuali'i had found his countervailing force.

Scheffer pledged to protect Kaumuali'i militarily and help him develop a navy, starting with a fine Russian ship. Kaumuali'i in turn pledged allegiance to Russia. Together they laid a plan to fortify Kaua'i and invade the islands of O'ahu, Moloka'i, Lāna'i, and Maui—in essence to drive the Hawaiians back to Hawai'i Island, from which they had come. Meanwhile, the ambitious Baranov was attempting to stage-manage events at a distance. At one point he ordered ships to prepare for a possible conquest of the Hawaiian Islands in the name of the emperor of "all the Russias," as he grandly phrased it.

Scheffer overreached. A contingent of Russian soldiers began building a small fort, or blockhouse, near Honolulu Harbor on O'ahu. On the north side of Kaua'i, Scheffer and Kaumuali'i built two earthen forts overlooking the Hanalei River. On the south side of Kaua'i, they built Fort Elizabeth, named in honor of the empress of Russia. It was in the shape of a five-pointed star, and its ruins—the Russian Fort—stand today on the banks of the Waimea River, where the Russian cargo ship was wrecked, and also where Cook had made his first contact in 1778.

While the Russian Fort was being built, yet another Russian ship anchored in the bay at Kailua-Kona on Hawai'i, where Kamehameha now resided. Kamehameha continued to fear a Russian invasion, but he agreed to sit while the ship's artist, Louis Choris, painted his portrait. During the sitting, he asked Choris for news of Kaua'i. What were the Russians doing with Kaumuali'i?

Choris must have drawn and painted furiously. He not only created the original firsthand image of Kamehameha, but also the most extensive visual record of the Hawaiians since James Webber had sailed with Cook thirty-eight years before. Occasionally Choris's brilliant drawings and paintings show groups of vigorous, beautifully formed people, as Webber had, but mostly Choris portrayed the chiefs and chiefesses. The *ali'i* cut brilliant figures, but the sense of the enormous numbers of people that Webber had captured was greatly diminished. In reality the population already had been reduced by at least half, mostly as a result of disease. The aging Kamehameha managed ably, maintaining his government and his military force, but he worried.

The Russian captain sailed away. He had probably deduced that Kamehameha was still very much in control of the Hawaiian Islands. He avoided Scheffer's eccentric operation on Kaua'i, and subsequently the Russian American Company refused to honor Scheffer's promised payment of naval vessels to Kaumuali'i. Kaumuali'i turned on Scheffer and ran him off.

Joesting contends, "The events of 1816-1817 should be known as the adventures of Georg Scheffer in Hawai'i and not as the work of the Russian government." It is an analysis that fits to a great extent with the way Native Hawaiians were to experience the aggressive behavior of foreigners. The person at hand might be mad, but their distant nation maintained a more stable and seemingly more principled course.

While the memory of Scheffer was fading, something extraordinary occurred at Honolulu Harbor on O'ahu. From the beginning, John Young had been suspicious of the Russians, suspicious of Scheffer, and suspicious of Scheffer's medical treatment of the great *mō'ī* and the *ali'i*. By this time John Young was a high chief of the Kingdom that had gently detained him, and Isaac Davis was in his grave. Young fueled suspicions against the Russian presence. With instructions from Kamehameha to fight if necessary, he and the war chief Kalanimoku took a contingent of Hawaiians to Honolulu to deal with the Russian blockhouse. The Russians awoke one morning to find themselves surrounded by heavily armed Hawaiians. They were allowed to leave peaceably. Their fort was torn down. For good measure, Kalanimoku burned down a warehouse on the waterfront filled with Scheffer's goods.

The Russian threat to Hawai'i's sovereignty passed into history, but Kalanimoku's work had just begun. To secure Honolulu Harbor, he built—at Kamehameha's direction—an enormous fort where the Russian blockhouse had stood. The Fort of Honolulu was located on the east side of the deep-water channel through the reef that allowed access to the harbor. The fort was 360 feet long from the ocean to the mountain side and 300 feet wide. The walls were a minimum of twelve feet high and twenty feet thick at the base. The outside and inside walls were made of cut coral block, and the interior was filled with rubble, dirt, and stone. It touched the water's edge, and the ocean side curved out into the sea. Cannon sat in notches in the wall along the arc, pointing at the arriving and departing ships.

If Kaumuali'i's fort at the Waimea River did not really address the issue of maintaining strategic control of Kaua'i, the Fort of Honolulu came much closer to controlling Honolulu Harbor, which was the most strategic feature of the Kingdom. To clear the narrow front channel, ships had to be towed into Honolulu Harbor by hand. Initially hundreds of Hawaiians assembled on shore for this job. Subsequently, oxen were used. The boats crept in under the range of the cannon. Clearly, for a time, the fort dominated what was not only the main commercial port, but the seat of government and the main urban center.

The Fort of Honolulu was yet another instance of the story of the Hawaiians being forgotten. In the early statehood period, the history of the fort was virtually unknown. In 1975, as interest in the Hawaiian past was being renewed, a book was published on the palaces and forts of the Kingdom.[3] Today the fort is not as unknown as it was, but the majority of Hawai'i's people, including Native Hawaiians, still know nothing of it. When the Aloha Tower area of the Honolulu waterfront was redeveloped in the early 1990s, the existence and location of the fort remained unmarked. The nominally historic theme

Hawaiians at the Fort of Honolulu (Drawing by Louis Choris.)

of the redevelopment was Boat Days, which harked to the time when wealthy *haole* arrived by ocean liner, when the band played, streamers flew, and dark-skinned males dove for coins in the water. A small scale model of the fort is on display at the nearby Hawai'i Maritime Center. A partial wall, made of the coral blocks of the fort, lies in the water unseen, a few feet from the traffic on Nimitz Highway. The uppermost of the coral slabs of the fort reemerges at low tide, and the black *'a'ama* crab sit on the wall and bathe in the sun.

Numerous sketches and paintings of the fort survive. Louis Choris produced a superb drawing of a waterfront scene that included the fort, documenting how quickly it was built. Detailed paintings were made of the interior of the fort. A lithograph exists of the wall and gate on the mountain side. The huge double gates opened onto what is today the intersection of Queen and Fort Streets, in the center of the business district of Honolulu.

A gun battery that was an adjunct to the fort was developed on Punchbowl Crater overlooking the harbor. It was in front of what is today the famous Punchbowl National Cemetery, the burial place of the dead from the Pacific War.

LILI'UOKALANI CAME OF AGE when the fort was a major center of activity in Honolulu. There was an odd, sad family connection. Her biological mother's father, Kamanawa, was convicted of poisoning his wife. Kamanawa was the grandson of the man of the same name who was one of Kamehameha's four uncles, along with Keaweaheulu. For his crime, the younger Kamanawa was hanged to death from gallows built into the parapet of the fort.

Lili'uokalani's biological grandfather on her father's side, 'Aikanaka, was the grandson of Keaweaheulu. 'Aikanaka was in charge of the gun battery on Punchbowl, which she knew by its original name, Pūowaina. As the American troops took up their positions in front of 'Iolani Palace and set up their guns on January 17, 1893, the queen might have thought of her ancestors. Perhaps she thought about 'Aikanaka and the guns of his battery, which had been imported from the island of Hawai'i. Perhaps she thought of the fort, and the way it once had served as a bulwark against the uncontrolled comings and goings of foreigners.

Kamehameha himself had served as a bulwark, even in his old age, as his meetings with the Russians in 1816 illustrated. He died of natural causes at Kailua-Kona in 1819 at the approximate age of seventy-one. Today he is represented by the statue that stands in front of Ali'iolani Hale. A duplicate is in the statuary hall in the rotunda of the American Capitol in Washington, D.C. The highway around O'ahu is named for Kamehameha, and Kamehameha Day is celebrated each June 11. The Hawaiian writer Malcolm Naea Chun, in describing the monarchs, conjured the question that Hawaiians of the sovereignty movement sometimes discuss today: "Perhaps during a night that is very rainy, when there is thunder and lightning, in what the people of old called 'Ikuwā, the season of the roaring surf, thunder and cloudbursts, the din and voices of the gods in the elements, another child will be born to the hushed whispers of, 'Is this the one? Is this the next Kamehameha?'"

IN THE ONGOING REWORKING of Hawaiian figures, a new feminist approach to history has caught up with the memory of Lili'uokalani. A contrast has been drawn between the ferocity of Ka'ahumanu, the favorite of Kamehameha's many wives, and the relative passivity of Lili'uokalani. It is true that Ka'ahumanu was something of a terror. After her husband's death, she tattooed his name on the inside of her biceps. She abandoned the ancient religion. She broke the *kapu* that forbade men and women from eating together. '*Ai noa*, free eating, symbolized the destruction of discipline and defiance of the ancient system. In a colossal coincidence of timing, the Protestant missionaries arrived six months after the breaking of the *kapu*. Ka'ahumanu progressed from eager student of reading and writing to Christian convert. She proclaimed the religion of the powerful Westerners as the religion of the nation. As she went, she positioned her family members, who were Maui chiefs, in high places in the government.

She also got Kamehameha II to sail to Kaua'i to set matters straight with Kaumuali'i. When the younger Kamehameha arrived on Kaua'i, Kaumuali'i greeted him warmly, as he had promised Kamehameha he would. He recalled his meeting with the king in Honolulu Harbor, and, in a replay of his speech in Honolulu, said, "You are his rightful successor, and you are my king!" He described his fort, guns, and abundance of muskets. "All are yours," he said.

Liholiho replied, "Kaumuali'i, I have not come to take your island." The two went off on a tour of Kaua'i for forty-two days. Kamehameha II took the handsome gentleman for a ride on his new yacht, but failed to return him to the shores of Kaua'i. Kaumuali'i was coerced into serving as Ka'ahumanu's husband for the duration of his life. He died on O'ahu and was entombed in Lāhainā, on Maui. The largest letters on his tomb spelled the name of his spouse, Ka'ahumanu.

One of Kaumuali'i's sons likewise was forced into marriage with Ka'ahumanu. A second son of Kaumuali'i rose up in revolt on Kaua'i and fought an expeditionary force of the Kingdom in the vicinity of the Russian Fort. The famous missionary Hiram Bingham was living there. He ran out of his house in time to hear one of the rebels yell from the top of the wall, in a burst of optimism, "The Hawaiians are beaten—the Kauaians have the fort!" In the aftermath of their defeat, the aristocracy of Kaua'i was scattered throughout the Islands, and their lands were redistributed to adherents of the conquering Kingdom, which prominently featured the family of Ka'ahumanu.

If Ka'ahumanu eventually became a devout Christian, she also was a fighter and a conqueror. It is perhaps true that with the passage of time Lili'uokalani had absorbed the Christian taboo against women being warriors. Perhaps she abhorred the shedding of blood, but a battle in 1893 would at most have been a ritualized sacrifice of native soldiers, for it was as Lili'uokalani said, the Hawaiians had no arms of consequence, and the whites were armed to the teeth. Lili'uokalani discarded her obvious options, which were to fight or surrender, and seized on a third. It was a less obvious but more ingenious option, and it was conditioned by an elaborate history that was influenced not only by Britain and Russia, but by France and, increasingly, by America.

CHAPTER SIX

American Expansionism

If Thomas Jefferson had lived another century, he would have been startled to learn what Theodore Roosevelt thought of him. Roosevelt wrote in his *Naval War of 1812* that Jefferson was "perhaps the most incapable Executive that ever filled the presidential chair."[1] Roosevelt said it would be difficult to imagine a man "less fit to guide the state with honor and safety through the stormy times that marked the opening of the present century." Rather than build up the navy and prepare for a second war with the British, Jefferson, along with his successor, James Madison, who oversaw the defeat in the War of 1812, had pursued a continental vision of the country.

In 1803 Jefferson paid eighty million francs to France for its claim to the Louisiana Territory. Overnight the land area of the United States doubled. From the Gulf of Mexico, the Louisiana Territory ran up through New Orleans, following the west bank of the Mississippi River north all the way to what is now part of Minnesota, North Dakota, and Montana. It included most of the future Wyoming, part of Colorado, and most of Kansas and Oklahoma.

The American traders in the Pacific at the time of Kamehameha might have agreed that America needed more of a navy to keep the British at bay, but most Americans were looking toward their continental frontier. In the year 1819, America annexed what are now the southern tips of Mississippi and Alabama and all of Florida. Prophetically, these areas were acquired as a result of the declining fortunes of Spain.

While the American government thus was engaged in taking control of the continent, the American Board of Commissioners of

Foreign Missions began sending companies of missionaries into the Pacific. The first mission to the Pacific was to Hawai'i in 1820. The whaling industry, which used Hawai'i as a port of provisioning and transshipment of whale oil, picked up dramatically because of Americans. The first experiments with sugar were started in 1835 by Americans. The Honolulu waterfront and the waterfront at Lāhainā, Maui, were becoming little urban centers, reflecting the encroachment of merchants—mostly Americans—into what had been the exclusive trading domain of the Hawaiian chiefs.

While the daily impact of Americans was relentless, the dramatic events of this period were caused by the British and the French, who were respectively the number one and number two naval powers of the day. At the urging of the Protestant American missionaries, the Kingdom had banned Catholic missionaries. The Kingdom had also placed a heavy tariff on French wine. In 1839, a year after Lili'uokalani's birth, a French warship arrived, intent on improving the position of France. The French captain forced the Kingdom to roll back the tariff and open its doors to a Catholic mission. He also demanded that any French citizen accused of a crime was to be tried by a jury of foreigners that met the approval of the French consul.

This affront to the dignity and effectiveness of the Kingdom was nothing compared to what would happen the year Lili'uokalani turned five, as she was attending the American mission's school for the children of chiefs. A British ship arrived, following up on a dispute over land tenure involving a British subject. When the outlandish demands of the British captain, Lord George Paulet, were not met, Kamehameha III ceded control of the Kingdom's government to the British captain under protest. Kamehameha III spoke from the wall of the fort, calling out to "chiefs, people, and commons from my ancestors, and people from foreign lands!" He said he had given away "the life of our land" for reasons that had been imposed on him. But, he said, "I have hope that the life of the land will be restored when my conduct shall be justified."

Perhaps he thought of Paulet as another Georg Scheffer. The students of the Chief's Children's School taunted the British and implored their American headmaster to fly the Hawaiian flag in defiance, and if not the Hawaiian flag then the American flag, but the missionaries forbade it. The youthful David Kalākaua threw rocks at British troops. After five months, a second British ship arrived, rebuked the ambitious captain, and affirmed the sovereignty of the Kingdom. Lili'uokalani would always remember marching with her classmates to the Protestant church for a yearly celebration of Restoration Day. "*Ua mau ke ea o ka 'āina i ka pono,*" said the king on the first Restoration Day. The gamble he had made in his speech from the wall of the fort had paid off. "May the life of the land be perpetuated in righteousness."

As a result of the turmoil of the ill-defined European ambition that occurred in Lili'uokalani's childhood, the Kingdom of Hawai'i crafted an international strategy in 1842 aimed at surviving as a nation in an uncertain, greedy, and bellicose time. It sought, and won, a joint declaration from France and Great Britain recognizing Hawai'i as an independent, sovereign country. Both countries promised to honor Hawai'i's sovereignty so long as the other did.

Simultaneously, Hawai'i also sought America's recognition. In response, America produced what became known as the Tyler Doctrine, which said in part that the United States desired "no exclusive control over the Hawaiian Government, but is content with its independent existence," so long as the European powers stayed their distance.

By the time of this first round of international negotiation, the sugar planters were seriously altering the Hawaiian landscape. The first immigrant laborers had been imported. The disastrous decline of the Hawaiian population, which had begun after contact with Western disease, continued. Yet all was far from lost. The Hawai'i of Lili'uokalani's childhood had survived epidemics, invasions, and incessant pressure. It had devised a course of international action that was cause for some optimism.

AS HAWAIIANS REFLECTED on their conflicts with the West, and as Lili'uokalani ultimately was to reflect on the arrival of the American troops, there was a pattern to the intimidation. The leaders of a powerful but distant nation set benign policies, but these policies were not necessarily followed by their national representatives who arrived on Hawai'i's shores. Even in the Hawaiians' dealings with the Russians, Georg Scheffer eventually had been isolated. The Russian American Company had turned its back on him, and the problems posed by the Russians went away. Lord Paulet of Britain clearly was not following British policy. France signed the treaty of 1842 guaranteeing Hawai'i's independence, only to have another belligerent captain arrive in 1849 and make outlandish demands on the government. Finally the French marched on the Fort of Honolulu, but only one person was there to receive them, the chief Kekūanao'a, governor of O'ahu.

"Where are your soldiers?" the French officer demanded.

"They have all been sent into the country," Kekūanao'a said.

"Where are their arms?" the Frenchman asked.

"Each man has taken his gun with him," Kekūanao'a said.

"I require you to surrender this fort and all the munitions of war," the Frenchman said.

"You have everything already," Kekūanao'a said. "There is nothing left to surrender."[2]

The French occupied the Fort of Honolulu for ten days, and then wrecked the interior of the fort as they departed. Between the construction of the fort in 1816 and the British and French incursions in the 1840s, the Hawaiians had made a sober estimate of the firepower of Western troops and Western ships and decided not to fight back. Minimize the damage. Chances are the problem would go away. In fact, this approach was to work for nearly a century. Troubles always did go away, and the life of the land was perpetuated.

Meanwhile, during the 1840s, America took a second enormous leap in size. The phrase "manifest destiny" was used in connection with the debate over the annexation of Texas. An expansionist magazine argued that annexing Texas was "the fulfillment of our manifest destiny to overspread the continent ... " The argument went on to site Providence and America's rapidly growing population. Texas was joined to America in 1845 and was followed quickly by the acquisition of the Oregon Territory in 1846 as a result of a treaty with Britain. Today's Southwest U.S. and California were acquired in 1848 as a result of a war with Mexico. By 1848, Americans stood on the Pacific shore of a new nation that stretched from Baja California to present-day Canada.

THE IMPACT ON Hawai'i of America's expansion to the West Coast was immediate. The California Gold Rush of 1849 intensified trade and migration in both directions. An observer in Honolulu wrote that immigrants from California included "many restless, ambitious spirits, some of whom came for the purpose of exciting revolution."[3] A second wrote that every day there were fewer Hawaiians and "the Americans in California more numerous and enterprising."[4]

The pressure of statehood for California added to the turmoil of Kamehameha III, who was by then thirty-five years old. He was born in 1814 and had ascended to the throne at age eleven after the untimely death of Kamehameha II. He had come of age under the regency of the imperious Ka'ahumanu, then under a second powerful female chief, Kīna'u. He had proclaimed Hawai'i a constitutional monarchy in 1840, at the age of twenty-six. He possessed a strong sense of the ancient system and its culture, but it often failed him in the immediate present. He was always looking for ways to adapt to change. Despite his successful venture into international diplomacy in 1842, in which the British and French guaranteed Hawai'i's independence, he had been humiliated by the British in 1843 and the French in 1849. That same year, through an elaborate process involving the Hawaiian chiefs and his Western (mostly American) advisers, he instituted fee simple ownership of land. It was the commodification of land that was familiar to Westerners and unfamiliar to Hawaiians.

In 1849, Kamehameha III also signed a Treaty of Friendship, Commerce, and Navigation with the United States. While the idea of treaties of friendship may stir little interest in most people today, this treaty remains an issue of active importance, because it promised perpetual peace and friendship between the two countries. It declared both sides "equally animated with the desire of maintaining the relations which have hitherto so happily subsisted between their respective states." The treaty resides on its expensive, highly durable paper, in all its solemnity, in the National Archives of the United States.

California became a state in 1850. In 1851, Kamehameha III, in desperation—fearing above all a return of the marauding French—began negotiating with the United States for protection. The agent of the United States at that time was referred to as a commissioner, who in 1851 was a publisher from Maine named Luther Severance. Severance originally was a printer. He migrated to Maine and founded *The Kennebec Journal* in Augusta. The newspaper is still published under that name, only today it is a morning daily. Severance wrote his opinions and stories as he set type by hand, bypassing the tedium of pen and paper. He rose to prominence as an editor and was appointed commissioner to Hawai'i by a Whig president, Zachary Taylor. He arrived in the aftermath of the annexation of Texas and the Mexican War, which added the Western territories to America.

In his introduction to Kamehameha III, Severance said that America's possession of the Pacific Coast "will necessarily induce a more intimate connection with your islands."[5] He alluded to the military vulnerability of the Kingdom by saying it was "accessible on all sides to the fleets and armies of all the world." Therefore, Severance went on, Hawai'i must derive its strength from "the moral power which is obtained by a wise policy and a strict regard for justice," which surely was an allusion to adopting the political and economic forms of the West.

Severance pledged to do all he could to aid "the permanent independence" of Hawai'i's government, but the situation almost immediately was confused by Kamehameha's apprehension of France. "I distrust France and fear her," Kamehameha wrote.[6] By summer, he had given Severance a letter placing the sovereignty of Hawai'i in America's hands in the event that France threatened the Kingdom directly. If France tried to take over, would America create a protectorate that provided security to the Kingdom? From this, a serious conversation evolved regarding annexation, in which Hawai'i was to become one of the "sovereign" states. Severance was receptive, but Secretary of State Daniel Webster directed Severance to return the letter. Webster acknowledged a special interest in the American settlers, but said they had ceased to be American citizens, and "any idea or expectation that the islands will become annexed" should not be encouraged.[7]

Severance's health failed and he returned to Maine. The discussion of annexation resumed between Kamehameha III and

Severance's successor, but the king's representatives held out for immediate statehood, apparently realizing this would foil the making of a deal. The American negotiators pursued the idea far enough to realize that serious reservations existed within the United States, and everyone backed off. Soon thereafter, Kamehameha III died, at the age of forty-one, after thirty years as king, and the conversation about annexation ended.

Kamehameha III was followed by a grandson of Kamehameha, who apparently looked at the world with a clear, calculating eye. Kamehameha IV turned his back on the statehood negotiations and substituted the idea of giving the Americans what they wanted, and also giving the sugar planters what they wanted, but not surrendering the sovereignty of the Kingdom. America's navy was to have the use of the Pearl River Lagoon, which was the only natural deep-water harbor in the Hawaiian Islands other than Honolulu Harbor. The sugar planters were to have tariff-free access to the American sugar market. And Hawai'i was to continue as a sovereign country, with its independence guaranteed by the United States. This was the essence of what would become known as reciprocity.

Negotiations dragged on for two decades, but, in the meantime, Kamehameha IV pursued a foreign policy through which he distanced himself from the Americans and cultivated the British. Today one may walk around the historic district of Honolulu and see results of Kamehameha IV's attitude toward the world. Next door to Washington Place, Lili'uokalani's mansion, and a block from 'Iolani Palace—in the exact opposite direction from the missionary church— is a perfect Anglican cathedral, Saint Andrew's. Its construction was started by Kamehameha IV and completed by his wife Emma, a granddaughter of the white war chief, John Young. In the stained glass windows at the entry of Saint Andrew's Cathedral, the visitor sees a tall, handsome Hawaiian man in royal uniform. With him is a stately woman who is visibly of a lighter skin tone. Together they revived the affinity of the Kamehameha dynasty for Britain. Their class structures of monarch, nobleman, and commoner were parallel. However powerful, the British were at a more comfortable distance. The British did not insist on sending missionaries who stayed forever and lectured their audiences on how to think.

If Kamehameha IV could have been transported around the globe to the colonial administration of the British in its entirety, he would have found a great deal of bloodshed and organized plunder, but the British approached their task with an inclination to leave the structure of colonized societies more or less intact.

At any rate, Kamehameha IV's embrace of the British was more about form than substance. The real issue was to which nation Hawai'i's economic system would be tied. At the time, Britain controlled Canada, Australia, and New Zealand. Among the Pacific islands it controlled Fiji and Tonga and was to come as close to Hawai'i as the Gilbert Islands and, finally, Johnston Island, only several hundred miles to the south of Hawai'i. Yet no effort was made to seek reciprocity with Britain, nor—contrary to the dark warnings of the pro-American lobby—was it ever seriously considered. The Hawai'i of Kamehameha IV faced the prospect of an Americanized economy with a fine Anglican church.

Only diplomacy was left in the arsenal. The Fort of Honolulu was dismantled during the reign of Kamehameha IV, its coral blocks rededicated to the building of commercial piers. At its peak of firepower it had seventy cannon, none of which were ever fired other than ceremonially. One of those cannon sits on the lawn of an office tower today, just below Fort Street. Another is a few hundred feet away. It sits vertically, its base in the concrete of the sidewalk. Conscientious citizens who are concerned with litter put cigarette butts and gum wrappers in it. The whereabouts of most of the Kingdom's cannon are unknown. The fourteen cannon of the gun battery at Punchbowl were dispersed, as were the thirty-eight cannon of the Russian Fort on Kaua'i. The result was a total absence of military defense. In 1866, the American minister wrote to his secretary of state, saying that Hawai'i was destitute of both army and navy and "without the power to resist aggression, to compel belligerents to respect the neutrality of her ports." The secretary of state was William Seward, who was early evidence that the new Republican Party, the party of Lincoln, was capable of simultaneously standing in opposition to slavery and in favor of aggressive overseas expansion at the expense of others. Seward wrote back to the minister in Hawai'i that when America's transcontinental railroad was completed,

Hawai'i would be needed as a base for both commercial and military purposes. A reciprocity treaty, he believed, would pave the way for "quiet absorption." America would have its naval base, and the anxieties of the sugar planters would be put to rest.

In the strategy of Kamehameha IV, reciprocity was a substitute for annexation. From his viewpoint, it was better to give the Americans what they most immediately wanted rather than to give them everything at some later date. The fact that reciprocity was less preferable than annexation to many influential Americans was illustrated by Seward, who wrote that "if the policy of annexation should really conflict with the policy of reciprocity, annexation is in every case preferred." A reciprocity treaty actually failed in the U.S. Senate in 1871 because senators voting against it were holding out for annexation. A senator from Maine, the state that recurs as a special source of jingoistic fervor, said it was "folly to pay for a thing we already have."[8]

THE STORIES OF DEATH among the Hawaiian people are alternately wrenching and numbing. The male heir of King Kamehameha IV and Queen Emma died at the age of four. The king died at the age of twenty-nine. He was succeeded by his brother, the fifth and last of the Kamehamehas, who died without designating a successor. As Kamehameha V lay dying, he asked Lili'uokalani's sister through adoption, Bernice Pauahi, to be queen. Bernice was a Kamehameha. She declined, and the Kamehameha dynasty was at an end.

As provided in the constitution, the office was to be filled by election. Unerringly the Hawaiians narrowed the field according to the dictates of high chiefly rank. William Lunalilo, the first elected king, won nearly all the votes in a contest with David Kalākaua. William died the next year. The subsequent election contest was between Kalākaua and Queen Emma, the widow of Kamehameha IV. In the course of the campaign, David promised to vigorously pursue reciprocity in return for the support of the planters, who were fearful of Emma.

The final choice was made by the Legislature. The Hawaiian supporters of Emma, enraged by the Legislature's endorsement of Kalākaua, stormed the building where the legislators were meeting.

In the old days, the Hawaiians who disputed authority either would have risen in successful revolt or been put down. The passage of power then would have been consecrated and order restored. Now Americans were called from a ship in the harbor to restore order. It was an ominous beginning for the reign of David Kalākaua.

The Reciprocity Treaty was approved by both Hawai'i and America in 1875. It was the key event in a year that should be understood on several levels. First, the signing of the treaty set off an explosion of growth in the sugar industry. Growth of the industry in turn triggered a massive importation of immigrant labor, mostly from Asia. Both of these events occurred in an environment in which colonialism and imperialism became an ever more frequent characteristic of the behavior of powerful nations.

When Kalākaua went to Washington, D.C., to lobby for the treaty, he became the first monarch to visit the United States. Over the course of his journey, he made a brilliant impression. He spent a week in San Francisco, then took a train to Washington. He met with the president, Ulysses S. Grant, and addressed Congress. Previously, reciprocity had floundered, so he was given major credit for its passage. Even one of his harshest critics wrote, "He made an excellent impression in Washington and throughout the United States, and did well for the treaty."[9] Kalākaua won a concession of sorts by not agreeing to give away Pearl Harbor in perpetuity. The United States was giving up tariff revenues, and, from the viewpoint of the Maine senator, was paying "for what we already have." But there was a conscious understanding that Hawai'i was being pulled more closely into the economic and military systems of America. While Kalākaua had opposed ceding Pearl Harbor, in the end he agreed to a proviso inserted by the U.S. Senate that during the life of the treaty he would not lease ports to any power other than America. For this diminution of Hawai'i's autonomy he was criticized by his sister, Lili'uokalani, among others.

MUCH HAS BEEN MADE of this treaty by historians, but relatively little has been made of the global environment in which it was written. Perhaps Kalākaua looked around the world and counted Hawai'i lucky. In 1857, the British ruthlessly put down a rebellion in India. In 1875, they took over the Suez Canal. Various European countries cut pieces from China, the most enduring of which was British Hong Kong. France was to take over much of Southeast Asia, including Vietnam. Virtually all of Africa was carved up, and most of the Pacific Islands were colonized, variously by the British, French, Dutch, and Germans. It was the orgy of national enslavement that resulted in the pre-World War II map, in which the European nations each had a color code that was sprinkled liberally around the world. It resulted in such familiar phrases as, "The sun never sets on the British Empire."

In this climate, the process of change accelerated in Hawai'i. Just as Native Hawaiians had panned for salt, they had grown a subsistence supply of a sweetener, *kō*, in clumps of a gigantic grass that became known in the West as sugar. The basis of the industrial growing and processing of sugar had been developed incrementally in Hawai'i as the nineteenth century unfolded. Fields, mills, labor, machines, financing, etc. were worked out in stages, starting in 1835. When the ancient Hawaiian land system was destroyed in 1849 in favor of a highly feudal fee simple system, huge tracts were bought up quickly by Westerners who were eager to plant sugar. The chronic anxiety of the sugar industry always had to do with paying tariffs to get its product sold into the American market.

With the Reciprocity Treaty finally signed and approved, the sugar industry grew at a wild pace. Where it had taken forty years for annual production to reach twelve thousand tons, it doubled in four years. Thereafter it doubled again and again and again by the end of the century. The plantations grew incessantly as the market developed, as more land was cultivated, and as more of Hawai'i's water resources were diverted to sugar. The clearing of fields, digging of water ditches, drilling of water tunnels, planting of vast fields, and milling of the ever-larger production—all were labor-intensive, so increasing numbers of workers were needed.

Before the signing of the Reciprocity Treaty, twenty-three hundred immigrants had arrived from Asia, most of them from China, with contracts to work on the plantations. In the four years after reciprocity, while sugar production was doubling, the number of immigrants quadrupled, and that was just the beginning. The labor agents of the planters searched the globe for low-cost labor, and in the end turned from China to Japan. Where Hawaiians typically had outnumbered the foreign community by more than ten to one (even in their greatly reduced state), in less than a generation they became an ethnic minority in their own homeland—with much of that change occurring in the first eight years of Kalākaua's reign.

The numbers are so stunning as to bear exploring in some detail. In the 1853 census, Hawaiians numbered about seventy thousand and made up 96 percent of the population. In the last census before the Reciprocity Treaty (1872), 86 percent of the population was Hawaiian, and another 4 percent to 5 percent were half-Hawaiian.

In the 1872 census, locally born "foreigners" were a minuscule part of the population. The missionary descendants who so immediately come to mind were a small part of this minority. Many of the 849 persons in the category of locally born "foreigners" must have been the offspring of Chinese, because Chinese were the largest immigrant group. Next came Europeans and then Americans. The American and American-descended population (that is, both immigrant and locally born) made up less than 2 percent of the total population of Hawai'i.

If one can imagine encountering ten people at random on a given day in 1872, nine were Hawaiian. The tenth person was most likely to be Chinese and next most likely European—meaning British, French, German, or Portuguese. The remotest possibility was that the tenth person was American.

By 1884, twelve years later, Hawaiians made up only half the population, with another 5 percent listed as partially of Hawaiian ancestry. By 1890, eighteen years after reciprocity, Hawaiians were only 38 percent of the population and part-Hawaiians another 7 percent. While the number of Hawaiians had declined from seventy thousand to forty thousand, they had become a numerical minority as a result of the migrations resulting from reciprocity.[10]

And what of the American colony, whose members had done so much to bring about this dramatic change? It is tantalizing in the extreme to realize that, although the influence of the American colony was growing by leaps and bounds, it still made up only 2 percent of the total population.

By 1890, the mix of the population was more complex. Now one must imagine encountering a hundred people on a particular day. Only forty-five were of Hawaiian ancestry. Seventeen were Chinese, fourteen were Japanese, and ten were Portuguese. Of the small remainder, the majority were likely to be from Britain, Germany, France or, lately, Norway. The remainder—two persons—were either American descendants or American immigrants.

If the Americans were such a consistently small minority, why had they succeeded in molding the Hawaiian situation? Why were Americans to so consistently determine the outcome of future situations? One explanation is that Americans were people of extraordinary ability, like the American Jacks who sailed the seas of Theodore Roosevelt's first book. Another explanation is that their country of origin had an extraordinary interest in dominating events in Hawai'i, and was forever doing things to become more dominant. That country was recovering from a civil war, and it was coming to believe it deserved a place among the Earth's great national powers.

The reign of David Kalākaua occurred in this increasingly American-dominated environment, and for all his problems Kalākaua proved remarkably inventive. With reciprocity in place and sugar booming, he directed that the old palace be torn down. Already he was the first monarch to travel to America, and now he departed Hawai'i to make a journey around the world. In his pursuit of the Reciprocity Treaty, he had wanted to go on to Britain and France to reaffirm, in a timely way, the relationships with the original guarantors of Hawai'i's independence. His cabinet had opposed his plan. Now he took off in the opposite direction, traveling west, albeit by way of an initial stop in San Francisco. He arrived in Japan having no idea how he would be received, but determined to make the best of it. To his great surprise, he was given an exuberant welcome. Cannons fired in Yokohama Harbor, and crowds gathered to stare at this dark, handsome *gaijin*, who was king of the distant island nation. Kalākaua not only met the emperor, which no foreigner had ever done, but shook the man's hand, which was taboo.

Kalākaua enjoyed himself, but this was more than a pleasure trip. At bottom, he was searching for ways for Hawai'i to survive. This is proven by his famous proposal to Japan's emperor: First, that the crown prince of Japan marry his niece, Princess Ka'iulani, who was one of the great beauties of her age; second, that the two nations sign a treaty of mutual support; and third, that Japanese workers be allowed to emigrate to Hawai'i. Kalākaua was seeking a way to check the rising domination of Americans while at the same time supplying their plantations with workers. The emperor, no doubt with a wary eye on America, tactfully declined. But he went to considerable lengths to say how pained he was to pass up such wonderful offers, and how he would think about these ideas again at a later time.

The opening up of such friendships dismayed the American government, which was nursing the idea of Hawai'i becoming a captive client state. James G. Blaine, in his first brief stint as secretary of state under President James Garfield, alerted American consulates around the world to keep an eye on Kalākaua.[11] What did he want? Kalākaua forged on through Europe, Britain, and America and returned to Hawai'i nine months later with plans for the reinvigoration of his Kingdom.

On his return, he supported the organization of a Board of Genealogy. He sent bright students abroad for study. He commissioned a statue of Kamehameha to honor the founder of the dynasty. He completed the palace that is such an attraction today. Next to the palace he built the gazebo where Hawai'i's governors today take the oath of office. Having originally taken a simple oath of office, he now held a coronation, at which Hawaiians danced the hula in defiance of the Puritanism of the missionaries. The statue of Kamehameha I was unveiled, and the party went on for two weeks.

Kalākaua was roundly criticized by the missionary elements of the white community for waste and extravagance, but he plunged ahead. Perhaps it was not only he who glimpsed the possibility of a Hawaiian revival, but the pro-American element as well. There was a slump in the economy in 1884 and 1885, as both sugar prices and government revenues fell, but Kalākaua persisted with his mixture of cultural revival and nationalism. He organized a charitable society called Hooululahui, a nationalistic name that translates *ho'oulu* (increase) *lāhui* (the race/nation). He organized a secret society, Hale Nauā, called the House of Science in English. The same year, 1886, Lili'uokalani established what came to be called the Lili'uokalani

Education Society, dedicated to the education of young Hawaiian girls. The landholding *ali'i*, who were criticized in life for being wealthy at the expense of the commoners, were demonstrating through their wills and estates a concern for the entire society. King William Lunalilo bequeathed his lands for the care of the elderly. Queen Emma gave her lands for the care of the sick, through what would become The Queen's Hospital. Bernice Pauahi gave her lands for the creation of Kamehameha Schools.

It was during this same period that King David Kalākaua oversaw the writing of his *Myths and Legends of Hawai'i*, which put him in active touch with the heroic stories of the voyagers and the early settlers. He had a vivid understanding of Hawaiian culture and the role of the Hawaiian chief, and he was determined that Hawaiians not perish.

Twice he had witnessed the incursions of France into the Kingdom, and when the British had taken over he had thrown rocks at the red-coated soldiers. He had listened to stories about the Russians. On his journey around the world, he had heard stories of the European powers gobbling up the lands of others at a horrendous pace. Europeans were everywhere in the Pacific, sometimes quarreling with one another over which country would get certain islands.

Along with trying to strengthen Hawaiian tradition, Kalākaua undertook to rekindle the relationships of Hawai'i with Polynesia. His actions were brutally criticized, but if the Hawaiians are acknowledged as having a long history connected to the even longer history of Polynesia, and his actions are analyzed geopolitically, then Kalākaua's behavior makes sense. In Japan he had attempted to create a relationship that would serve as a countervailing force to America. In the Pacific he attempted to minimize the rampant spread of colonialism and create a zone in which the sovereignty of native people was the rule rather than the exception. In the archives of Hawai'i there is an undated document of the Department of Foreign Affairs that protests the annexation of Polynesian societies as "subversive of those conditions for favorable national development which have been so happily accorded the Hawaiian nation." It goes on to say that the Hawaiian people appreciated the blessings of national independence, which they attributed in part to the support of the great powers.

Could not other Polynesian societies maintain their sovereignty as well? Why could the great powers not accord the same support to those islands from which the first voyagers had sailed—such places as the Society Islands, which included the legendary island of Raiatea, and the Samoan Islands, which included the vast island of Savai'i? Kalākaua had proved himself to be an extraordinary Polynesian. He had concluded the Reciprocity Treaty with America, and he had dealt with many heads of state on his journey, including the monarch of Britain. The Samoans were beset by the British, the Germans, and the Americans, each with an interest in either military or commercial uses of the Samoan Islands. They were interested in Kalākaua's ideas. He bought a British warship and sent it to Sāmoa to assert Hawai'i's presence, but the crew fell into disarray, and the mission floundered. Criticism from the American colony in Hawai'i grew even louder. Kalākaua was wasteful. He was corrupt. He was a poor imitation of European monarchy. His *haole* advisers, particularly Walter Murray Gibson, were worse than devils. They were white, yet they approved of the licentious, wasteful behavior that Kalākaua was encouraging in the natives, who now again danced the hula.

CHAPTER SEVEN

A Two-Layered Conspiracy

Viewed from a distance, there is a crushing pattern to the death rate of the Hawaiians, the drastic change in the makeup of the population, the spread of sugar, the revival of American expansionism, and the fixation of the U.S. navy on Pearl Harbor, to say nothing of the closing of the American frontier and the American habit of moving west. Yet at closer range the patterns give way to specific conspiracies organized by specific individuals. The conspiracies break out into two layers, one operating in pro-American circles in Hawai'i, one in expansionist circles in America. These two groups seek one another out like unstable molecules, and they bond on contact.

When Lorrin Thurston was a small boy, he made a trip from Honolulu to Kōloa, Kaua'i, which is situated on a south-facing plain that has an abundance of rich soil, sunshine, and rain. It is known as the site of the first sugar plantation in Hawai'i, but Lorrin would remember it as the place he first saw Sanford Dole. Lorrin was a rambunctious little boy, and Sanford Dole was a big upright boy, and over a lifetime Lorrin Thurston would devote a part of himself to making sure that everyone saw Sanford Dole the way he first saw him.

Sanford's father, Daniel Dole, was from a small town on the Kennebec River, which runs into the sea partway up the Maine coast. The little town was called Skowhegan, and it is situated immediately northwest of the small capital city of Augusta. Sanford's mother, Emily Ballard Dole, was from Hallowell, which is immediately south of Augusta. One day Daniel visited Emily and asked her to be his wife and go on a Christian mission. Ethel Damon was to write that "a sudden light shone over her and her heart cried, This … is the awaited call!"[1] When the newly married couple arrived in Hawai'i, the mission board asked them to organize a school that was to become central to the legend of an Americanized Hawai'i, Punahou School. This task, Damon says, "seemed manifest duty." Sanford, their second son, was born in 1844 while they did their work at Punahou. Four days after his birth, Emily Dole died. The missionary chaplain Samuel Chenery Damon preached at her memorial service the next day.

When Sanford Dole had reached old age, he opened up sufficiently to Ethel Damon for her to write a surprisingly intimate portrait. The missionary milieu described by Damon's biography suggests the missionaries were no less clannish than the Hawaiian *ali'i*. The original members of the company addressed one another as Brother and Sister. To the next generation, they became known as Mother and Father (as in Father Castle, Mother Cooke, etc.) The descendants addressed one another as Cousin. The closer they were in the chain of generations to their original mission, the more likely they were to overflow with Christianity. Just after young Sanford learned to read, his father called him into his room and handed him a new Bible. Sanford burst into tears, then calmed himself and began to read. By accomplishing a little each day, he completed his first reading of the Bible in several years. When he had finished, he started over. He read it the second time in one year.

When Sanford was eleven, his father was reassigned to the sugar country of Kaua'i. The plantation had been founded by William Ladd, who was from Hallowell, Maine, the hometown of Sanford's mother. One of Ladd's partners was Peter Brinsmade, also of Hallowell. Ladd was married to Lucretia Goodale of Hallowell, and Brinsmade was married to her sister, Elizabeth. By the time of Daniel Dole's arrival in Kōloa, a Dr. R.W. Wood of Augusta, Maine, was living there as well, as one of the plantation's new owners.

Dr. James W. Smith, a missionary doctor, was another significant figure in the small community. When the Reverend Dole's school began to thrive, Smith gave him an additional ten acres of land. Dr. Smith's son, Will Smith, was a student at Dole's school, and he would become a lifelong friend of Sanford Dole. When Lorrin Thurston arrived on his outing to Kaua'i he likely saw not only Sanford for the first time, but also Cousin Willie, or W.O. Smith, his future law partner and co-conspirator.

By the time of Thurston's interisland jaunt, it was 1864, the third year of the American Civil War, and Kōloa was thriving. The cane sugar of Louisiana that normally had been shipped to Northern markets was cut off by the war, and island-grown sugar cane was suddenly more lucrative as a result. Sanford sat up nights during this period talking to his father about the meaning of the war. He prayed for the reelection of Abraham Lincoln. During the day—for reasons that are not apparent—he rode about on horseback, drilling a group of Hawaiians. His little militia was armed with muskets left over from the battle at the Russian Fort between the Kauaians and Hawaiians in 1824. Some of the muskets, it is said, were stained with blood.

The day of Lorrin's visit, Sanford Dole rode about on his horse, then rode off to Kōloa landing and disappeared on a whale boat. "My principal recollection is not of the incongruity of foot soldiers being mounted on horseback, or of their going on a boating trip," wrote Thurston, "but of my resentment that I was not allowed to go also, for I was a superfluous small boy."[2]

Sanford Dole subsequently worked for a nearby plantation long enough to save money to study in America. The first steam-powered ship arrived in Hawai'i from the West Coast carrying the storyteller Mark Twain, and Sanford Dole rode the steamer back. There he boarded a second vessel for Panama, where he crossed the isthmus of the American continents by train in three hours. He then caught a second ship to New York. While his parents had taken six months to sail to Hawai'i, Sanford made the trip in five weeks. He wandered New York City with a missionary offspring from back home, Bill Castle, a future conspirator, and bought a suit from the uncle of Cousin Willie Smith. At Williams College he was delighted to entertain yet another future conspirator, Samuel M. Damon, son of the Samuel C. Damon who had preached at his mother's funeral. Ethel Damon wrote that while Sanford was "as indigenous as a Hawaiian tree," nothing so mysteriously affected him as New England "emerging from its dark, frozen winter of leafless trees into the glow and bloom of spring."

After a year at Williams College, Dole studied with a lawyer in Boston who was connected to Hawai'i. "Were I not a Hawaiian," he wrote to his father, "I would be a Bostonian." While in New England, he visited the Doles of Maine. He helped his grandmother celebrate her eightieth birthday. He swam in the Kennebec River. He also must have read *The Kennebec Journal*, which already had a long record of favoring the annexation of Hawai'i.

After two years, Sanford Dole returned to Hawai'i to practice law in Honolulu. On the day the Legislature voted to make David Kalākaua the seventh king of Hawai'i, he was one of the two white men who stood shoulder to shoulder in the hallway and attempted to hold off Queen Emma's angry supporters. By 1884, he was so disturbed by the reign of King Kalākaua that he decided to go into elective politics.

LORRIN ANDREWS THURSTON was Dole's junior by fourteen years. He was born in 1858, the same year as Theodore Roosevelt. While Dole was of the second missionary generation, Thurston was of the third. On his father's side, he was the grandson of Asa and Lucy Thurston, who built the large stone church that is a landmark to this day in the town of Kona, Hawai'i. On his mother's side he was descended from Lorrin Andrews, who was remembered kindly by the Hawaiians for helping to launch the work of the young Hawaiian scholars at Lahainaluna School on Maui. While Dole had prayed over whether to become a preacher or a lawyer, Thurston left no such record of uncertainty. He not only had wanted to run off with Sanford at Kōloa, but had succeeded in running off from Punahou School on the day that William Lunalilo became Hawai'i's first elected king. He also skipped school the day of the fracas over Kalākaua's election, and he watched as Sanford stood strong and upright in the path of the outraged supporters of Queen Emma.

He studied law at Columbia University, which allowed him to not only live on the U.S. mainland but to be a part of New York City at a time when the fortunes of America were ascending. Thurston preceded Roosevelt in the law program, but they experienced many of the same influences. The post-Civil War reconstruction of the South had ended. Alexander Bell was introducing the telephone, Thomas Edison was introducing the electric light, and the belief of whites in their racial superiority had been elevated to college course work and learned discussion.

Thurston returned to Hawai'i at the age of twenty, law degree in hand. In 1884, when Sanford Dole and other critics of Kalākaua won a block of seats in the Legislature, Thurston ran for clerk of the House. Although he lost, opportunity loomed. He took a job as editor of one of the English language newspapers, the *Bulletin*, and then Sanford Dole called him to a meeting of *haole* to work at increasing their influence in the government. In September 1885, young Thurston was chosen to be one of three people on the executive committee of a new political organization called the Reform Party, a name that reflected their belief that they were right. The other two were Sanford Dole and Bill Castle. The next year, at the age of twenty-eight, Thurston stood for election to the House of Representatives of the Kingdom of Hawai'i.

Thurston's story of his campaign reflects a genius for legitimizing himself on the move. His little *haole* group guided him into running from the islands of Moloka'i and Lāna'i, essentially from Moloka'i, as the more populous of the two. This in itself was an interesting choice that presumably reflected a belief that Hawaiians on the perpetually impoverished island of Moloka'i were disgruntled with the royalist ticket. Thurston wrote that he had never been to Moloka'i until he went to campaign. The outing began with a church service and was followed by a political rally and lū'au that ran on for two days. He went in the company of Bill Castle and one of his two law partners, William A. Kinney, who he was to describe later as "the most intense man I have ever known."

The part of Kinney's oration at Sunday school that Thurston remembered was, "Look up and not down! Look forward and not backward! Look outward and not inward!" Kinney, Thurston said, was greeted with a roar of applause. They were hosted on Moloka'i by a John Kalua, who was regarded as a brilliant orator. Kalua had grown up on Moloka'i and then gone into politics. He launched Thurston at the political rally as a "young lion who was to bring salvation and liberty to downtrodden Moloka'i." Said Thurston, "What it meant to have this introduction by Kalua can hardly be realized by the present generation." A choir from Maui followed Kalua's introduction with a song that wove Kalua together with Kamehameha's conquest of Maui at the Battle of 'Iao Valley.

When it was Thurston's turn to speak, he talked about a fisherman who found a corked bottle on the beach. Inside the bottle was an imp who promised grandiose rewards to any person who would release him. The imp in the bottle was the famous sugar baron, Claus Spreckels, an enormously influential crony of Kalākaua. The Hawaiian fisherman could not resist. He pulled the cork. "An immense column of flame and smoke roared forth, filling the sky," the young Thurston said, "and the imp, changing into a demon, with giant gnashing teeth and blazing eyes, devoured the fisherman and everything else in sight." Thurston spent a month living among the Hawaiians of Molokaʻi. At one point he had to push his way past the local politicians to address the victims of leprosy who were impounded at Kalaupapa, on the northern tip of the island. Father Damien, who in the late twentieth century would be a candidate for sainthood, chastised Thurston as a "son of Belial." What Thurston did not explain was that in the Bible the son of Belial helped steal another man's vineyard, so the name had become synonymous with the word scoundrel.

"I bear Father Damien no ill will," Thurston said. "He doubtless was acting on orders from higher authority."

Thurston's campaign was a clever play on the frustrations of an island of people who perpetually felt themselves squeezed between Maui and Oʻahu. He criticized the absentee sugar baron, Spreckels, who was widely thought of as corrupting the monarchy, rather than criticizing the monarch head-on. Thurston gave no clue that he sought to reorganize the government, let alone turn the government over to another country. Nonetheless, Thurston not only won the election, but also won a majority vote of the leprosy victims.

While Thurston's grandfather, Asa, and grandmother, Lucy, peer out from their portraits with broad foreheads, strong cheeks, prominent noses, and strong jaws, young Lorrin was more refined. He had sharper features. He dressed in a three-piece suit. Of his many portraits, the most striking would show him seated in the exact center, framed by his white comrades. Beneath his chair was a huge animal skin.

Whenever something important happened, Thurston was there—often as the organizer. He had an understanding of timing and an instinct for action. His opinion counted among his colleagues far more than that of any other person. If you were to read the correspondence, memos, and minutes of the men who decided they would take over Hawai'i, you might imagine the others asking, "What does Lorrin think?"

By the 1886 election, Thurston, Dole, and W.O. Smith were all members of the Legislature of the Kingdom. All had worked on plantations, and all possessed law degrees. Thurston represented Moloka'i and Lāna'i, Dole represented Kaua'i, and Smith represented Wailuku, Maui. It is here that the traditional histories begin to refer to the Reform Party, and to recite the fortunes of a bewildering array of small, constantly changing political parties.

Essentially there were at first two and eventually three competing elements. The first were the loyalists, or royalists. The royalists relied on the votes of the majority of Hawaiians who supported the monarchy. The second were those who were loyal to the nation of Hawai'i but were no longer thoroughgoing royalists—either because they disliked the monarch's cabinet and preferred other potential cabinet members, or because they disliked the monarch and preferred another monarch, or because they disliked the native government but preferred another form of native government, such as a Hawaiian republic. Then there were the annexationists and annexationists-in-the-making, represented by Thurston, Dole, Smith, Castle, and others.

Kalākaua fell under the attack of Thurston and other critics of the government in much the same way that Tammany Hall fell under the attack of Theodore Roosevelt—and at virtually the same time. Kalākaua was portrayed as wasteful and corrupt. He was debt-ridden. He had taken at least one large payoff from a Chinese rice farmer who wanted the government license to sell opium. He was in the grip of people who were portrayed as scheming and evil, such as his militantly pro-Hawaiian but white prime minister, Walter Murray Gibson. A schism with the surviving Kamehameha, originating in his electoral battle with Emma, also weakened Kalākaua. In this environment the self-appointed white reformers made political headway, but most of the Hawaiian electorate continued to support Kalākaua.

It was at this juncture that Thurston leaped the bounds of electoral politics into the realm of conspiracy. He said the idea came

Life on the Kennebec River in Maine

Luther Severance, founder of The Kennebec Journal, *minister to Hawai'i*

Missionary Daniel Dole, founder of Punahou School and father of Sanford

James G. Blaine, partner of John Stevens in the Journal, *future secretary of state*

John L. Stevens, partner
of James Blaine, future
minister of Hawai'i

KENNEBEC JOURNAL.

AUGUSTA, JULY 6, 1855.

PUBLISHED EVERY FRIDAY MORNING, BY
STEVENS & BLAINE,
EDITORS AND PROPRIETORS.

JOHN L. STEVENS . . . . JAS. G. BLAINE.

TERMS—Two dollars per year, to which fifty cents will
be added if not paid prior to the expiration of the year.—
When paid *strictly in advance*, one dollar and fifty cents
will be received for a year's subscription.

Handbills, Blanks, and all other kinds of Job and Book
Printing done at short notice at the Journal Office.

The masthead suggested a co-equal relationship between
Blaine and Stevens.

The Kennebec Journal, *Augusta, Maine, ca. 1890*

to him one day while he was standing at the gate of his home. A Dr. S.G. Tucker went by. "Thurston," Dr. Tucker is said to have asked, "how long are we going to stand for this kind of thing?"

"What kind of thing?" Thurston asked.

Tucker replied, "The running away with the community by Kalākaua, his interference with elections, and running the Legislature for his own benefit, and all that." Tucker suggested "an organization, including all nationalities, which shall force him to be decent, and reign, not rule, or take the consequences."

Thurston went down Judd Street to the home of his law partner, William Kinney, who had told the Hawaiians of Moloka'i, "Look forward and not backward!" Kinney was not only enthusiastic, but "more belligerent than Dr. Tucker or I." Kinney pulled a book from his library on the French Revolution and pointed to a revolutionary who "called upon citizens in sympathy with the revolutionists to declare themselves."

The Damon biography of Dole says that Thurston's next step was to call a group together to meet at Dole's house. It was the first of many instances in which Thurston turned, almost as a reflex, to the shelter of Dole. Where Thurston always pushed for fundamental changes in the distribution of power and control, Sanford Dole provided an aura of moderation, tempered by Christian piety and expressions of concern for the Hawaiian people. Even though Dole had convened the Reform Party, his speeches in the 1885 Legislature were described by the *Pacific Commercial Advertiser* as "the most moderate and logical of any of the opposition."[3] Dole was superintendent of the Sunday school of Kawaiaha'o Church, where the princess of the realm, Lili'uokalani, was the organist and director of the choir. Dole had been urged by his father to master the Hawaiian language so he could preach to Hawaiians, and as a result he was bilingual, which brought him into more intimate and repeated contact with Hawaiians.

Thurston's conversation in the street, and the subsequent meeting at Dole's house, was the beginning of a long process of insurrection against the Hawaiian government. Dole remembered Thurston, Bill Castle, and Dr. Tucker attending, and "perhaps others," the most likely being William Kinney. Dole intimated there was a great deal of talk about overthrowing the government and annexing Hawai'i to the United States that he could not countenance. He therefore withdrew from the organizing committee, but he obviously was never more than a breath away.

"Politics are getting warm," he wrote to his brother George on Kaua'i. "The rifle companies are filling up with good men evidently induced by the possibilities of genuine work ahead."[4] Shortly thereafter he sent George a hunting rifle, ammunition, and an ammunition belt. While reiterating he did not favor an armed uprising against the government, obviously Dole knew what was really going on.

The original group had expanded to an underground committee. It was led by Thurston and had thirteen members. It had written a new, secret constitution that was designed to greatly reduce Kalākaua's powers and expand its own. Thurston and his colleagues changed their place of meeting nightly. Recruits to the cause were charged with memorizing the constitution but never copying it. The executive committee brought in a larger shadow organization they called the Hawaiian League, with members again swearing to protect the group's secrecy.[5] Thurston said he and William Kinney were in charge of recruitment, and that he swore in most of the members in his office on Fort Street, above where the Fort of Honolulu had stood around the time Thurston was born. According to Thurston's ledger, which was labeled "Accounts for Collection, Honolulu," the Hawaiian League grew to 405 members.

One need only overlook a few things to believe this was democracy working at a heroic level. While Thurston claimed the League was open to all, it was in fact a race-based organization. Entry was at Thurston's personal invitation, or Kinney's. Members were sworn to secrecy. Not only were all the surnames of the executive committee of European origin, but so were all—or virtually all—of those in the League. What may seem like a sizable grassroots organization represented only a tiny fraction of the citizenry. Unable to win control of the government at the ballot box, and likewise unable to bring about a mass uprising, Thurston and his friends turned to the selective exercise of force in the few square blocks that constituted the harbor, business, and government districts of Honolulu.

The League developed its military arm in a roundabout way by demanding that League members exercise a primary loyalty to white people. The oath found in Thurston's ledger by his editor said, "... I will not, in my position of a member of any military organization, oppose or oppress the white citizens of this Kingdom (and) ... I will stand by and support my military superiors in their necessary efforts to protect the white community of this Kingdom ... " With this tactic, Thurston subverted the white military force known as the Honolulu Rifles, which had been organized long before, in 1846.[6] From his boyhood, Lorrin Thurston remembered the Rifles being called out to police a squabble among the king's guards. They had a history of their own that sprang from the white American and European enclaves, but they were also a voluntary reserve force of the Hawaiian Kingdom. In 1887 they were commanded by a man named Volney V. Ashford, who had recently arrived from Canada. Ashford had fought in the American Civil War and then served as a captain in the Canadian army. As the Hawaiian League grew, the Honolulu Rifles became a vigilante force with a nominal allegiance to the government.

Kalākaua saw the outline of the conspiracy coming, but seemed powerless to stop it. In 1886, Kalākaua and Walter Murray Gibson had made an attempt to develop a stronger military force, but the Rifles were the most proficient and enthusiastic volunteers. When Queen Victoria invited Kalākaua to London to the fiftieth anniversary of her reign, he sent his wife and Princess Lili'uokalani in his place. He again may have told Gibson to strengthen the defense force but, if so, Gibson failed to follow through. The Hawaiian Kingdom was as defenseless as the American minister had described it to be in 1866. As the tension increased, the white Honolulu Rifles were actually posted for security by the Kingdom government, but were looking out for the interests of the white Hawaiian League. On June 30, the whites held a mass rally. Appropriately enough, it was at the armory of the Honolulu Rifles, which once had been on the second floor of one of the sugar agencies' offices,[7] and which now stood on the mountain side of the government district just above where the state capitol of Hawai'i stands today.

Although Sanford Dole claims to have distanced himself from the organizers, he called the meeting at the armory to order. Lorrin

Thurston read the demands they were to give the king. The king was to agree to their new constitution and be done with Gibson. When it was Dole's turn to speak, he said, "From the talk I hear along the street, opposition to political reform is in the public mind something akin to treason." That is, on the brink of treason, he was suggesting the treason lay with the supporters of the government. In the speeches that followed, one of the planters said they should not try to force changes on the government by such tactics, but rather make changes through the legislative process. No one agreed.

That week alone, nine hundred new rifles arrived in Honolulu from San Francisco, passing into the hands of the people who had expropriated the word "reform." Merchants ranging from hardware dealers to sugar agents channeled the guns to the white militia. Kalākaua would specifically complain about two of the future Big Five firms, then doing business as Brewer & Co. and Castle & Co., as well as E.O. Hall and Son (hardware) and J.T. Waterhouse. They had, Kalākaua wrote, "distributed promiscuously the arms to everybody."[8]

Sanford Dole had written to his brother that if Kalākaua refused to sign the new constitution, "he will be promptly attacked, and a republic probably declared." The king let go of Gibson before the rally. When he was presented with the new constitution, Kalākaua brooded, argued, and capitulated. On July 6, he signed what aptly became known as the Bayonet Constitution. The relationships of power changed drastically. Native government—diluted as its power had been previously—was at its lowest ebb.

The League installed a new cabinet that included, over the king's objections, Lorrin Thurston. It also created a property qualification for voting so high that mostly it was the sugar-rich *haole* who could qualify. Thurston complained that Kalākaua had an "uncanny ability of knowing when to quit," as if he were disappointed.

The Hawaiian League dragged Walter Murray Gibson from his house, along with his son-in-law. A University of Hawai'i historian of territorial days[9] wrote, "Threats to hang Gibson were made by Lieutenant Colonel Ashford and other noisy radicals, but any such purpose was promptly vetoed by the executive committee of the Hawaiian League." He said "threatening demonstrations" were made against Gibson's daughter. Lili'uokalani's account said that

Gibson and his son-in-law were forced onto the wharf, "where hung two ropes with nooses already prepared, and a man of widely known missionary ancestry, led the outcry, vociferating loudly and lustily, 'Hang them! Hang them!'"

She asked how a son of one of her missionary teachers could have come to this. Lili'uokalani said the noose was around Gibson's neck when he was saved, not by the Hawaiian League but by the British consul. As for Gibson's daughter, another missionary boy entered her home, "threw a lasso over her head, as though the gentle woman had been a wild animal, and avowed his intention of dragging her into town." Thereafter, Gibson was forcibly deported, and his cabinet was replaced by the organizers of the white crowd that at times functioned as a vigilante mob.

Subsequently, it was often written that the Bayonet Constitution "stripped" Kalākaua of his power and fated him to "reign but not rule." At least on paper, that was not quite true. It reduced his powers to roughly that of a monarch whose cabinet is not really his cabinet, but the Legislature's. From the viewpoint of the traditions of a Hawaiian chief, it was intolerable even on paper, and the reality that followed was worse. The cabinet demanded total control. At one point it demanded in writing of Kalākaua that he "sign all documents and do all acts" required under the constitution, whenever the cabinet wished. He balked. The cabinet appealed to the Supreme Court, which ruled in its favor.

A British man named W.L. Green headed the new cabinet, and the attorney general was the Canadian Clarence Ashford, a uniformed officer of the Honolulu Rifles and brother of the commander, Volney Ashford. The American missionary descendant, Lorrin Thurston, became minister of the interior. He administered roads, trails, wharves, harbors, government lands, leases, land awards, water development, and the management of immigration— in short, all those things that so possessed the thoughts of the sugar planters. After a dispute over the administration of the military, the military was reassigned to Thurston's department as well.

Thurston opened a road to the Halema'uma'u Fire Pit on Hawai'i Island.[10] The most spectacular tube-cave formed by lava is renamed for Thurston. The Hawaiians already had named it, as they had named

Sanford Ballard Dole   *Lorrin A. Thurston*   *W.O. Smith*

everything of any significance, but if Thurston had thereafter tended to his work, he might be thought of in Hawai'i today as a farsighted man who helped create parks—much as most people would remember his friend, Theodore Roosevelt, whose image is on Mount Rushmore.

Where Kalākaua had successfully resisted giving America exclusive rights to Pearl Harbor in perpetuity, the cabinet of the Bayonet Constitution quickly gave the U.S. navy the right to build and maintain a coaling station. The new cabinet also struck a blow at Kalākaua's cultural revival by closing the Board of Genealogy that supported the Hale Nauā. The writer Samuel Kamakau had warned that Hawaiians were in danger of becoming a race without a history. He said they might be seen as having blown before the winds onto Hawai'i's shores. As an act of oppression, the closing of the Board of Genealogy was perfect, since the genealogies bound Hawaiians across millennia to their gods and demigods, to the voyagers, the early settlements, and the formation of districts, island kingdoms and, finally, to the Kingdom itself.

The new cabinet also stopped Kalākaua's program of educating promising young Hawaiians abroad, a move that was to have repercussions in the years ahead, as some of the brightest, most ambitious young men of the Kingdom returned to Hawai'i and were thrown into the middle of the widening conflict.

The cabinet that was formed under the Bayonet Constitution served as a preview of white oligarchic rule over the Hawaiian Islands. Through the cabinet, various members of the oligarchy displayed their repressive natures and their willingness to resort to the gun. They were conspiratorial. They had a deep antagonism for Native Hawaiian culture if it reinforced native nationalism. Their alliance with the United States navy was further developed and reinforced. Nonetheless, this small white elite continued to coexist with the institution of the Hawaiian monarchy. Kalākaua's free flow of communication continued with the Hawaiian population. The sugar industry grew constantly, and the planters continued to import laborers, now almost solely from Japan.

Thurston acknowledged that some people believed the constitution of 1887 was not legally enacted. Neither did he. "Unquestionably," he wrote, "the constitution was not in accordance with law; neither was the Declaration of Independence from Great Britain. Both were revolutionary documents, which had to be forcibly effected and forcibly maintained."

Late in 1887, the cabinet of the Bayonet Constitution forced Kalākaua to appoint Sanford Dole to the Supreme Court. While Thurston labored over the development of roads and ditches, Dole was tucked neatly away in the respectability of the judiciary. By 1887, Dole was forty-three. His flowing beard had turned white. He was married to a woman who had visited Hawai'i from Maine. Although he had ascended to the dignity of the court, his key relationships with the white elite continued just as certainly as they had during the uprising. In the spring, Dole bought a small yacht with a young attorney named Francis M. Hatch, who was soon to emerge as an ardent annexationist. They sailed to the Pearl River Lagoon along with Thurston, W.O. Smith and several others. "Camped on Ford's island," Dole told his brother, "caught eels by torch light, sailed next day, Saturday, and raced home."

WHILE LORRIN THURSTON HAD BEEN PREPARING the Bayonet Constitution, Queen Kapi'olani and Princess Lili'uokalani were on a triumphant tour. They sailed to San Francisco and rode a train to Washington, D.C. There they met with the president, Grover Cleveland, who was the first Democrat elected since the Civil War, having defeated James Blaine of Maine.

They visited George Washington's Mount Vernon, visited friends in New York and Boston, and then sailed to the Golden Jubilee of Queen Victoria, monarch of Great Britain, which was still the most powerful nation on Earth. Their visit to London extended the special relationship that had begun with Kamehameha I and the explorer Vancouver nearly a century before. Kamehameha II and his wife had died in London of the plague. The British had signed the 1842 treaty guaranteeing the independence of Hawai'i. The British government had set straight its rogue sea captain George Paulet and restored Kamehameha III to his throne. Subsequently, the Duke of Edinburgh had visited Hawai'i. The British consul in Honolulu was consistently helpful and considerate.

Now, even though London was brimming with nobility from around the globe, Victoria displayed a special interest in Queen

Kapi'olani and the heir apparent, Lili'uokalani. The Hawaiian royalty were scheduled immediately to call at Buckingham Palace. Victoria sat on a couch with Kapi'olani. They conversed through Kapi'olani's interpreter, Curtis Iaukea. Victoria then turned to Lili'uokalani, and they spoke in English about school life in Hawai'i. Victoria introduced her children. As they departed, everyone kissed—as they had on entering. The king of Denmark and the crown prince of Germany waited in the anteroom. Victoria assigned royal guards to Kapi'olani and Lili'uokalani. At the jubilee celebration they sat between a cousin of Queen Victoria and the queen of Belgium. On their return from a garden party, a telegram awaited them with news of the Bayonet Constitution.

They cut short their tour and returned quickly to Honolulu. People assembled on the dock to welcome them, but there was, in Lili'uokalani's words, "an undercurrent of sadness as of a people who had known with us a crushing sorrow." Some people had tears in their eyes. "They knew, and we knew, although no word was spoken, the changes which had taken place while we had been away, and which had been forced upon the king." Among those greeting their ship was the new, all-*haole* cabinet, prominently including the young Lorrin Thurston, minister of the interior. The king came. He was well-dressed and handsome, but Lili'uokalani believed she saw on his face "the terrible strain through which he had passed."

BENEATH THE SURFACE, what was going on? In his dissertation, the Hawaiian historian Dr. Jonathan Osorio traced the cultural content of government and politics between the years 1842 and 1887. As part of his complex thesis, he described the evolution of the missionaries. They arrived believing they had been chosen by God to save the Hawaiians. It was but a short step for them to begin undermining the cultural basis of native rule, which rested on the mutuality between the commoner and the *ali'i*. As the Hawaiians were pressured into adopting Western institutions, it was the Westerner who readily grasped the nature of these institutions and manipulated them. Briefly stated, in Osorio's view, Western religion opened the door to Western education, which opened the door to Western governmental institutions and destruction of the ancient land system, which in turn allowed for the rampant, nearly all-pervasive development of the plantation economy.

The children and grandchildren of the missionaries could no longer stand to be mere preachers, or teachers, or advisers, or even mere tycoons. With their superior knowledge of the world, they were compelled to take charge. As time passed, all things Western were given an ever-higher value, and all things Hawaiian were devalued, then sentimentalized, or crushed and discarded altogether.

As this process went forward, what was occurring in America? What had Lorrin Thurston learned at Columbia, and what had Sanford Dole learned from his journey up the Kennebec River? In fact, the missionary descendants—already so prepared to believe in the superiority of their knowledge and position—were being influenced by American culture and American public life to take over direct control of Hawai'i. It was their job and their—the word that will recur—destiny. Between the first constitution in Hawai'i in 1840 and the Bayonet Constitution in 1887, a systematic theory of white supremacy had been developed that came to be described in the intellectual history of America as Social Darwinism. The keystone of Social Darwinism was the teaching of white supremacy.

In *The Expansionists of 1898*, the historian Julius W. Pratt began a description of Social Darwinism with Charles Darwin's theory of the survival of the fittest. Darwin wrote that nowhere did he see his idea so clearly at work as among the vigorous people of the United States. Darwin in turn was followed by white nativist adapters—such people as the Reverend Josiah Strong, who wove Darwinism together with Christianity, and John Fiske, who said that "the work which the English race began when it colonized North America is destined to go on until every land on the earth's surface that is not already the seat of an old civilization shall become English in its language, in its religion, in its political habits and traditions, and to a predominant extent in the blood of its people."[11]

Next in Pratt's description came John W. Burgess, who was not only a Columbia University professor but the founder of Columbia's political science program. Burgess was yet another figure who was enormously influential in his time but is today conveniently forgotten. He particularly taught Teutonic supremacy in the art of government. The countries of northern Europe and the United States exemplified Burgess's definition of a Teutonic genius for self-government, a trait closely intertwined with the "Aryan" craving—his word for free enterprise. These fine qualities were in sharp contrast to the Celts of Ireland and the Slavs, Czechs, and Hungarians of central Europe, all of whom, in Burgess's mind, lacked self-control and tended toward collectivist thinking. In this hierarchical order, where people of color fit was not hard to imagine.

Today Burgess is interesting not merely as intellectual history in the abstract, but because of his immediate influence over people who would determine the fate of Hawai'i. Lorrin Thurston studied at Columbia about the time that Burgess began attracting a wide audience. In his scant appearances in history today, Burgess is recorded as keeping a watchful eye on his brash young student, Theodore Roosevelt. Roosevelt, Burgess said, "seemed to grasp everything instantly (and) made notes rapidly and incessantly." Finally, Burgess was to become a correspondent and adviser to Sanford Dole.

CHAPTER EIGHT

Trade-off for Pearl Harbor

As time went on, the white community of Hawai'i had invested more and more money in opening up fields and mills. It imported an ever-increasing number of immigrant workers from Asia and shipped an ever-increasing amount of sugar to America. All of this was in response to the opening of America as a tariff-free market. For the small white elite that reaped most of the benefit from the sugar market, anything that might diminish its access to that market struck terror.

In fact, the threat of losing the American market was ever-present, as competing sugar crops were increasingly grown in the continental United States, and congressmen increasingly asked why America was enriching the sugar planters of Hawai'i. The answer to their question always had to do with the future of the American navy, and the plan to build, at some unnamed future date, a base at Pearl Harbor. That is, the answer was always geopolitical, and not simply economic.

The original Treaty of Reciprocity had run for seven years, then was to run from year to year until renewed or canceled. The planters, along with their agents and attorneys, kept an anxious eye on renewal of the treaty. From planting to harvest, their crops were on a two-year cycle. The cycle of raising capital, paying off loans, importing workers on three-year labor contracts, leasing land, and rearranging the landscape, was even more complicated, yet during the 1880s the all-important American market could disappear in a year's time.

In the negotiations to renew the treaty, while many Americans wondered why they were subsidizing the sugar planters of Hawai'i, a coalition of expansionist United States senators took the issue of America's naval interests into their own hands. In January 1887, before voting to renew the treaty, they inserted a clause giving the United States the exclusive use of Pearl Harbor and the right to build a coaling station and other improvements there. In response, Thurston and other American-descended politicians of sugar were ready to agree to America's terms, but Hawaiians generally were not. While Thurston bitterly criticized Kalākaua's character, it was against the backdrop of chronic anxiety over reciprocity that he successfully staged the coup of 1887. Thurston's cabinet took over in the summer. By fall, after haggling the meaning of terms, the Thurston-led cabinet approved the new treaty, as amended by the U.S. Senate.

Dr. Edward Crapol, a historian of the College of William and Mary, described the 1887 Pearl Harbor amendment as the handiwork of James Blaine, even though Blaine held no office at the time.[1] Blaine mobilized the support of several key expansionists, who were soon to become more actively involved in determining the future status of Hawai'i—William P. Frye of Maine, a protégé of Blaine; Benjamin Harrison, who was soon to be president; and John T. Morgan, the Alabama senator who was the Democratic anchor of American expansionism.[2] If it is debatable whether the Pearl Harbor amendment indirectly brought on the coup of 1887, it is indisputable that American expansionism in general was creating intense pressures on the Kingdom of Hawai'i that triggered drastic changes in the status quo.

In the years between 1887 and 1893, the turmoil increased dramatically. Members of the American colony and their European friends had gone so far toward destroying the sovereignty of Hawai'i that an elaborate reaction set in, in which Hawaiians significantly retrieved control of their government. As this conflict was developing, American policy on tariffs began to change again, compounding all the existing conflicts.

The story of America's change in tariffs begins in the late 1880s. The U.S. treasury had piled up an embarrassingly large surplus, part of it from tariffs paid by other countries to get into the sugar market. This did not go entirely unnoticed, because as a result of the tariffs American consumers paid artificially high prices for sugar. A plan addressing this situation began to take shape that was to bear the name of the congressman from Ohio, William McKinley. The plan was to completely abolish all American tariffs on sugar, while giving

American sugar growers a subsidy of two cents a pound.[3] In the narrowest of terms, the Reciprocity Treaty of 1875 as renewed for seven years in 1887 would remain intact, because the Hawai'i growers still would not have to pay tariffs, but other foreign countries would not have to pay tariffs either. Without the two-cent subsidy, Hawai'i growers would no longer be on an equal market footing with American growers. The prosperity of Kalākaua's years would be seriously eroded, if not destroyed. The loans of money, the labor contracts, the rerouting of fresh water, the rearrangement of the land—all would be thrown out of kilter.

The McKinley tariff plan was part of a larger picture, in which the American economy was producing surpluses of both agricultural and industrial products. As a result the Republican Party, traditionally protectionist, was seeking to open up or expand foreign markets while, if possible, protecting the domestic market to the benefit of domestic producers. In other words, it sought to have things both ways.

Increasingly the McKinley tariff proposals seemed certain to become law. The question for Hawai'i was whether it would be treated as an exception to the new law or merely as another foreign country. While traditional Hawaiian society was struggling to free itself from the Bayonet Constitution, the stage was set for the arrival of John Stevens, and looming behind Stevens was the large figure of James G. Blaine.

Blaine was the single most influential Republican on the expansionist side of policy-making. Blaine also happened to have been thinking for the preceding thirty-five years about what America could do with Hawai'i. As a young man, he had been a schoolteacher, but in 1854 he had migrated to Augusta, Maine, where he became known thereafter as Blaine of Maine. In Augusta, he became closely acquainted with Luther Severance, who had returned from his service as U.S. commissioner to the Kingdom of Hawai'i. Blaine took over the newspaper that Severance had founded, *The Kennebec Journal*. He found a partner in John L. Stevens, a minister who was noted for advocating the abolition of slavery.

While everything to do with Hawai'i was to become infinitely more complicated, it is noteworthy that as early as 1854 or 1855,

Stevens and Blaine had absorbed Luther Severance's enthusiasm for gaining control of a chain of islands one quarter of the globe away that neither had seen. As a tribute to Severance on his death, Blaine published a thirty-three-page obituary pamphlet. John Stevens was to write that Severance was a light that "still shines on us like the rays of the sun on the mountains, ere it goes down."[4] Severance not only influenced their thinking about Hawai'i, but how they lived their lives. Just as Severance moved in stages from newspaper editor to elected official to diplomat, so would both Blaine and Stevens.

In the years to come, when the American government would sidestep responsibility for Stevens's actions in Hawai'i, the nature of the relationship between the mighty Blaine and the odd figure of Stevens took on a much-discussed historical importance. In point of fact, their relationship was not only close but, at least in the earlier years, one of equals. On the masthead of *The Kennebec Journal*, Blaine and Stevens listed themselves on the same line—that is, as apparent equals. The next line described them as "Editors and Proprietors." Both were among the original members of the Republican Party. Blaine represented Maine at the first Republican Party national convention in 1856, and the next year he was elected to the Maine Legislature. In 1862 he was elected to the U.S. House of Representatives, leaving John Stevens to publish the *Journal*.

A correspondent for the *Chicago Tribune* said Blaine was "surcharged with nervous energy," which caused his engine to race at more than three hundred revolutions per minute. "He darts hither and thither across the hall, up and down the aisles, or through the lobby, with incessant activity."[5] Blaine was credited with shaping the language of the Fourteenth Amendment to the U.S. Constitution, which guarantees equal protection of the law to all citizens, regardless of their state. In support of the Fourteenth Amendment he argued that if slavery had not taught Americans "to do justice to all of God's creatures without distinction of race or color, we must expect a still more heavy vengeance of an offended Father."

He was a spellbinding orator who drove people to intense emotional heights, and he quickly became speaker of the U.S. House of Representatives, a position he held when Kalākaua arrived in Washington and addressed Congress, asking for reciprocity. By the age of forty-six, Blaine was the leading candidate for the Republican nomination to succeed Ulysses Grant as president. Since the Republican Party at this point had never lost a presidential election, its nomination was the next thing to being president. Blaine was close to his prize when his opponents alleged that he had made a windfall by influencing the award of land grants to a venture called the Little Rock and Fort Smith Railroad. He defended himself by saying his payments were commissions. As a result of the scandal he lost the nomination to a little-remarked man, Rutherford Hayes, who proved the staying power of the Republican Party by winning the election.

Blaine tried again four years later, but again he lost, this time to James Garfield. Garfield nonetheless made Blaine his secretary of state. Shortly thereafter Garfield was assassinated, and Blaine again was out of work, but as the next election came around he resumed his quest.

In the meantime, the precocious New York assemblyman, Theodore Roosevelt, became involved in the presidential nominating process. Roosevelt was a political wisp in comparison to the powerful Blaine, but their encounter was nonetheless interesting. As the leading young Republican in the New York Legislature, Roosevelt became a member of the New York delegation to the 1884 nominating convention. He was among those in the Republican Party who were not inclined to forgive Blaine for the quick money he was said to have made on the Little Rock Railroad. For a comparatively well-to-do warrior such as Roosevelt, Blaine's interest in additional and effortless income was a sure sign of decadence. Roosevelt opposed Blaine.

To drum up support for an alternative candidate Roosevelt turned to a leading member of the Massachusetts delegation, Henry Cabot Lodge, who would soon become his most important ally in perfecting a strategy of American expansion. Blaine won the nomination anyway. An Ohio congressman pushed his way through the crowd to plead with young Theodore to make a unity speech. It was the protectionist William McKinley, who in the not-too-distant future was to get his tariff bill through Congress and thereafter become president himself. Roosevelt told McKinley no. The purists of the party bolted the Republican ticket, backing the Democratic nominee, Grover Cleveland. They wanted Roosevelt to join them, but Roosevelt and Lodge returned to the Republican fold. Calming themselves, they stumped for Jim Blaine, further offending the purists, but it all came to nothing. In Maine to this day it is written that if Blaine had gotten another 1,041 votes in New York state, he would have been president.

It was at this point that Roosevelt went West, not only recently widowed but at odds with his political party, having managed to offend both the regulars and the reformers. He stayed in the Dakotas long enough for the image of the closing of the western frontier to fix vividly in his mind, just as it was fixing vaguely in the mind of the American public. He then returned to New York, remarried, and got back into politics. He also wrote books at an amazing pace. *The Winning of the West* was a big success. In 1888, a year after Lorrin Thurston imposed the Bayonet Constitution on the Hawaiian chieftain, David Kalākaua, Roosevelt again became involved in a presidential campaign. He stumped the country for Benjamin Harrison, who successfully challenged the incumbent Democrat, Cleveland. It was the first of the fateful presidential elections with regards to Hawai'i.

Blaine, then one of the most prominent American expansionists, became secretary of state for the second time. Henry Cabot Lodge, an expansionist as well, suggested to Blaine that his young friend Theodore Roosevelt—also an avid expansionist—be named assistant secretary of state. Would not Blaine let bygones be bygones? Blaine wondered aloud what would happen if young Roosevelt was in Washington running the shop while he was out of town. "I do somehow fear," Blaine said, "that my sleep at Augusta or Bar Harbor would not be quite as easy and refreshing if so brilliant and aggressive a man had hold of the helm." Roosevelt, now thirty, had to settle for being one of three civil service commissioners in the Harrison administration. This job would turn out to be no small thing, because it would allow him to turn his domestic face to the public and be an advocate of reform, tearing into the working of political machines, including Harrison's own postal department.

But while Roosevelt was getting ready to make history, Blaine— twice Roosevelt's age—actually was making history, even if he was not to be widely remembered for it. He was single-minded and seasoned, and he was in charge of American foreign policy. Who he recommended to be the American minister to Hawai'i was a highly sensitive matter, because Hawai'i was ascending on the American agenda. To manage the relationship with the Kingdom of Hawai'i, Blaine turned to John L. Stevens, with whom he had worked thirty-five years earlier, when both had sat together at the weekly newspaper in Maine and made the acquaintance of Luther Severance.

IT IS TEMPTING TO THINK OF John L. Stevens as a caricature of crankiness and paranoia, but the paradoxes of Stevens would be lost in the process. While it is true he was both ill-tempered and inclined to fight demons, he was also diligent and accomplished. The author of a thesis on John Stevens remarked repeatedly on what she perceived as his "compassion" for others.

He, too, was from Maine, specifically from Mount Vernon, which is a few miles west of Augusta. He was born in 1820, the year the first missionaries departed for Hawai'i and Severance arrived in Augusta with his printer's stick. As a young man Stevens studied with a minister in Hallowell, the hometown of Sanford Dole's mother, and he became a minister of the Universalist, or Unitarian, Church.

Historians of the Kennebec River valley begin their story by saying that in 1625 the pilgrims—after only five years in their new land—sent an expedition from Plymouth to the Kennebec. They traded corn for furs. Thereafter the landscape was accented with church spires, and Maine society was dominated by the tenets of Puritanism. The Maine Anti-Slavery Society started in Hallowell, and a temperance society forced a ban on the sale of liquor. While Sanford's father, Daniel Dole, was preparing to migrate to Hawai'i, he was an active opponent of both slavery and whiskey.[6]

Where America's land-based images of Maine have to do with moose, lakes, and lighthouses, life in Maine is shaped considerably by the long, cold winter. The Kennebec Valley is frozen for long periods, and it is littered with granite. The land is forbidding, but the sea beckons. Both Hallowell and neighboring Augusta were ports, even though located forty miles inland, because the river runs so deep and wide that it forms a sort of inland sea. The Kennebec in turn is one of the many waterways and harbors that allowed Maine to become a leading force in navigation, shipbuilding, and, finally, America's adventure into the Pacific (John Stevens's father-in-law, for example, was a ship's captain based in Hallowell). If there is an apparent combination of climate, geography, and zealotry at work here, the question is nonetheless not adequately answered: Why would this one stretch of land, only several miles long, originally five months' distant from Hawai'i by sea, produce an interconnected network of people who would play such prominent roles in American expansionism?

The process was transforming. John Stevens got a foothold in politics by writing antislavery tracts that were to the liking of Blaine. In the original organization of the Republican Party in the state of Maine, Stevens served as party chairman from 1856 to 1860 and was succeeded in that position by Blaine. A critic of the day complained that Maine was controlled politically by "the Augusta ring," first listing Stevens, then Blaine and several others.[7]

If there is an early clue to the dark side of Stevens, it may be found in an opposition newspaper published in Augusta in 1855. It said that Mr. Stevens of *The Kennebec Journal* was a leader of the Republicans by day and the Know-Nothing Council by night. The Know-Nothings, this account went on, were also known as the Supreme Sons of the Star-Spangled Banner. The "test sign" of the secret organization was a forefinger (presumably one's own) under the top button of the vest. The correct response was a thumb under the top button, the hand facing down. Stevens, by participating in the secret, xenophobic organization, was part of a "dark-lantern oligarchy" subverting the intentions of the Republican Party.[8]

Over decades, Stevens was one of those who transformed the antislavery party into a party dedicated to imperialism. Such behavior may seem puzzling today, as people have come to think of slavery and colonialism as evils of a similar sort, but such was not the case in the early days of the Republican Party. When Stevens and Blaine went to the Republican national convention in Chicago in 1860, Stevens backed William Seward, one of his lifelong heroes, while Blaine backed Abraham Lincoln. William Seward became Lincoln's secretary of state, attacking slavery on the basis of "a higher law" than the Constitution. Seward was probably the most important expansionist of his day. He oversaw the purchase of Russia's claims to Alaska, and he inquired none too gingerly about the possibilities of annexing Hawai'i. Barring annexation, Seward vigorously advocated a treaty of reciprocity with Hawai'i.

Following Blaine's early departure from *The Kennebec Journal*, Stevens served as editor and publisher. He also served in the Maine Legislature from 1865 to 1870, and he became a leader of a successful movement to abolish capital punishment. His pamphlet, *The Death Penalty*, was reprinted repeatedly. It took as its text the commandment, "Thou shalt not kill," quoting Cicero, Montesquieu, and Ben Franklin to make its case.

In 1870 President Grant appointed Stevens ambassador to Paraguay and Uruguay. On his return to the United States, Stevens pushed for Blaine for president, only to see Blaine derailed by scandal. He then served as ambassador to Sweden and Norway for six years. In a lull he wrote a book about Swedish history and received a doctorate of law from Tufts College. He returned to writing for *The Kennebec Journal* in 1887—he was then sixty-seven years old—and renewed some of his old acquaintances. Maine's U.S. Senator William P. Frye, a member of the Senate Foreign Relations Committee, wrote Stevens a note saying, "I am under great obligation to you for the kindly manner in which you speak of me and my services."[9]

In this state of semiretirement, Stevens dropped by the home of his old and valued friend, Blaine, who had yet to give up on his great political ambition. Blaine House is an enormous mansion that directly faces the state capitol of Maine, and one may imagine Blaine and Stevens meeting there and discussing Blaine's last run at the presidency. The intensity of their tie is reflected in Stevens's papers during 1888, when he wrote glowing articles about Blaine and corresponded on Blaine's behalf with politicians in states as far away as Kansas, Ohio, Maryland, and West Virginia.

The Republican nomination and subsequent victory went instead to Benjamin Harrison, who then acquiesced to the influence of Blaine by appointing him secretary of state. Stevens wrote Harrison, "I feel it is my duty to open to you my heart and mind in a revelation to be known only to God and yourself," etc.—that Blaine should serve. By the summer of 1889, Blaine was running the U.S. Department of State, and Stevens was headed for Hawai'i for his final diplomatic assignment. Although their mentor Luther Severance was long gone, he shone like a light on a high mountain.

This close relationship between Blaine and Stevens is of historical importance precisely because it supports the impression that

Stevens's subsequent behavior reflected the attitudes of Blaine (and Harrison) as the creators of U.S. policy, and that Stevens therefore was an extension of the highest levels of policy-making by the United States government.

Blaine had openly endorsed the idea of taking over Hawai'i and stated his willingness to abandon American tradition in order to do so. While Blaine left no trail of direct instructions to John Stevens, most historians agree at least with the view that "it must be supposed that a close personal understanding existed with (John) Stevens as to the nature of his duties and the policies to be pursued."[10]

Blaine and Stevens were not only like-minded individuals, but part of a directory of people of like mind reaching between Hawai'i and the Kennebec River. After Stevens arrived in Hawai'i to take up Severance's old assignment, he seems to have been well aware of the special impact that people from his neighborhood had made on Hawai'i. He wrote a newspaper editor in Hallowell, H.K. Baker, asking for details. Baker wrote back describing the Goodale sisters of Hallowell, who had married William Ladd and Peter Brimsmade of Hallowell, organizers of Hawai'i's first sugar plantation at Kōloa, Kaua'i, where Sanford Dole had grown to adulthood.[11]

H.K. Baker could also have added—or perhaps Stevens already knew—that he and his brother, Joseph Baker, had grown up in Skowhegan, Maine, Daniel Dole's birthplace, and that his brother Joseph had attended Maine's Bowdoin College with Daniel Dole. At that point, the circle of connections was complete, because it was from Joseph Baker that Stevens had bought his interest in *The Kennebec Journal.* In other words, John Stevens originally knew Daniel Dole's boyhood friend and college classmate, Joseph Baker, as a co-owner of the *Journal* in Augusta, along with Blaine.

The names of the Maine towns may sound confusing, but an understanding of their small size and their proximity to one another helps clarify the story. Hallowell and Augusta not only lie next to one another but were once part of the same town. By 1840, the population of Augusta was 5,314 and Hallowell was 4,654. Most of the leading citizens were Whigs, then Republicans. They were involved in not only the antislavery movement but the temperance movement.[12]

Those who formed the directory of Maine-based relationships within Hawai'i had founded the sugar industry, founded Punahou School (which was to dominate education in Hawai'i thereafter), launched the original discussion of annexation, and crafted the American policy of expansionism in the late nineteenth century. By 1889, that left John Stevens on the scene to forge ahead with Sanford Dole and Dole's missionary cousins, such as Thurston, W.O. Smith, and W.R. Castle.

How much Sanford Dole knew about this web of relationships is not known precisely, but it can be safely generalized that he knew a great deal and was influenced by it. He liked Maine, and he thought of his family in Maine. He married a woman from Maine. He discussed events and people from past days with his father, who either knew, or knew about, not only Ladd and Brimsmade but Severance, Stevens, and Blaine. In Dole's photographic album, he kept a picture of Luther Severance's son, Henry W. Severance, as well as his children. In all likelihood Dole attended Punahou with Henry before the Severance family returned to Maine. Thereafter Henry became the San Francisco consul general to the Kingdom, and by the time of John Stevens he had returned to Honolulu to work under Stevens as consul general. While influential people subsequently would distance themselves from John Stevens in the writing of history, it seems logical that Dole would have taken a special interest in Stevens as the newly arrived minister from Maine.

At first Stevens professed to favor a protectorate rather than outright annexation, a position that was in line with James Blaine's thinking. But in either event Stevens was unabashed in announcing his belief that America must control Hawai'i. When John Stevens was to call the American troops into Honolulu, was he doing what he was supposed to do, or had he lurched out of control? That must have been what Lili'uokalani asked herself as she stood on the balcony of 'Iolani Palace. That also was what the U.S. House of Representatives eventually would ask, as it reviewed a resolution to censure Stevens. Finally, it is a question that has confronted modern-day Native Hawaiians, at times when the American government has sought to evade responsibility for the overthrow.

LILI'UOKALANI DESCRIBES her and her brother's lives during this period as nightmarish. She contends Kalākaua was not merely treated badly but threatened with assassination. Representatives of the *haole* elite appeared at her door to ask if she would take over the monarchy from her brother. The suggestion was that she be more pliable than he.

Five different political parties contended for power—with names that serve to confuse rather than clarify. There was the Reform Party, led by Dole and Thurston; a National Reform Party, which supported the monarchy; a Liberal Party made up of Hawaiians who sought change in the government; a new nativist party called Native Sons, which also supported the monarchy; and for those who did not otherwise fit, an Independent label.

The situation can be simplified by focusing on the fact that while Hawaiian royalists were regaining political influence, the threat of the McKinley tariff was causing further instability. After John Stevens's arrival in 1889, he wrote to Blaine in Washington warning that the McKinley tariff "would be the virtual annulment of the reciprocity treaty and the destruction of the prosperity of the islands." Worse, from Stevens's viewpoint, it would weaken Hawai'i's "fraternal relations" with America. The Kingdom's ambassador to Washington, H.A.P. Carter, engaged Secretary of State Blaine in earnest conversation to the same effect.

Blaine began throwing out pieces of what he wanted—the right to speak for Hawai'i in foreign affairs, the right to land troops to quell disturbances, and the right to veto any and all treaties between Hawai'i and any other country (for example, Britain, France, and Japan). In return, America would guarantee the continued existence of Hawai'i as a country and give the sugar planters whatever subsidies were given to American sugar growers. Kalākaua, who awoke each day to the cabinet imposed by the Bayonet Constitution, wrote in the margin of his copy of the treaty draft, "This amounts to a Protectorate." He turned to the British ambassador for an analysis of Blaine's proposal. The British minister agreed. He urged Kalākaua not to sign it. At one point, Thurston's cabinet reminded the king that he was supposed to sign whatever was placed in front of him, but the king said no, not in the realm of foreign affairs.

While Kalākaua stalled, he looked for ways to improve his anemic position, and it was in this environment that the monarchist organization Hui Kālai'āina developed as a political force. It was dedicated to reawakening Hawaiian support for the monarch as the embodiment of tradition, as well as to maintaining Hawaiian control of the nation. It formed an alliance with a mostly white organization, the Mechanics and Workingmen's Political Protective Union, and together they made up the National Reform Party, borrowing the key word of the white missionary Reform Party. In the election of 1890 the mostly Hawaiian National Reform Party made serious strides toward recouping Hawaiian control of the government—but not before a great deal more turmoil ensued.

Among the young men sent overseas to study by Kalākaua, and then forced home when the Bayonet Cabinet cut off their means of support, one had studied military strategy. His name was Robert Wilcox, and his story grew to legendary proportions. Wilcox was of mixed Caucasian and Hawaiian ancestry. He was handsome and articulate. On his return, he stayed initially in one of Lili'uokalani's several homes, and there he began to plot a revolt to abolish the Bayonet Constitution of 1887.

To destroy the Bayonet Constitution was a clear enough goal. What was unclear was whether he also wished to unseat Kalākaua and put Lili'uokalani on the throne. Around three o'clock on a midsummer's morning in 1889, he set out for 'Iolani Palace with eighty men. Among them they had thirty-five rifles, a few pistols, and some small guns that Chinese rice farmers had imported to frighten away birds. Where the Honolulu Rifles and Thurston's crowd had brought in nine hundred new rifles in the week before imposing the Bayonet Constitution, Robert Wilcox set out with less than one tenth their number of arms to reverse that action.

Wilcox marched through the gates of the palace and set up a defense that lasted a day. Several people were killed, and Wilcox was forced to surrender. He initially was charged with treason. The charge was reduced to conspiracy. By a vote of nine to three, a native jury found him not guilty.

Wilcox inflamed the imagination of many Hawaiians in the late nineteenth century, much as he inflames people's imaginations today.

He can be tracked wandering widely over the political landscape, but in one thing he was consistent. He dreamed of, and took risks for, effective native control of Hawai'i. His slogan was "Hawai'i for the Hawaiians." His thoughtful side was marred by impetuosity, but he touched the native longing to adapt and maintain Hawaiian control of the Hawaiian Islands.

Like the culture heroes of Hawaiian story, he had the audacity to stand and fight against impossible odds. From ancient time Hawaiians had a tradition of periodic revolt. Typically the low-born revolted against the high-born. 'Umi, as the commoner son of Līloa, had revolted against Hākau, Līloa's high-born son. Kamehameha, as the war chief, had revolted against Kiwala'ō, who had the most rarefied genealogy. A successful revolt established a new order. Unsuccessful revolts became minor items in the great skein of the Hawaiian story. In Western time, the exciting possibilities of revolting against chiefly authority had been largely suppressed. Only those who knew history well were aware that one of Kamehameha's sons had revolted after Kamehameha's death against the anointed heir. He lost.

It is possible—indeed probable—that Robert Wilcox reflected a growing schism in the traditional leadership system of the Hawaiians, the extent of which should be the subject of further research, because it bears not only on what was confusing then but is confusing now as nationalist-minded Hawaiians attempt to redefine their relationship with America, its political institutions, and its culture.

One thing is indisputable. Wilcox was immensely popular, not only with Native Hawaiian voters but with Native Hawaiian jurors. His closest ally was John E. Bush, also of mixed ancestry. Bush wrote long essays that described the evolution of a Native Hawaiian political culture. In Bush's view, Kamehameha and the monarchy had been a necessary step. Constitutional monarchy likewise had been a logical development in its time, but now, he argued, the institution of the monarchy itself was archaic. What was needed was a Hawaiian Republic. He and Wilcox repeatedly used the words "by the people, of the people, and for the people." Where they may be regarded by some as betraying the idea of tradition that hung so heavily over the Hawaiians, from another viewpoint they were advocates of a genuine native democracy, fighting the autocracy of the Hawaiian *ali'i* system on the one side and the budding oligarchy of the white combatants on the other.

Enhanced rather than tarnished by his armed revolt of 1889, Wilcox immediately launched a campaign for a seat in the House of Representatives, as did Bush. In their campaigns, they complained bitterly about ambassador H.A.P. Carter and his negotiations with James Blaine. They also deftly exploited the schisms within the white militia and the Reform Party.

The fault lines in the Euro-American coalition in Honolulu appeared as Blaine more aggressively pressed American terms. The American-descended missionaries became more transparently pro-American in their politics. The German and British communities became more wary. The cabinet splintered.

Although American missionary descendants clearly were the driving force in the Reform Party campaign of 1884, and Thurston clearly instigated the 1887 coup, the American group had made no effort up to this point to control all the positions of power. Two of the cabinet members were British and one, Clarence Ashford, the attorney general, was Canadian. Only Thurston was an American annexationist.

Thurston and Ashford were the most keen on creating a more heavily militarized state in which Ashford's brother, Volney Ashford, would (and finally did) serve as commander of the army. Thereafter the military was placed under Thurston in the Ministry of the Interior, which is where armies usually are placed administratively when the domestic hold of the government rests on the power of the gun. Thereafter Thurston became estranged from the Ashford brothers and Clarence actually left the country for an awkward period to shop for friends and ideas in Canada. On his return he began to work an alliance with Robert Wilcox.

In yet another sector of dissatisfied people, the less-privileged Americans complained that the Bayonet Cabinet was a government by the few in the interests of the few—expressing a dissatisfaction that Hui Kālai'āina tapped in its alliance with the Mechanics and Workingmen's Union.

In this increasingly chaotic environment, the National Reform Party won the election of early 1890, if barely. After skirmishing in the Legislature to determine where the votes lay, the cabinet that had been formed under the Bayonet Constitution resigned, Thurston included.

The new Legislature officially disbanded the Honolulu Rifles, but revising the despised constitution of 1887 was another matter. In midsummer 1890, Bush and Wilcox organized a rally in Palace Square that was intended to launch a grassroots movement for a new constitution. It resulted in a call for a constitutional convention that was presented with ceremony to Kalākaua, who in turn presented it to the Legislature. In response, John Stevens appeared before the king and told him he should not support the movement for a new constitution. The Bayonet Constitution had become an item of national policy for America, even if it had been imposed by means that were ruthless, untraditional, and illegal.

By the fall of 1890, the conflict over the constitutional future of Hawai'i had reached a standoff. Thurston was out of the cabinet, Kalākaua was regaining influence, the Hawaiians were getting better organized politically, and Robert Wilcox's star was rising. As for reciprocity, Ambassador H.A.P. Carter talked earnestly with Blaine about the McKinley tariff bill that was now moving quickly through Congress. Carter was led to believe that Blaine would look out for the interests of the sugar industry of Hawai'i. The device was to be a catchall provision that the bill would not impair existing treaty obligations. This was not a straightforward solution, because the government of Hawai'i nonetheless would have had to haggle for a subsidy. But the point became moot, because the catchall language was absent when the bill came out of the House Finance Committee. The bill was silent on Hawai'i, and as a result Hawai'i's market advantage came to a crashing halt.[13]

The planters' worst nightmare had come true. Their competitive advantage was gone. American planters got their two-cent subsidy, and the planters of Hawai'i got nothing.

The historian Ralph Kuykendall portrayed this as an omission that went unnoticed until after Congress adjourned. He quoted Blaine as saying he regretted the omission, as if in his busy life Blaine had lost track of a detail. It is an interpretation that fails to take account of Blaine's extraordinary abilities and extensive influence. It also fails to address the possibility that Blaine purposely neglected the interests of the sugar industry in Hawai'i.

What if Blaine was letting go of "fraternal relations" with Hawai'i in favor of something bigger? What if Blaine was letting the planters, their lawyers, Ambassador Carter, and even Stevens squirm, by brutally reminding them of how dependent they had become on the deal with America? What if Blaine was using the McKinley tariff bill as leverage for effectively taking control of Hawai'i?

American historians since Kuykendall have been revisiting that possibility. Walter LaFeber wrote that Blaine made his move for a protectorate when McKinley's sugar proposals "became a probability." It seems indisputable that Blaine was trying to use the vulnerability of Hawai'i's cash economy to take perpetual control of Hawai'i. The only question is whether he purposely let go of reciprocity when he failed to get his way—that is, did he purposely destabilize the economy of the United States as an antecedent to expanding America's control of Hawai'i?

When the McKinley tariff passed as written, an economic downturn set in, followed by a sense of panic. Investment in the plantations of Hawai'i began to dry up even before the tariff went into effect.

King Kalākaua, in his fine moment in the American spotlight, had seemed to provide the crucial difference in the campaign for reciprocity. Now, despite the abuse he had suffered, despite failing health, he was ready to go back to work on behalf of reciprocity. He went to San Francisco, where he met with Carter and several *haole* businessmen. When he realized that he was dying, he made a voice recording on one of the early wax cylinder recording machines, urging Hawaiians to persevere. He died in San Francisco on January 20, 1891, at the age of fifty-four. U.S. navy Admiral George Brown was at his bedside, along with several other *haole* and two Hawaiian companions. The sugar baron Claus Spreckels hovered in the room, as did Charles Reed Bishop, husband of the late Bernice Pauahi Bishop. His casket was carried past large crowds in the streets of San Francisco to the S.S. *Charleston*. As the ship approached Honolulu, the Hawaiians could see it was draped in black, and the chants of grief arose even before the *Charleston* tied up at the dock.

Lydia Kamaka'eha succeeded to the throne as Her Royal Highness, Lili'uokalani of Hawai'i. Under intense pressure from her inherited cabinet, she haltingly swore an oath to uphold the Bayonet Constitution, which she despised.

DURING THE TIME LORRIN THURSTON was railing against corruption in the regime of David Kalākaua, Theodore Roosevelt was railing against corruption in the U.S. Civil Service. In 1890 he read a new book by Captain Alfred Mahan, *The Influence of Sea Power upon History, 1660-1783*. Having written the definitive history of the naval War of 1812 with Britain, Roosevelt was in a unique position to evaluate Mahan's work. He wrote a glowing review that appeared in the *Atlantic Monthly*, calling it the "best and most important" naval history in many years. To a country that was looking for ways to develop overseas markets for its glut of industrial and agricultural products, Mahan provided a scholarly variation on Roosevelt's original message, which was that America needed a powerful navy.

Few people today know who Mahan was, but he should be remembered for his extensive influence in the American expansionist movement, and above all for his impact on people's thinking about Hawai'i. Other members of the imperialist group talked grandly about a two-oceans strategy and building an isthmian canal, but it was Mahan who drilled home—over and over, in crucial moments— the primary importance of Hawai'i to America's global strategy. Whenever the issue of Hawai'i arose, Mahan would grab his pen, write furiously, and almost instantly find publishers for his views.

By the time his first major work was published, he was fifty years old. He was still on active naval duty. He had a reputation for being vain, intellectually arrogant, and an inept seaman, but he captured a large public following. People in the top reaches of the navy, Congress, and the national administration were all sensitive to his thoughts. If a congressman was wavering on whether to support the expansionist agenda, Roosevelt's ultimate weapon was to become a note from Mahan.

CHAPTER NINE

An American Coup

From the moment of taking the oath of office, Lili'uokalani had balked at the idea of serving as a mere figurehead. In essence, she rejected the Anglo-American definition of a monarch as it was evolving in the late nineteenth century. In doing so, she adhered in a general way to the tradition of the Hawaiian ruling chief, who not only reigned but ruled.

On a personal level, in light of all that had transpired, her determination to assert her will and to reassert the powers of the native citizenry was remarkable. She had lost not only King David but most of her family. She soon was to lose her husband, and she was surrounded at every turn by critics, and by men whose real loyalties lay not with the nation of Hawai'i but with the ambitions of other nations.

The execution of her plans might be faulted as uncertain, but she operated in a world of extreme uncertainties. It was uncertain whether she would be immediately subjected to the same treatment as Kalākaua, whether an exercise of power on her part would bring retaliation, and even whether she would come quickly to a violent end. It was uncertain how far Robert Wilcox and John Bush would pursue their idea of a Hawaiian Republic, and, finally, it was uncertain how far the Harrison Administration would go in pursuing its demands for control of Hawai'i.

In the Hawaiian Renaissance of the 1970s and 1980s, as a result of the work of the playwright and author John Dominis Holt, and subsequently the play of Aldythe Morris, and the documentary films *Act of War* and *The Last Queen*, Lili'uokalani has come to be a more accessible figure. Yet so much of this recitation has revolved around her personality that the all-important context tends to be lost—namely, the mood, tactics, and aspirations of the United States government.

Again, the answers lie with James Blaine and John Stevens, and in a general way with the president, Benjamin Harrison. On the death of Kalākaua, John Stevens appeared before Lili'uokalani to offer condolences, then proceeded to lecture her on America's expectation that she not try to run the government. As he had told Kalākaua in so many words, the constitution that had been adopted at gunpoint—the constitution that Thurston was to proudly describe as illegal—was regarded by the American government as the law of the land, and any move against it was wrong-headed and illegal.

At the Fourth of July celebration after Kalākaua's death, John Stevens attacked monarchs who "claimed to be above the sovereignty of the people." By early 1892 he had discarded the idea of a military protectorate in favor of outright annexation. He wrote Blaine that "the time is not distant when the United States must say yes or no to the question of annexation ... " He was talking with Thurston. He also wrote Thurston a letter of introduction to carry with him to Washington. By the fall he was writing detailed dispatches to Blaine that he was showing to Thurston before they went into the State Department diplomatic pouch.

Stevens outlined the alternatives of a military protectorate or annexation and recommended the latter. Not long afterwards he wrote an unsigned article for his and Blaine's old newspaper, *The Kennebec Journal*, saying the time was at hand to decide "who shall hold these islands as a part of their national territory." It apparently was recognized as his work and was widely reprinted around America. The alternatives Stevens posed were for either America or a European power to take over Hawai'i. The continuation of native government was not an option.

In the aftermath, historians have searched for evidence that Stevens was operating on orders from Blaine. Kuykendall searched, and found no such orders, nor has anyone else. The significance of this line of inquiry is enormous, because the facts of history have been twisted to reinforce the idea that Stevens was operating on his own, or at least that the United States was not responsible for his actions. After this history again became an issue in the late 1970s and early 1980s, the non-native majority of the presidentially appointed Native Hawaiian Study Commission squelched the Hawaiian claim for reparation, substantially on the contention that no one could prove the intent or malice of the U.S. government. They sent the Native Hawaiian members of the commission on a fruitless search for a "smoking gun," as it was called, focusing on the narrow specific rather than the broad pattern.

Stevens at one point wrote to Blaine, asking, "... are you for annexation?" In the diplomatic correspondence, there is no record of a response. However, to interpret this silence as a lack of agreement is in error, given the nature of their long-standing relationship, and particularly given that Stevens had his hands on one of the most delicate issues of U.S. foreign policy. The most likely distinction Stevens sought was whether Blaine had shifted his thinking from a military protectorate to outright annexation.

"Did Blaine favor annexation?" asked the historian Charles S. Campbell. "Absolute silence reigned in Washington. A highly intelligent man, the Secretary obviously saw the drift of his protégé's queries and comments. Had he disapproved he should have sent a strong caution. By not doing so Blaine ... incurred a clear responsibility for Stevens's actions ... "[1] The absence of official communication, Campbell said, was "almost as meaningful to Minister Stevens, who knew his chief well ... "

That Stevens and Blaine shared the same vocabulary, definitions, and attitudes is undeniable. As early as 1868, a quarter-century before the overthrow, Blaine as a young congressman had argued for America to turn from the problems of the Civil War to world affairs and "the extension of our flag and our sovereignty over insular or continental possessions." The insular possessions naturally would have been Hawai'i.

As early as 1881, in the first of his two terms as secretary of state, Blaine had said that Hawai'i must become part of the American system. Ten years later, in his second incarnation at the State Department, he was telling President Harrison that Hawai'i was "of value enough to be taken." He said America should break with its tradition as a continental Republic and take possessions overseas, and that the value of Hawai'i made this worth doing.² Blaine convinced Harrison there was "mischief brewing" in Hawai'i, and by 1891 Harrison responded by saying that the Europeans were a threat. It was less than a month after this conversation between Blaine and Harrison that the United States navy, in the fall of 1891, indefinitely stationed a warship in Hawai'i, to Lili'uokalani's dismay. A newspaper report said the navy intended "to keep a United States vessel there from this time on to guard American interests in the islands."

Harrison, for his part, had been one of the senators who pushed through the Pearl Harbor clause in the 1887 renewal of the Reciprocity Treaty, and he was more than ready to believe what Stevens and Blaine told him. In the fall of 1891, as Hawai'i felt the bite of the McKinley tariff, and as the queen struggled to finance the government despite the recession, Harrison wrote to Blaine saying that reciprocity was "an interesting subject for a little work ... " but that the more important question was control—as he phrased it, "the necessity of maintaining and increasing our hold and influence in the Sandwich Islands ... "³

While America calmly maintained its pressure, it watched as political turmoil in Hawai'i became more pronounced. The five political parties were churning away, and the partisan press competed for attention and readership. Acrimony worsened in the Legislature as people fought over how to finance the government in light of the economic depression induced by America's new tariff law. An already polarized situation became moreso, and Native Hawaiian fears of losing their country were heightened.

During an attempt to renegotiate reciprocity, Minister H.A.P. Carter died. As Blaine began to work on Hawai'i's new minister, Stevens wrote, "... now is a good time to secure Pearl Harbor in practical perpetuity." Blaine maneuvered for a free trade treaty in which Pearl Harbor would be under the control of America indefinitely, provided it invested in facilities. This amounted to a cession with a built-in pressure on the United States Congress to get on with the development of a naval base in the northern part of the central Pacific Ocean. Hawaiian legislators again objected, Bush and Wilcox most vociferously.

In the 1892 elections Bush and Wilcox bolted from the National Reform Party they had led with such success and formed yet another party, called the Liberal Party. Marshaling Bush's argument that the monarchy was obsolete, they attacked the new queen. What was needed, they contended, was a Hawaiian Republic that would fully realize the ideals of democracy. They flirted with the idea that this sovereign republic should be a state of the United States. In midsummer, Wilcox briefly tried out the idea that Pearl Harbor should be ceded to the United States as a means of settling the status of Hawai'i once and for all. "If we give away Pu'uloa to America," he said, "we will fear no longer about annexation, for America does not want another inch of our land ... " Amid intense cries of protest, he abandoned the plan.

Rumors are said to have circulated that he planned to overthrow the queen. Certainly his criticisms were so harsh as to cause speculation of a revolt. "I believe no woman ought to reign," he said. "They have no brains. They are generally weak."[4] She arrested him and more than a dozen of his close cohorts, while thinking aloud about smashing John Bush's printing press. Volney Ashford was deported, but Wilcox was set free without trial and returned to his forum in the Legislature.

After the 1892 election, the queen's National Reform Party initially had enough votes to form a cabinet, but just barely. In November, her cabinet was displaced by a coalition of Thurston's Reform Party and Wilcox's Liberal Party. In the subsequent deal-making, Wilcox came up on the short end and responded by destroying the opportunistic coalition. As a result, the Hawaiians were split into two competing camps. The annexationists in Hawai'i by now had held power not once but twice—from 1887 to 1890 and briefly at the end of 1892— only to be turned out of office both times.

Stevens warned Blaine of a possible overthrow from within the ranks of the Hawaiians. It was an idea that Blaine apparently took seriously, as did President Benjamin Harrison. The intense conflicts among Hawaiians were apparently much on the minds of not only Lorrin Thurston and John Stevens in Honolulu, but James Blaine and Benjamin Harrison in Washington. "The present political situation is feverish," Stevens wrote to Blaine, and he saw no way it might settle down until Hawai'i became a part of America. While accounts of the overthrow have usually focused on the fanatical tone of Stevens, he was part of a broad pattern, in which he, Blaine, and Harrison had all worked to reduce Hawai'i to an American protectorate. Having been rebuffed by the continuing strength of various native nationalist political forces, they had abandoned the idea of a protectorate in favor of annexing Hawai'i outright. In late 1892, Stevens wrote that the "golden hour" for resolving the future status of Hawai'i was at hand. He sent copies not only to Blaine, but to the secretary of the navy, B.F. Tracy, to his other influential friend from Maine, Senator William Frye, on the Republican side of the Committee on Foreign Relations, and to Senator John T. Morgan of Alabama on the Democratic side.

Within this web of American communication, the United States navy consistently played a contributing role. Officers assigned to Honolulu socialized with the wealthy Americans, absorbed their views, and relayed them to Washington. The resulting quasi-diplomatic nature of their relationship gave "the naval officers a sense of responsibility for supervising and reporting upon the affairs of the Islands second only to that enjoyed by the American Minister."[5]

Under the weight of such pressures, in the tormented course of the nineteenth century, the essential workability of traditional Hawaiian society had all but been destroyed, and Hawaiians had fallen into increasing conflict with one another over the nature of their adaptation to Western modes of governance. As Blaine, Stevens, and Thurston increased the American pressure, these conflicts became more pronounced and became, in turn, a further rationale for extending America's power.

The traditional process of changing chiefs had not only been suppressed by the centralization of power in the Kingdom, but increasingly was suppressed by the interference of Americans. Outside force—specifically the force of the American navy—had quelled the opposition to Kalākaua's election as king, and now Blaine was pressing for the right to send troops ashore whenever America determined that a disturbance had to be put down. In the century-long view, it was the Hawaiian system that was being put down. In the short term, Blaine was guaranteeing that one way or another,

Wilcox and Bush would not succeed. While the American government might not like the new queen, it was infinitely more antagonistic to the idea of a Hawaiian republic animated by the slogan, "Hawai'i for the Hawaiians."

To understand the nature of America's pressure as exerted by Blaine and Stevens is also to understand the events of 1893 in a new way. The queen and her National Reform Party were caught in the middle, with the Americans on one side and the rising popularity of Wilcox and Bush on the other. The Hawaiian demands for a new constitution were ongoing, dating at least from 1889, and the queen was compelled to devise and pursue strategies that seriously incorporated those demands. Indeed, it was only by incorporating the furies of the native opposition that she could hope to keep the Americans at bay, redefine the Hawaiian nation, and perpetuate Hawai'i as she knew it into the twentieth century. As a patriot and nationalist herself, she was compelled to do so. By early 1893, she attained her first glimpse of potential success.

IN LORRIN THURSTON'S STORY, the coup of 1887 had resulted from a chat with Dr. Tucker. He was to write a second story about a chat in early 1892 with an attorney who had just arrived from America, Henry Cooper. Thurston said he was walking down the street one day when he ran into young Cooper. Cooper asked him, "Thurston, if Lili'uokalani attempts to subvert the constitution of 1887, what do you intend to do about it?" Thurston replied that he would oppose her. Cooper asked who agreed with him. Thurston said he lacked specifics. "Well," Cooper said, "I think that you should know in advance who can be depended on, and what you propose, should action become necessary." Thurston said he thought that was a good idea. And that was how, Thurston said, the Annexation Club was born.

As part of his posture as a revolutionary, Thurston never thought these thoughts on his own, but in kindly discourse with his fellow citizens. The Cooper story places the onus on Lili'uokalani for what she might do, not on what the Annexation Club intended to do. It also refers to the 1887 constitution as inviolable, when in fact it had been forced on the king at gunpoint, and Thurston himself would later boast that it was illegal.

The story of meeting Cooper on the street contains the germ of the oligarchy's propaganda campaign—that Lili'uokalani was a willful person who brought trouble upon herself. She deserved what she got. By extension, the Hawaiians deserved to lose what they lost. The situation was intolerable. With better leadership, it almost certainly would never have happened, etc.

Thurston said he previously had been a supporter of independence for Hawai'i. Further, the purpose of the Annexation Club "was not to promote annexation." Rather, the club's purpose was to take quick action in case Lili'uokalani reverted to what he called "absolutism"— a favorite word within the little American colony.

The historian Kuykendall felt obliged to take issue with Thurston's story, even though he did most of his work at the University of Hawai'i during the territorial period. "Thurston's account," he wrote, "has somewhat the character of a rationalization after the event." Kuykendall's gentle critique deserves to be quoted at some length: "... it is well to keep in mind that Thurston was by nature an enthusiast on any subject in which he became genuinely interested; he was a lawyer skilled in writing briefs and arguing a cause, and like other lawyers he was not in the habit of understating his case; he was a fluent writer, a forceful speaker, and a resourceful debater. He was also a practical politician and an opportunist in the sense that he believed in being ready for opportunity when it came; he could provide a plan or draft a proclamation on short notice to suit the existing circumstances."[6]

Although the Kingdom was forced to cut its spending to cope with the economic problems induced by the McKinley tariff, Thurston went off in the spring of 1892 to plan Hawai'i's participation in the Chicago World's Fair of 1893 (known as the Columbian Exposition for its celebration of the 400th anniversary of the arrival of Christopher Columbus in the Americas). Thurston traveled with a sugar man, Ed Walsh, who gave an interview in Salt Lake City, saying that interest in annexation had increased, and citing the economic damage of the McKinley tariff.

From Chicago, Thurston went on to Washington, D.C., arriving on May 5, 1892. He represented the secret Annexation Club and carried a letter of introduction from Minister Stevens. He met first with a member of the Senate Foreign Relations Committee, Cushman Davis, then with Representative James H. Blount, chairman of the foreign relations committee in the House. Blount, who would soon play a prominent role in events in Hawai'i, was to testify under oath that Thurston said, "I mean to endeavor to bring about the annexation of the islands."

Most importantly, Thurston then met Secretary of State Blaine. By this time, Blaine had been advised by his lifelong political ally, John Stevens, to abandon a protectorate in favor of outright annexation. He had also been advised that the monarchy might be overthrown by Hawaiian nationalists. For decades, Blaine had been prepared to create an overseas empire if the opportunity arose, and now, in Thurston's words, "he did not see how the application could be rejected."

Blaine sent Thurston on to B.F. Tracy, secretary of the navy. An insight into Tracy's thinking can be found in his maneuvering to keep Captain Mahan ashore so Mahan could continue his writings (a move in which Theodore Roosevelt also was involved). B.F. Tracy took Thurston to the White House, but President Harrison said he was uncomfortable with meeting Thurston face to face. Thurston was, after all, taking a reading on what would happen if he and his club overthrew a small, friendly government that had a treaty of friendship with the United States, as well as a treaty of reciprocity. Tracy said the president authorized him to say that "if conditions in Hawai'i compel you people to act as you have indicated, and you come to Washington with an annexation proposition, you will find an exceedingly sympathetic administration here."[7]

Thurston was frustrated that Blaine had not been well enough to spend more time with him. On his way home, he wrote a long letter to Blaine. In his list of reasons for annexation, he began with the economic effects of the McKinley tariff. He went on to predict that Native Hawaiians would become supporters of annexation. While this statement may be interpreted as further evidence of his disregard for truth, another possible interpretation is that Thurston had been watching Wilcox's agitation for a Hawaiian republic, and then jumped to the erroneous conclusion that Hawaiians would come around on the issue of annexation.

The little-known but able historian, Sylvester K. Stevens, said Thurston's conversations with the American government showed the willingness of both to engage in "extra-legal methods" to achieve the annexation of Hawai'i. To this he added: "A relatively ruthless and unscrupulous conspiracy existed in 1892 against the autonomy of the kingdom."[8]

It was a two-layered conspiracy that was carried out not only within Honolulu, but within the few square blocks of Capitol Hill, the State Department, and the White House. A higher level of understanding had been reached in the meeting between Thurston and Blaine, but the ideas were more powerful than either of the bearers.

In the course of his long career, Blaine of Maine typically had posed for his portraits with his arms folded, as if awaiting the answer to his demands, or else in a Napoleanic stance with his forefinger under the top button of his vest, but now a photographer induced him to hold his hand to his cheek, as if he were actually pondering a question for which he did not have a ready answer. Thurston's time with him had indeed been cut short by illness. Blaine resigned in the spring of 1892 and died on January 27, 1893, without ever knowing what happened in Honolulu.

He was replaced by a John W. Foster, and the annexationists of Hawai'i had direct access to Foster just as they previously had direct access to Blaine. The connection to Foster was through a man named Archibald Hopkins. Thurston described him as a clerk in a U.S. court of claims in Washington, D.C. He was introduced to Thurston during his 1892 trip by a missionary descendant, William N. Armstrong, then practicing law in New York and later to write extensively for the *Pacific Commercial Advertiser* on annexation. Armstrong said it was important for the annexationists to maintain unbroken contact with the U.S. government, and he helped set up Hopkins as the conduit. Hopkins was paid seventy-five dollars a month. He talked with people, checked rumors, and counted votes. That a court clerk could talk with the U.S. secretary of state underscores the fact that this communication had nothing to do with the status of the persons, but with goals. That someone at Hopkins' level could have quick access to the highest levels of the United States government reflected the extent to which the U.S. government was involved in systematically pushing the annexation of Hawai'i. In November 1892, Hopkins wrote Thurston that he had just talked with Secretary of State Foster, and that the Harrison Administration was willing to put up a quarter million dollars to buy out the queen's claims to Hawai'i.

The national administration was continuing to push for annexation through the conversations of Hopkins, even though Thurston and Stevens were advising that because of the coming presidential election, the timing was wrong. Thurston wrote to Hopkins saying that the pendulum had swung temporarily toward the queen. The $250,000, he said, was not nearly enough to cover what she would lose. He advised it was best not to attempt paying her off because her spirits were up.

Thurston had just read the dispatch from Stevens to Foster. He suggested that his agent, Hopkins, try to nose around and read it. Hopkins ran down to Foster. He reported to Thurston that he and Foster agreed that time was running out to overthrow the government of Hawai'i during the Harrison Administration. Hopkins said if anything unexpected happened that caused Thurston to act immediately, "everything possible to second your plans will be done at this end of the line in the short time that remains." His letter arrived on January 11, three days before the queen intended to proclaim a new constitution.[9]

THE DISCUSSION OF Lili'uokalani's new constitution had begun during Kalākaua's lifetime. Discussion had intensified with the successes of the National Reform Party, and with the subsequent partial success of Wilcox's Liberal Party. In the summer of 1890, when Wilcox and Bush staged their rally to promote a constitutional convention, Hawaiians came to Honolulu from the Neighbor Islands to participate. Petitions circulated, and the idea was debated extensively in the Legislature. Although the proposal was narrowly defeated, individual amendments to the constitution continued to circulate in the Legislature. One example was a provision to restrict voting to citizens of the Kingdom.

The queen was approached by various influential figures to proclaim a new constitution in 1892. She held a meeting, asking advisers to express their thoughts. Drafts were advanced. The political party Hui Kālai'āina petitioned for a new constitution. The queen calculated that the registered voter list at the time was over nine thousand, and that two-thirds had signed petitions for a new constitution. The petition still exists, apparently in two different formats. The more formal, printed petition has about 1,600 names, mostly male, reflecting the Western practice of restricting political participation to men. A simpler format has several thousand more names. The importance of the petition to the queen is demonstrated by the fact that she kept it in her personal desk. As to the resulting draft constitution, its essential feature was strengthening the native government through the person of the queen, which was the basis of the annexationist's charge of absolutism.

Although the political atmosphere was chaotic, the queen appeared to be developing a greater mastery of the situation. The cynical alliance between her opponents, the Reform Party and Wilcox's Liberal Party, crumbled in late 1892, and the queen formed a new cabinet that she had reason to believe would be more actively loyal to her. She was a formidable figure. She was not so concerned as Kalākaua that she be liked. She was determined to restore some measure of the native rule lost to the Bayonet Constitution. She said it was her duty as a Hawaiian chief to respond to the petition of the citizens.

The problem was that neither she nor Kalākaua had strengthened the military resources of the Hawaiians after the Kingdom had been overrun in 1887, and the people she had to deal with most immediately—the *haole* politicians in town, and the sugar planters in the countryside—were more on edge than ever as a result of the economic depression. Business was bad.

And so the story came down to what a few people did within a few square blocks of Honolulu during the several days of mid-January 1893. Following the close of the Legislature, the queen attempted to promulgate her new constitution. It was the event Thurston and Stevens had been waiting for. Accounts of what happened over the next four days typically cover the comings and goings of the queen's cabinet, the writing and reading of statements, interactions primarily between the Committee of Annexation and the cabinet, and secondarily between the cabinet and Minister Stevens.

Here, in brief, is an outline of the most widely accepted accounts:

January 14, Saturday: The queen sets out to announce her constitution, but the cabinet balks. She wavers. The Annexation Club approves a plan to form a provisional government. Thurston meets with John Stevens, who has just returned on the S.S. *Boston*, which had been at sea for gunnery practice. Stevens tells Thurston that if the annexationists control three buildings—'Iolani Palace, Ali'iolani Hale, and the Archives—he will announce American recognition of a new government.

January 15, Sunday: Thurston, after meeting far into the night at his house with the military subcommittee, announces that the monarchy must be abolished.

January 16, Monday: The queen circulates a statement retreating from her new constitution. The Annexation Committee asks Stevens by letter to do what it already knew he would do—call out the American troops. They hold a rally at the armory at two o'clock, attracting fifteen hundred or so people. Stevens calls the troops from the S.S. *Boston*.

January 17, Tuesday: Stevens tells the queen's cabinet that he will protect the annexationists if they are attacked or arrested by government police. Sanford Dole agrees to serve as chairman of the executive council of a provisional government, resigning as a justice of the Supreme Court of the Kingdom of Hawai'i. Thurston rises from his sick bed to draft a proclamation asserting control of the government. Dole and the Annexation Committee walk into Ali'iolani Hale, which is unguarded. They announce to the clerks that they are taking over. Henry Cooper reads the proclamation at the back door of the government building to no one in particular, as white militia belatedly move through the city toward Ali'iolani Hale.

Stevens recognizes the Committee of Annexation, now renamed the Committee of Safety, with its inclusion of Dole, as a provisional government.

Out of all that has been written about these four days, the question today is, what determined the outcome of events? How did a particular circle of people within the 2 percent American colony come to dominate the situation? Without underestimating the nature or skills of Thurston, Smith, Dole, Cooper, and the others, clearly the answer is the American government's relentless pursuit of control, beginning with the Pearl Harbor amendment of 1887 and continuing through the election of Harrison, his selection of James Blaine, and the resulting actions of Stevens and the American troops who mobilized at Stevens's direction.

While the most obvious proof of America's paramount importance is its firepower, the answer likewise lies in how unprepared Thurston and the Committee of Annexation were for the specifics of 1893. This was not a reprise of 1887, when Thurston's Hawaiian League had taken the time to draft and share among themselves a new constitution, systematically subverted the Honolulu Rifles, organized a mass meeting, and brought events to a head on June 30, close to the Fourth of July.

In contrast, they had no paperwork ready in 1893, no letters, and no proclamations. Most significantly, they were not prepared militarily, as they had been in 1887. Thurston, who typically had been several steps ahead of others, was a step behind. The power the missionary descendants had gained in 1887 had drifted away from them. Only in one regard were the insurgents ready to do in 1893 what they had not done in 1887, and that was to say clearly that they wanted to take complete control, and not to share power with Hawaiians.

The composition and dynamics of their group had shifted substantially. Where Thurston had been the only American descendant in the cabinet of the Bayonet Constitution, Americans now played all the key roles. The more numerous Europeans—the British, French, and Germans—were either on the periphery, or were sometimes in outright opposition to the grab for control by the American colony. Where the Americans and American missionary descendants in 1887 had wanted a new constitution, they now wanted to annex Hawai'i to their country of origin.

They knew firsthand that if they overthrew the government, they would be welcomed in Washington. Stevens and Thurston were in close communication with one another, and this ease of communication allowed the dual layers of conspiracy to work in an environment of crisis. It was the clarity of the annexationists' goals, and the security they derived from their relationship with Stevens, that carried them along, not their preparedness.

It was not until well after the U.S. troops had landed that the annexationists held their mass meeting at the armory of the Honolulu Rifles, in what Stevens was to describe as a meeting "worthy of the best American towns, the best American days,"[10] as if it were the Fourth of July in Hallowell, Maine. The annexationists mobilized a substantial force of riflemen, but they still represented a small element of the total population in their desire for annexation. Up to this point the Annexation Committee had operated in secret. It had thirteen members when it surfaced, and Kuykendall believed that in secret it had only seventeen members. Kuykendall's description of political opinion prior to the overthrow provides riveting information in light of the question of who was ultimately responsible for the events of January 17.

"Study of the debates in the legislature leads to the conclusion that the Hawaiian members were nearly unanimous in opposition to the idea of annexation, and that a majority of the *haole* members were likewise opposed to it," Kuykendall wrote.[11] Kuykendall refers particularly to a survey of the Legislature made in the late fall of 1892 by a writer for the *San Francisco Examiner*, Thomas T. Williams. Opinion was overwhelmingly opposed to annexation to the United States, although on most other issues the legislators agreed with one another.

"There was a consensus that the McKinley tariff act was unfair to Hawai'i, that close commercial relations with the United States by means of a free-trade treaty were desirable, and that closer relations, either commercial or political, with Great Britain, were not a matter for practical consideration."[12] The latter is particularly interesting, since the imagined threat of Great Britain was President Harrison's rationale for the frequent presence of U.S. warships in Honolulu Harbor.

Nonetheless, Thurston would insist that the takeover was a revolution for life and liberty, and not for the two-cent subsidy for sugar. As proof of this, some historians have noted (awkwardly for the oligarchy) that sugar planters were not indisputably supportive of the coup. They wanted their two-cent bonus for sugar, but they did not want to lose their control over low-cost labor, which would occur as soon as they came under U.S. law.

While it is much clearer today what the white lawyers in Honolulu thought than what the planters in the countryside had on their minds, it is true that planters played little direct role in the overthrow. They did not converge on Honolulu, nor did they raise their voices loudly. Let us say the sugar planters were divided, even though they had been damaged economically by the McKinley tariff. There also was a semi-organized class of Americans who were mechanics, saloon keepers, skilled tradesmen, etc., and they sometimes exhibited skepticism about the privileged class that had grown from the missionary community. The result was that the Committee of Annexation represented virtually no Hawaiians, only part of the white foreign community, and only a part of the American and American-descended community. It seems possible that Dole and Thurston represented as little as 2 percent of the population, and never more than 4 or 5 percent. This was what Thurston described as the popular revolution that became the stock subject of so much written history.

The little annexationist group was not only sheltered by Stevens but was cued by him as well. It was to follow a scenario of time, place, and action sketched by Stevens. The annexationists took no significant risk of life and property because they were protected by John Stevens, who virtually guaranteed the outcome of the actions taken against the queen. Therefore the real leader of the overthrow of the native government of Hawai'i was not Lorrin Thurston or Sanford B. Dole but John Stevens, originally of Mount Vernon, Maine, later of Augusta, Maine, operating as an ambassador of the Harrison Administration in his capacity as America's minister to the independent nation of Hawai'i. America overthrew Hawai'i's government.

Stevens was able to assert such influence because an American warship was in the harbor armed with marines, rifles, side arms, machine guns, ammunition, and cannon. The ship was in the harbor as an ongoing feature of American foreign and military policy, as defined most particularly by U.S. Secretary of State Blaine, Stevens's ally of thirty-five years, and as sanctioned by President Benjamin Harrison.

As Kuykendall records, Stevens had commenced his relationship with the queen with his lecture, in which he alluded to the Bayonet Constitution as being among the "free and enlightened constitutions" of the Earth. At a point when a wide spectrum of the community spoke of her with high praise, Stevens wrote Blaine that she was surrounded by bad characters and "persons of native and foreign birth," which by definition took care of everyone.

Thurston would say in his memoirs that Lili'uokalani's unexpected move brought the overthrow on herself. This contention became one of the most essential features of the American mythology regarding the overthrow. However, Kuykendall's research points to a conclusion that the proposed constitution merely triggered a course of action that the annexationists, of both Washington and Honolulu, were predisposed to follow. Only their timing and preparation were thrown off by the queen's unexpected move. The eagerness with which Thurston and Stevens reached their positions on January 14, in spite of Lili'uokalani's pulling back from her plan, is further proof that Lili'uokalani's reach for added power was the excuse they had been waiting for.

During the much-remarked four days in January, Thurston, Dole, and the other annexationists poked along at a remarkably slow pace. Thurston was ill part of the time. Dole only slowly decided to preside over a provisional government. Together they evidently moved too slowly for Stevens, because he forced their hand. He told them he would bring in American marines at five p.m. Monday, January 16, the third day of the crisis. They asked him to wait. They were not ready. The marines actually landed two hours ahead of Stevens's schedule. Stevens had said that if they did the most minimal things— if they held 'Iolani Palace, the legislative building (Ali'Iolani Hale), and the Archives, and if they exercised control over the streets—he would recognize them as the rightful government of Hawai'i.

Even with the marines ashore, after nearly four days of preparation, the annexationists failed to meet Stevens's definition of control. Nor did they come close. They took over one building from clerks of the Kingdom—Ali'iolani Hale. Henry Cooper mouthed a declaration out the back door to no one in particular.

Stevens then announced that the United States recognized the Committee of Annexation, renamed the Committee of Safety, as the provisional government of Hawai'i. Thurston could not restrain himself from winking at their name, saying they had gone public "in the guise of the committee of safety."[13] Why had Thurston, Dole, and the others not been arrested? One reason is that two of the queen's cabinet had heard Stevens say that if Dole and Thurston were taken into custody, he would intervene. In fact, the queen's marshal, C.B. Wilson, went to Thurston's law office and attempted to warn him off from an overthrow. Subsequently he was to tell Thurston[14] that he argued for his arrest at that point but that the cabinet said no, it would cause John L. Stevens to bring in American troops, which indeed Stevens did anyway just hours later.

From her balcony, Lili'uokalani turned to history for an answer on what to do. Bloodshed was not an option. To simply give up was not an option. But as a Hawaiian attempting to survive in a world of great naval powers, she had learned that the rogues running loose from supposedly respectable governments would eventually be isolated. It had been so when Georg Scheffer had run out of the control of Russia, and when Lord Paulet had run out of the control of Britain. The French likewise had run out of control in the port of Honolulu, in violation of their treaty, but they, too, had pulled back. Surely a nation of such lofty intentions as the United States of America would set straight the knotted zealot who represented them as ambassador. Was John Stevens not a rogue? From Lili'uokalani's viewpoint, he was indeed. Perhaps he was waging a private war. Accordingly, Lili'uokalani yielded not to the Committee of Annexation, but to the "superior force" of the United States government, until such time as it reviewed the situation and returned her to her rightful office.

THE FIRST NIGHT the Provisional Government held control, it stationed armed men inside Ali'iolani Hale. They sat up singing. One of their songs was the *Battle Hymn of the Republic*. In 1848, America had taken over California, and soon thereafter Luther Severance had engaged Kamehameha III in a conversation about annexation. The Civil War had disrupted the westward movement of America, but by the 1890s the wounds of the war had healed significantly, and the most strategically located combination of islands and ports in the Pacific had been grasped with the goal of annexation. The Americans inside Ali'iolani Hale had lived to see glory of a sort.

Two days later the Provisional Government sent a three-man delegation to Washington, D.C. With Sanford Dole as president,

Lorrin Thurston unerringly followed his instinct for action, leading the way to Washington. He found the officials of the Harrison Administration to be hardworking people who were men of their word, but they had a time problem. Harrison had been defeated by the Democrat he previously had turned out of office, Grover Cleveland. He had only until March 4 until Cleveland was sworn in as president.

In the meantime, the Provisional Government appealed to its friend—its virtual creator—John Stevens, to declare Hawai'i an American protectorate. Stevens did so. For the first time, the American flag flew at the top of the government buildings in the Hawaiian Islands. The same day, Stevens wrote the State Department his most concise reduction of Hawai'i to a piece of fruit: "The Hawaiian pear is now fully ripe and this is the golden hour for the United States to pluck it."

Because American accounts and American beliefs about the overthrow were so distorted, the question of whether Stevens represented American policy recurs. On January 18, 1893, Blaine's replacement, John Foster, wrote to Stevens reinforcing his decision to recognize the new American government. "Your course in recognizing an unopposed de facto Government appears to have been discreet and in accordance with the facts." He said Stevens had followed the American rule of dealing with "any actual Government in full possession of effective power with the assent of the people." Foster said he trusted Stevens's actions would draw Hawai'i and America closer. He instructed Stevens to stay in close contact with the navy. Thereafter Foster hedged, saying that some of the events of the overthrow were unclear, and that if Stevens indeed had overstepped his authority, then his behavior could not be condoned. However, the most telling evidence of all is that Stevens's friends—those who had overthrown the Kingdom's government—were welcomed by the Harrison Administration in Washington, D.C., with open arms.

The all-white Honolulu Rifles became the strongest, best-armed military organization in Hawai'i.

Sanford Dole (sitting, left) and his friends sailed to Pearl Harbor for fellowship and relaxation.

Major John Schofield traveled to Hawai'i in civilian attire, analyzing its strategic significance. He pinpointed Pearl Harbor as of utmost importance to the United States.

Pearl Harbor before its development as a U.S. naval base

President Benjamin Harrison

Navy Secretary B.F. Tracy

Secretary of State James G. Blaine

U.S. Minister John L. Stevens

Dole with Thurston

Thurston was the centerpiece of the delegation that pursued annexation in Washington, D.C.

Hui Aloha 'Āina women's committee petitioning James H. Blount. Kuaihelani Campbell, seated on left; Emma Nāwahī, standing fourth from left.

Hui Aloha 'Āina men's committee petitioning James H. Blount. Joseph K. Nāwahī, seated third from left; James K. Kaulia, seated second from left; J.A. Cummins, seated, center; John E. Bush, seated fifth from left.

Joseph Nāwahī, president of the resistance organization Hui Aloha ʻĀina.

Newsboys

CHAPTER TEN

Hawaiian Resistance

The day of the overthrow, the queen wrote a brief diary entry noting that she had given up control of the government under protest, and also that a Hawaiian policeman had been shot. The next day she wrote, "I mean to go to ride and then return to Washington Place to stay." Her impulse to withdraw gave way to a more powerful desire to battle on. She visited the tomb that housed the remains of David Kalākaua, as well as the Kamehamehas and the high chiefs of Hawai'i Island. She went to Waikīkī to bathe. Then she wrote President Harrison, appealing for a review of Stevens's actions and for her restoration to the throne.

Not receiving a reply, she sent her own delegation to Washington. She was assisted by an attorney, Paul Neumann, who wrote a case for the reversal of America's actions. Her delegation of three followed the annexationist delegation by two weeks.

While there was obvious room for doubt, the queen believed in the possible success of her appeal. The great powers previously had supported Hawai'i's efforts to remain independent. Americans had said over and over they did not want to colonize Hawai'i, and for substantiation Hawaiians needed only to review their previous impressions of America. To own colonies overseas violated—a little too obviously—the American tradition, for which Americans had fought and died in their rebellion against the British. Although the queen was pressed financially, she had resources with which to fight the battle for American public opinion. She also had a strong moralistic bent, which made her well-suited to engage in a battle that revolved around an issue of conscience.

On the fifth of February she wrote a note on the gloom of the weather. "It rains, rains, rains." She was repulsed by the thought of going to church with the missionary descendants. They were, she said, "so uncharitable as to abuse me in the manner they do from the pulpit." She instead attended Saint Andrew's Cathedral next door to Washington Place. The British-style cathedral constructed by Kamehameha IV and Queen Emma now was guided by a rector who prayed for the queen. The bells of Kaumakapili Church rang at four each morning, calling commoner Hawaiian parishioners to pray for the queen's restoration.

In the second week of February, the rain stopped and the queen went for a carriage ride. Passing the palace, she turned her head to avoid the sight of the American flag flying over it. "Time may wear off the feeling of injury by and by," she wrote, "but my dear flag, the Hawaiian flag, that a strange flag should wave over it. May heaven look down on these missionaries and punish them for their deeds."

She worried about money. In addition to financing her delegation to Washington, she helped finance a royalist newspaper, *Holomua*. She was beset by requests from Hawaiians who were in dire financial straits. A Hawaiian cabinet member, on her instruction, sold sugar stocks at a sacrifice, raising $9,500. He took a third of the money to pay off one of his own creditors, then asked for the rest to pay other creditors. When the queen said no, that she needed what remained of the money to deal with her own debts, they quarreled. "He was very angry," she wrote.

Another Hawaiian warned her to stop supporting the Hawaiian language press. She told him she did not read the newspapers, that she considered herself "entirely removed from politics and was living in complete retirement." After the overthrow, the Provisional Government had at first left her with personal guards, but quickly Dole had written her a letter saying he had heard that people were coming to Washington Place in the night, and that the Provisional Government therefore was compelled to withdraw her guards. She was torn between the advice of her attorney, who believed she should stay in seclusion, and a reporter from a mainland newspaper, who thought she should challenge the untrue things being said about her.

As the days went on, she became less than a free person. Where initially she felt she could move around, she wrote, "now I could not." According to the queen's notes of one of her meetings with an American official,[1] he asked if she felt in danger.

"Yes I do," she replied.

"Why?" he asked.

Because, she said, of "the spies that still continue to creep or prowl about in the next yard and into the school house at night, equipped with loaded revolvers and belts full of cartridges—also in the streets around us."

In another passage she wrote: "… we are without arms. And they are armed to the teeth."

While side arms and spying violated the image that the Provisional Government was trying to project, Lili'uokalani was merely recording fragments of a larger picture. Spying was widespread. In addition to the armed men who roamed or patrolled the streets, the marshal's office formed a network of sixteen paid snitches who spied on royalists.[2] Top pay for a spy was $75 a month. The spies turned in written notes to the marshal with code names such as "Buffalo," "J.B. Adams," and "JLX."

THE HAWAIIAN RESISTANCE to annexation was quick to form. It was carried on by political *hui*, or associations. Hui Kālai'āina already was in place. The English name for this group was the Hawaiian Political Association. The words mean a gathering or group, a *hui*, dedicated not merely to politics but to dividing up the land, which is an interesting definition of politics. Hui Kālai'āina was a male organization, just as voting then was a males-only right in Western democracies.

The second *hui* was Aloha 'Āina, literally meaning the group that loves the land or—in its English translation—the Hawaiian Patriotic League. It was backed by a Hawaiian language newspaper of the same name, *Ke Aloha 'Āina*. The second *hui* had both male and female organizations that were equally active and broadly based.[3] It was a mass protest organization. While it staunchly supported the queen and recognized her as the leader of the Hawaiians, its focus was not on the monarchy so clearly as it was on indigenous control of the land and government. The *hui* reflected a trend of more than half a century in which the Hawaiian people had developed as an active political force regardless of their ranking at birth.[4]

The political *hui* were led by Joseph K. Nāwahī, a person who is reemerging in history in the context of the contemporary Native Hawaiian sovereignty movement. Nāwahī was the subject of a biography originally written in Hawaiian and recently translated into English.[5] He also was the subject of a chapter in the queen's book, in which she described him as an unrelenting advocate of an independent Hawai'i.

He reappears after a century of obscurity as a thoughtful, even prophetic man. He was born in 1842, the year of the treaties with England and France. He was educated by missionaries at the Hilo Boarding School on Hawai'i Island. After his graduation he stayed on as a teacher, then principal. He studied law on his own and appeared before Supreme Court Justice Albert F. Judd to be interrogated. Was he fit to practice law? Nāwahī answered questions for nearly an hour. Finally Judd asked who his teachers were. Nāwahī said he had none. He was given his license. He was elected to the Legislature of the Kingdom in 1872, on his second try, at the age of thirty. He represented the Puna district south of Hilo on the Island of Hawai'i. Thereafter he was elected over and over, even though his boast was of "benefits not acquired." That is, he brought nothing special home for his district because of his fierce independence. Why should he be reelected? Because, he said, he was a person of high principles who was above petty politics. No doubt to the dismay of the Hawaiian monarchy, he was among those who favored the creation of a Hawaiian republic.

When King Kalākaua's prestige was on the line behind the Reciprocity Treaty, Nāwahī vigorously opposed reciprocity. "This is a nation-snatching treaty," he said, "one that will take away the rights of the people, causing the throne to be deprived of powers that it has always held as fundamental." He predicted reciprocity would be "the first step of annexation later on, and the Kingdom, its flag, its independence, and its people will become naught."[6]

Nāwahī served in the Legislature of the Kingdom through the time of Kalākaua and Lili'uokalani. He then served as minister of foreign affairs in one of the queen's short-lived cabinets. To protest the overthrow, resist the Provisional Government, and seek the return of the Hawaiian nation, he organized Hui Aloha 'Āina. He also founded *Ke Aloha 'Āina* newspaper, in which he constantly editorialized on behalf of an independent Hawai'i. Along with Wilcox and Bush, he had realized that the ability to influence others lay not only with oratory but with the mass communication afforded by the press. When Cleveland's minister, Albert Willis, asked Nāwahī to name three important Hawaiian leaders, he mentioned the vociferous Wilcox and Bush, to which he added ("modestly," in Willis's description), "I am a leader."

His wife, Emma Nāwahī, was one of several leaders of the Women's Patriotic League, along with the queen's adopted daughter, Lydia Aholo, and Abigail Kuaihelani Campbell. In their statement to the Americans in the wake of the overthrow, the women said they particularly resented being "transferred like a flock of sheep or bartered like a horde of untutored savages by an unprincipled minority of aliens who have no right, no legal power, no influence over us, not even a claim of conquest by fair-handed warfare ... " Along with the queen, they trusted that the "great and just American nation" would not tolerate annexation by force against the wishes of a majority of Hawaiians.[7]

A DIARY HAS BEEN TRANSLATED from Hawaiian that gives a rare glimpse into life on the Neighbor Islands during this period. The diarist was a man from the small island of Moloka'i named Solomon Kamaha Kaulili.[8] Kaulili had worked at 'Iolani Palace as a servant up to the time of the overthrow, then followed the queen to Washington Place, where he slept on the porch at night for two weeks until he was paid his final wages.

He took the steamer to Moloka'i and stayed with his father's family during two days of heavy rain. ("Rain, rain, rain," the queen had written.) Then he found his parents. "... when I arrived," he said, "it was a thing of joy." On the second Sunday in February he attended church services on Moloka'i, where people talked about restoration of the queen. The church met Monday and Tuesday nights as well and took up a collection, to which Kaulili donated the not insignificant sum of a dollar and a half.

The queen recalled him to work, but within six weeks he again was laid off, this time for good. He nonetheless went to the queen's place in Waikīkī to help give it a good cleaning. He said they tried to make it "outstandingly glorious," as would befit an *ali'i*.

He wrote, "My thought increased again to return to work on the land, to devote myself to farming, getting 'opihi and fish, and working in business, and so strong was my thought, that I went to tell the Queen of my wishes, and she consented ... "

Kaulili worked and studied for nine months and then was sent to Kawaihae on the island of Hawai'i, where Kamehameha had built his great war temple. When he disembarked, church members asked him, "On whose side are you?"

"On the side of God," Kaulili said.

"Then, you don't have any love for the Queen?" they asked.

"I do in fact love the Queen," he said. "She is the one standing on the side of God."

They replied, "If so, then it's all right for you to stay with us."

CHAPTER ELEVEN

Battle on the Potomac

When Thurston arrived on the mainland, he initially set off a wave of excitement and support for the Provisional Government. The reporters flocked around him in San Francisco. They boarded his train across the country to hear him expound on the great things that would ensue from the annexation of Hawai'i. Although he was a relatively lowly U.S. Civil Service commissioner, Theodore Roosevelt was among the enthusiasts for expansion who called for immediate annexation.

On Thurston's arrival in Washington, the State Department rushed to write an annexation treaty. In less than two weeks Harrison gave the treaty his blessing. The queen's delegation arrived in Washington to find the treaty was already in the hands of the Senate. The delegation went immediately to the president-elect, who was Grover Cleveland—again.

Grover Cleveland was both the twenty-second and twenty-fourth president of the United States. He had been elected sheriff of Buffalo, New York, mayor of Buffalo, governor of New York state, and president of the United States. He served as governor of New York while Theodore Roosevelt was a young leader of the Republicans in the New York assembly. He became president by defeating James Blaine, breaking the hold of the Republican Party on the presidency from the time of Lincoln. After four years in the White House, Cleveland lost to the nondescript Benjamin Harrison, then made his comeback at Harrison's expense. In the exercise of ranking presidents, historians allow Cleveland to creep up to, and sometimes above, the mid-level, but then seem to struggle to explain why.

Perhaps it was his capacity for stunning honesty. He is remembered for his response to the allegation that he had fathered the child of a woman to whom he was not married. Very possibly that was true, Cleveland said. He might also be remembered for his stunning honesty about America's role in the takeover of the Hawaiian Kingdom.

After reading the appeal presented by the queen's representative, he let it be known that he was disturbed. Thereafter members of the Democratic Party in Congress began to drag their feet on the immediate rubber-stamping of the annexation treaty. On March 4 Cleveland took the oath of office for the second time (the inauguration then occurring nearly two months later than it does now).

Cleveland appointed James Blount to investigate Hawai'i. Blount previously had been chairman of the House Foreign Relations Committee, and also one of those who Thurston had met in his tour of Washington, D.C., in 1892. When Blount's ship arrived in Honolulu Harbor, both the royalists and the missionaries turned out in hopes of convincing him of their point of view.

Sanford Dole expected to shape Blount's thinking by exposing him to the better classes in Honolulu and chatting over cigars after dinner. Instead Blount put the Dole government at arm's length and dismissed its bosom friend, John Stevens, as minister. He ended the American protectorate, sent the encamped troops back to their ship, and ordered the American flag lowered. Obviously Blount's actions were cause for the Hawaiians to be more optimistic. Perhaps this was the first step in what had occurred when the British restored self-rule to Kamehameha III. After removing the American flag, Blount withdrew into a long round of interviews that resulted in a report of over a thousand pages. It was an unprecedented critique of America's behavior overseas.

In America, the Blount report was to be forgotten with relative haste, and it was to be forgotten by most people in Hawai'i during the twentieth century as well. References to the Blount report in the written history of Hawai'i were either superficial or altogether lacking until Blount began to be read again in connection with the revival of Native Hawaiian culture in the late 1970s. By the 1993 centennial observance of the overthrow of the monarchy the Blount report was again being widely cited, at least in Hawai'i, as were the thoughts that Grover Cleveland formulated in response to the report.

In a subsequent (and greatly delayed) message to Congress, Cleveland was concerned first of all with the haste of the annexationists. He pointed out that the events of the coup took four days. Thereafter Thurston and his party spent fifteen days in transit. On their first day in Washington they met with Blaine's replacement as secretary of state, John W. Foster. Over the next eleven days they worked with the State Department to draft a treaty of annexation. On the following day, which was the thirty-second day after the queen had attempted to proclaim a new constitution for the Hawaiian Kingdom, President Harrison submitted the treaty to the United States Senate.

Harrison told the Senate the American government had nothing to do with the overthrow. Further, Harrison said Stevens had not recognized the Provisional Government until it completely controlled the government buildings and the queen had abdicated—that is, until she had entirely given up her throne, which she never did. These were two of the most blatant misstatements of fact recited by the Harrison Administration with the help of Minister Stevens and his cohort Thurston. Cleveland concluded Stevens was "watchfully waiting" for the opportunity that was presented by the queen's intended proclamation of a new constitution on January 14.

Was there, Cleveland asked, a popular basis for the Provisional Government? First and most obviously, the Provisional Government was not willing to hold free and fair elections. Second, Thurston's Committee of Annexation had not cleanly stated its goal of annexation even as late as the *haole* rally at the armory on the third day of the crisis, January 16. Supporters of the secret Committee of Annexation never knew to what extremes the committee planned to go. Further, Cleveland noted, the Committee of Annexation wrung its hands while American troops went into action. It had no effective military preparations and actually appealed to Stevens for more time before he called in the troops.[1] Cleveland noted that when the troops marched with the alleged purpose of protecting American property and lives, Honolulu was in its customary state of tranquillity. Cleveland also took notice of the Provisional Government's timid proclamation of itself, even while the men commanded by the marshal of the Kingdom continued their occupation of 'Iolani Palace, the royal barracks, and the police station.

"The lawful Government of Hawai'i was overthrown without the drawing of a sword or the firing of a shot," Cleveland said, "by a process every step of which, it may safely be asserted, is directly traceable to and dependent for its success upon the agency of the United States acting through its diplomatic and naval representatives."

Not once but twice, Cleveland characterized America's actions as an "act of war." The United States, he said, was in danger of setting up a "temporary government on foreign soil for the purpose of acquiring through that agency territory which we had wrongfully put in its possession." He went on, "The control of both sides of a bargain acquired in such a manner is called by a familiar and unpleasant name when found in private transactions." Although he did not recite the unpleasant name, the gist of his description was clear enough. The United States had created a provisional government, then rushed to accept that government's proposal to annex Hawai'i to the United States.

Cleveland held out for a reversal of this situation. "... if a feeble but friendly state is in danger of being robbed of its independence and its sovereignty by a misuse of the name and power of the United States, the United States cannot fail to vindicate its honor and its sense of justice by an earnest effort to make all possible reparation."

Thurston and the other commissioners of the Provisional Government saw they would get nowhere with Cleveland and began to wander off. Thurston went back to the World's Fair in Chicago and set up a promotion to generate interest in traveling to the Kīlauea volcano on Hawai'i Island. As part owner of the Volcano House Hotel, he had a direct personal interest in developing tourism in Hawai'i. The promotion itself was a semicircular panoramic painting of the volcano of such size that it was intended to create a "you are there" sensation—a cyclorama, as it was called. As dear to Thurston as was his annexation scheme, he stalled Dole while Dole urged him to accept the position of minister to the United States. Dole offered him the role on April 6, 1893, and Thurston accepted on April 23, provided he could stay until the fair ended.

Meanwhile in Hawai'i, the new American minister, Albert Willis, acting on Cleveland's instructions, demanded that Sanford Dole step down, dissolve the Provisional Government, and restore the queen to power. The hopes of the royalists soared, but the Provisional Government refused. The year dragged on. Little happened.

IN SEPTEMBER, SANFORD DOLE fell ill and retreated from his government position to live with a Hawaiian family on the island of Hawai'i. The image of Dole as president had been perfect for Thurston's ends, at least in part because of Dole's relationships with Hawaiians. Now Dole was sick, perhaps in part because of the stress resulting from his relationships with Hawaiians. The story begins with a Hawaiian woman named Pāmaho'a, who had a large number of children, one of whom was named Puiki, or—as she was to be known subsequently—Lizzie. At the age of six, Lizzie appeared in Sanford's Sunday School class. When she was thirteen, Sanford asked Pāmaho'a if he could adopt her as "a friend and companion" (in Damon's words) for his wife, Anna, who often was in frail health. Pāmaho'a would not agree to a Western adoption but did agree to a Hawaiian *hānai* relationship. Although Lizzie frequently ran away from Sanford and Anna's house, each time Sanford would find her at Pāmaho'a's and patiently explain to her why she was cared for and needed. [2]

During the period when Sanford was pleading with Lizzie to join him in his otherwise childless family, he was known in the community for his ability to speak, read, and write Hawaiian. He had written knowledgeably and sympathetically about the brief reign of King William Lunalilo, whose father, Charles Kana'ina, was a cousin of Pāmaho'a. Dole had served as a translator between Hawaiian and English at public meetings. On a scholarly level, he had translated such works as the Hawaiian writer Kamakau's accounts of Polynesian voyaging.

By the time Dole first worked with Thurston, Lizzie was reaching adulthood. By the time of the overthrow of the crown she was married to a part-Hawaiian rancher on Hawai'i Island, Eben Low. Sanford's wife, Anna, was uncomfortable with the relationship,[3] but she nonetheless wrote Sanford a letter in care of Lizzie and Eben

Low's house in Kohala, Hawai'i, instructing him, "Get strong and well, Sanford ... do not use your head at all." Anna told her friends that Sanford was suffering from overwork. He also was described as "seriously ill with 'brain fever.'" Lili'uokalani said he was suffering from an attack of conscience.

When he recovered sufficiently to go out, he went hunting rather than return to Honolulu. With a party that prominently included Hawaiians, he rode up the east slope of Mauna Kea, the enormous peak that dominates northern Hawai'i. He described riding through groves of native trees and seeing native bird species, such as the 'I'iwi, with their orange-red bodies and black wings, about which he had written in his earlier life with scholarly assuredness. "All our cooking was done at the fireplace," Dole wrote, "and we had good appetites for the good food ... I went on one cattle hunt—unsuccessfully, but shot a number of wild hogs and some plover."[4]

In Honolulu, a protégé of Dole, Francis Hatch, who held the title of vice president, served in Dole's place. It was a period of standoff between the royalist Hawaiians and the Provisional Government, and finally in mid-October Dole returned to his job as president, after an absence of more than six weeks.

THE QUEEN spent New Year's Eve of 1894 in seclusion at Washington Place, making notes in her diary. She wrote that the missionary descendants were gathered at their coral church to sing praises to God "while their spies are lurking." Fifty armed men roamed the streets, she wrote. Rumors circulated that someone intended to assassinate her. A worried British ambassador asked the American ambassador to tell the Provisional Government to rein in the armed bands of men, or Britain and Japan would land troops from their ships. Lili'uokalani dozed off, then was awakened by fireworks and the ringing of bells.

She resumed her writing: "All that transpired in 1893 is of the past. We commence anew with the New Year, thankful to our Creator for all we have enjoyed during the past and hoping for all that is good for the future—that our Nation may be restored by President Cleveland and Congress is my earnest prayer and of my people."

When Cleveland had told Dole to step down, Dole responded by arguing that the United States had no business interfering with Hawai'i's affairs. Members of the oligarchy decided among themselves to fight if the U.S. troops came ashore—the closest to physical courage they were to ever come. They trained their troops and expanded their armory, but Cleveland was unwilling to fight for the restoration of the queen. His moralistic comments were forwarded to Congress. In mid-December, Lorrin Thurston arrived in Hawai'i for the holidays. He told the cabinet of the Provisional Government not to worry. Cleveland was being swamped by criticism.

(2) the restriction absolutely to those who can speak, read and write the English language.

In this connection I would call your attention to the constitution of Mississippi adopted in 1891, which provides as a qualification the ability to understand any section of in the constitution. I rather think that some addition should be made to the section as I have drafted it, as the ability to read, write and speak the English language is rather indefinite, and leaves too much to the discretion of the election officers.

(7) As to the name of the new government, I think that what - ever else it is called, it should have the word "Republic" in the name. It seems to me also that to call it the "Republic of Hawaii gives it more character and distinctness than to call it the Hawaiian Republic or other similar name.

Excerpts from Thurston's letter to Dole on a new constitution

CHAPTER TWELVE

A Republic in Name

Despite the enthusiasm with which the Provisional Government first was received in America, the oligarchy had failed to reach its goal. The queen had succeeded in blocking annexation and generating serious doubts about the nature of the overthrow, but she had failed in her attempt to reverse the situation and be restored. Cleveland had made his speech, then turned the issue over to Congress. From the Native Hawaiian point of view, the United States—after participating so heavily in the overthrow—now was saying it had no right to involve itself in righting the situation.

In this climate of uncertainty, the imperative of the Provisional Government was to maintain itself as a coup d'etat government with as much of a veneer of democracy as possible. In the words of the attorney general of the Provisional Government, the problem was "to combine an oligarchy with a representative form of government so as to meet the case."[1] The author of this thought was W.O. Smith, the same Will Smith who was Sanford Dole's childhood friend and Thurston's law partner. W.O. Smith was an essential part of the leadership of the oligarchy. That he was to slip into anonymity in history may suggest he was part of the second tier of leadership, but in determining the course of events he was in a league with Thurston and Dole. If he was a follower, he was the sort of follower who kept others on track, and he often seemed to possess the clearest mind.

The lengths to which Smith, Thurston, and the others would go to maintain control at the expense of democracy speak volumes today regarding the Native Hawaiian claim that not only the coup of 1893 was illegal, but their five-year government was illegal. On the last day of 1893, they met as the council of the Provisional Government to assess their situation. The cabinet consisted of Dole, Smith, P.C. Jones, who came from the C. Brewer plantation company; and Captain James A. King, a pioneer of interisland shipping (of which sugar made up the bulk). The fifth person at the meeting was Lorrin Thurston.

They had held power as a provisional government for nearly a year, and now they had an American president-elect who was hostile to their plans. The new secretary of state, Walter Q. Gresham, seemed to personally despise them. They somehow had to hang on, continue their annexation campaign, and wait for a change in the political climate. The meeting was one of many occasions in which Thurston played an extraordinary role, as the executive council talked earnestly with him about creating a government structure that would allow them to shed the word "provisional." They agreed to write a constitution.

The next day, which was New Year's Day, W.O. Smith went to the queen's door. He acknowledged the rumors of violence that had circulated through the town. While he was soon to refer to her in correspondence as "the old lady," on this day he was solicitous, offering her armed guards from the Provisional Government. She declined, perhaps thinking she had enough problems already.

A MAJOR EFFORT to improve their image and institutionalize their government was set in motion, with Thurston designated as the lead person for drafting the document. With his new assignment, Thurston returned to Washington and the problems posed by an unfriendly national administration. The Senate Finance Committee reported out a bill that would impose a stiff tariff on sugar from Hawai'i.

To Thurston, the tariff bill was a frightening reminder of why annexation was their only possible course. As long as Hawai'i was outside the Union, such a bill might actually pass, "wiping us out of existence inside of a year thereafter."[2] The statement rings across a century of history. Annexation was not merely a nice idea but a necessity for the oligarchy, because it would guarantee access to its sugar market.

Thurston turned to people who wanted to maintain business as usual. He asked a San Francisco sugar agent, W.H. Dimond, to act as an intermediary. Dimond, who was also a descendant of the missionaries, wrote to a United States senator from California, George C. Perkins, saying that while some reflection of the Cleveland Administration's displeasure over Hawai'i was expected, "we were hardly prepared for so startling a step as this." The port of San Francisco was about to lose all of Hawai'i's business, he said, and the Canadians would jump in to "take advantage of so fatal a mistake."

Perkins wrote Thurston, reporting his conversations with a coalition of Republicans and Democrats, and predicting the bill's defeat. Perkins rephrased Dimond only slightly. The bill would "be most disastrous to the people of the Pacific Coast ... as undoubtedly British Columbia will stand ready to immediately make a more favorable Reciprocity Treaty with the Islands." It was a matter of wringing the last possible ounce of imagined threat from Great Britain, but the expansionist coalition won. The proposed new tariff was defeated, and the economy of the plantations that supported the Provisional Government was saved.

The spring of 1894 was particularly crucial to the fate of the oligarchy. In broad terms, the old trade-off of sugar markets for Pearl Harbor was being renegotiated, and in the process Cleveland was shifting his position. Military and economic considerations—the main elements of expanding America's power in the Pacific—were overtaking moral and political considerations. In late May, Thurston wrote Hatch, saying he believed the secretary of state, Walter Gresham, however unfriendly, was concerned that Native Hawaiians would be upset by the writing of a new constitution and the creation of a permanent government. Thurston said his sources in the navy "seem to think that the administration has experienced a change of heart concerning Hawai'i and is disposed to be friendly to us."[3] An Admiral John Walker was appointed to build a naval coaling station at Pearl Harbor. This drew attention because it was a step in developing America's navy, and also because it was an exercise of America's rights under the Reciprocity Treaty, even though America had violated the spirit of that treaty. For good measure, Walker did not bother to conceal his enthusiasm for annexing Hawai'i.

The Hawai'i legation in Washington, which consisted of Thurston and Frank Hastings, forwarded the views of the *London Times*, which described Walker's appointment as a "precipitate descent from the pinnacle of virtue on which President Cleveland took his stand a short time ago." It was not that the *Times* objected to the end result of American control of the north central Pacific, but rather, "What seems perplexing is the contrast between this concession to sordid expediency and the lofty resolution expressed by President Cleveland hardly three months ago."[4]

Two days after Thurston wrote Hatch, his second-in-charge, Hastings, wrote Dole a note describing Admiral Walker as an example of Cleveland's shifting position. "Our cause," Hastings said, "has been so popular with the masses in this country and his course unpopular that it is thought he has very wisely commenced to swing around."

John Stevens, now back in Augusta, Maine, was excited. Ever the conspirator, he wrote Thurston a note marked *Confidential*. "I have more than a Yankee's curiosity to know what is on the tap in the sending of Admiral Walker to Honolulu," he said.[5] Could Thurston find a reliable clue from the State Department as to the meaning of this? Stevens said Thurston could trust him to keep his answer a secret.

When Walker arrived at his new job in Hawai'i, he took Sanford Dole for a ride on his yacht. The American ambassador, Alfred Willis, was offended. He refused to join them. It was a case of Cleveland's moral indignation being in temporary conflict with the underlying American policy, which was to build up America's navy and expand westward into the Pacific. In this regard, the day-to-day influence of the U.S. navy was perhaps the most consistent factor in nurturing the alliance between the oligarchy and America. Unerringly, top navy officers and members of the oligarchy gravitated toward one another and entered into friendly discourse.

In hundreds of little ways, the mere fact of controlling the government apparatus and maintaining an office in Washington also worked to the advantage of the oligarchy.

From the Hawaiian legation, Minister Lorrin Thurston and his assistant fueled America's fascination with the idea of possessing distant islands. A soldier wrote Thurston asking how he could serve in Hawai'i's army. A cigar maker asked if Hawai'i needed someone who could make cigars. A bookkeeper wrote from Kansas City, "I am thinking I would like to locate in or near Honolulu. I am twenty-six years old. I would have no capital." A man from Larwill, Indiana, asked Thurston if he was his lost cousin, because his uncle had gone to Hawai'i as a missionary in 1827. "After my Father died all correspondence between the Brothers ceased," the man wrote. A woman named Grace Miller of Lincoln, Nebraska, repeatedly asked for pamphlets on Hawai'i.

A publisher in Philadelphia sent Thurston a copy of John Stevens's book, *Picturesque Hawai'i*. "If you find this work worthy of a word of commendation," he said to Thurston, "it would be highly appreciated." A promoter named Harry W. Foster organized the first Hawaiian hula show in America. "The only Troop of Hawaiians Ever in America," his letterhead said. "The Greatest Sensational Attraction of the Season." The photograph showed three Hawaiian women in grass skirts, cloth tops, and flower lei. They were accompanied by a male drummer, who knelt.

People wrote asking for the U.S. government reports that had been issued on Hawai'i. The legation chased down material favorable to its cause and sent it out to wherever it seemed the most needed. Thurston talked constantly to newspaper reporters—at a time when print media were far more influential than today. Publishers were a high priority. Thurston also talked often with navy officers, various business interests, the State Department, and members of Congress. He said George Perkins of California was so responsive it was as though he represented Hawai'i in the Senate.

The Republicans were extremely supportive. Thurston met Henry Cabot Lodge of Massachusetts and correctly recognized him as being crucial to the cause of expansion. "He has not thus far appeared on the surface much," said Thurston, "but he is a growing man and I think will prove a valuable friend to us." In fact, Lodge was to become perhaps the most influential figure driving American imperial expansion, other than Theodore Roosevelt, remarking that as of the 1896 Republican convention "foreign affairs were put entirely in his hands."[6]

Thurston's office was concerned simultaneously with an impoverished Hawaiian who was having problems in the hula troop, and also with researching the latest in weaponry that might be needed to maintain the oligarchy's control. Thurston wrote Dole, "Until the principles of government under which we live are definitely established we are in a state of warfare with them (the Hawaiians), whether we are actually using gunpowder or not."[7] Should they buy the Krag rifle (which soon was to be famous in U.S. military circles), or the Mannlicher rifle? The Hawaiian consulate in Belgium said they could buy lots of fifty or a hundred Mannlichers on two to three weeks' notice. The ammunition was loaded with smokeless power, a refinement of the projectile technology that the Hawaiians first had witnessed at Kealakekua Bay. Now someone could not only be killed at a great distance from his opponent, but without anyone ever knowing where the shot had come from. The office in Belgium said the ammunition "can be held in perfect condition in any climate, as the powder contains neither nitroglycerin nor any other volatile substance ... "[8] Thurston solicited an opinion from a naval officer, who said that the Mannlicher was preferable to the Krag.

As the members of the oligarchy devised their longer-term strategy to hold onto power, the question of what to do with Lili'uokalani came up again. W.O. Smith wrote Thurston that in light of Congress's opposition to Cleveland's position, the queen might be bought off. The main thing, he said, was "to eliminate the old lady from the case." He favored paying her $10,000 a year in return for her publicly relinquishing all claims to the throne. Barring that, Smith said they should ship her to Kaua'i. (Smith had cut in half the amount that originally had been in the draft Treaty of Annexation in 1893.) In either case Smith evidently was in a minority in Honolulu and looking for support from Thurston. The council majority, he told Thurston, thought "it would not do to approach her now; that it would only encourage her and make matters worse; that if we pursue our course the proposition will come from her ... "[9]

The meaning of pursuing their course with the queen is ambiguous. But clearly the attorney general referred to consciously pressuring her, and in fact the Provisional Government had created an environment in which she often heard rumors that she was to be forcibly shipped away or killed. She feared the gunmen who roamed the streets.[10]

The stream of propaganda, the constant analysis of guns, the discussion of the queen, all had to do with the small club of annexationists having no popular support and failing to quickly achieve annexation. As a result, it was the plan for a new constitution, hatched on the eve of 1894, that loomed largest in Thurston's mind. While battling the tariff bill in Washington, he took time out to write a draft. At a time when most people, including the secretary of state of the United States, wrote their correspondence in longhand, Lorrin Thurston announced to Dole that life was too short for such a thing. "In the role of a reformer," he said, "I have therefore initiated my correspondence with a typewritten dispatch, and unless I receive positive orders to the contrary will continue to communicate in that civilized fashion."

Thurston told Dole he wanted to dash off a few crucial thoughts about the new constitution before he missed the outbound mail. He then clattered away on his typewriter for twenty-four pages. The naming of the new government was profoundly important. "I think that whatever else it is called," wrote Thurston, "it should have the word 'Republic' in the name." The Republic of Hawaii gave it "more character and distinctness" than the Hawaiian Republic or other similar names.

The word Republic would provide cover for Thurston's plans for running a no-nonsense government that put down its opposition. "I hope," he said, "that those who are drafting the constitution will not allow fine theories of free government to predominate over the necessities of the present situation."

He proposed "a radical departure from the freedom of speech clause" by prohibiting anyone from advocating restoration of the queen. He also omitted the usual trial by jury clause. "Under our conditions," he said, "if a jury trial is required in all cases, we may get into such a condition that all trials will be a farce." The president of the Republic should be empowered to suspend the writ of habeas corpus without consulting anyone, even the cabinet. Rather than putting the office of president up for election, the constitution should name Sanford Dole as president. "I do not think," Thurston said, "that under existing conditions we are safe in leaving election of President to a popular vote."

He had several other ideas for restricting the vote. The simplest was to list royalists by name who would not be allowed to vote or hold office.[11] A constitutionally prescribed oath of loyalty to the new Republic also was of utmost importance. It would "finally impress upon the *kanaka* mind that the monarchy is *pau* (over)," while insofar as possible shutting out "those who are not with us."

To further reduce as many of "the more undesirable voters" as possible, he favored a five-dollar poll tax. To exclude the Japanese and Chinese immigrants from voting, language restrictions alone would not be sufficient. He called Dole's attention to the 1891 constitution of Mississippi, which required the prospective voter to understand and explain any and all sections of the constitution. Along with the poll tax, this was one of the most notorious laws of the racially segregated South, and it would plague the development of American democracy until the 1960s.

The Chinese, Thurston thought, "specifically by nationality, should be debarred." The Japanese could be kept out by giving only citizens or "those who have voted heretofore" the right to vote. "This," he said, "would let in all of the voters whom we desire to vote and who are not willing to become citizens, and at the same time will exclude all Japanese who are not willing to become citizens." Specifically, it would allow the Americans and Portuguese to vote, even if they held back from being dual citizens of Hawai'i and their respective countries of origin. Thurston said he was aware that Japanese were studying English to gain voting rights, but "I have no fear that many of the evening school population could get on to the voting list." Thurston apologized for being hung up on the tariff bill, but lectured Dole on the importance of forging ahead on the new constitution without further delay for any reason whatever.

While Thurston's letter may strike us today as the work of an extremist, it is important to remember that he was the most influential member of the coup. He spoke for the controlling group, and he reflected the tenor of its thinking. In fact, various members of the oligarchy wrote to one another repeatedly about the urgent necessity of denying the vote to Native Hawaiians and also of denying the vote to immigrants from China and Japan, regardless of their length of residence. One of the prominent annexationists of Hawai'i, W.D.

Alexander, who was to write a widely read history about this period, advised Thurston by letter, "Better to fight than submit any question about the form of government to an election." While they could talk about voting, the idea was to delay any real voting until annexation had been accomplished. "The government should hold no election under pressure, or until a considerable time," Alexander said. "Meanwhile it should perfect the organization of the Annexation Club." Will Smith told Thurston that when they had forced the Bayonet Constitution onto Kalākaua six years earlier, they had made a mistake. "Too much was yielded to the plea of fairness," Smith said. It was during their meeting just before the new year that Smith had defined the essential problem of the constitution as "how to combine an oligarchy with a representative form of government ... " In retrospect the writer Albertine Loomis, also a missionary descendant, would say, on the key issue of voting rights, the dilemma was "how to make concessions that would concede nothing." She explained that the men of the Provisional Government knew, from reading history, "that moderate makers of revolutions all too often had lost control to wild-eyed extremists." The implication was that the oligarchs were men of moderation who stood against more violent and radical forces loose in the land, but in truth the oligarchs represented the most extreme, antidemocratic views extant in Hawai'i. While they engaged in the rhetoric of democracy, they lived in fear of democracy.

That their minutes and correspondence survived to document their antidemocratic views is a mark of their self-righteousness. Far from considering whether to burn their papers, they carefully preserved all the scraps. They kept meticulous records. They were not merely smug about what they were doing, but proud of their hard work. As a result, evidence of their plotting has been handed down across time in great abundance, although it scarcely ever has been read, and never has been described candidly.

Their admiring historian, William Russ, who actually read a part of their correspondence, explained their constitution by saying, "They had to establish and preserve a stable nation with themselves in power, when they represented only a small minority of the citizenry..." They had to "maintain a government encompassing a semblance of democratic principles to convince the United States Congress and the American people that Hawai'i was worthy of joining the Union." If today this sounds like doublespeak, the members of the oligarchy were perfectly serious. They were determined to hold meetings, keep minutes, pass laws, study government theory, and write constitutions—until they reached their destination.

They also were concerned that their work be dignified by prestigious thinkers. Sanford Dole wrote for the advice of Professor Burgess of Columbia University, who was widely renowned for his writings on the doctrine of Social Darwinism, and particularly the political superiority of Anglo-Saxons and Teutons to all other peoples.

Dole first asked Burgess for guidance on creating a strong executive, then on dealing with ill-informed voters. Dole cited not only the Hawaiians but the Portuguese. All were people "who are comparatively ignorant of the principles of government, and whose vote from its numerical strength as well as from the ignorance referred to will be a menace to good government." Burgess replied that if the Teutons of Hawai'i, including not only the Americans but the English, Germans, and Scandinavians, were united, they would prevail. Burgess endorsed property qualifications for voting. He urged that the direct election of a president be avoided. The president's powers should be broad, and the president should be appointed, Burgess said. Judges, he said, should be people with proper Teutonic backgrounds and should sit for life.

Thurston pulled himself away from Washington in time for the discussion of the new constitution. In general the Provisional Government approached democracy as chemists approach titration, a drop at a time. Dole squirmed at the thought of being designated by name as president. "It savors too strongly of South Americanism,"[12] he said. Who should sit in the constitutional convention? They settled on nineteen appointed members, essentially themselves, and eighteen elected members.

Who was to elect the elected members? The answers reflected Thurston's thinking about the constitution itself. First, the vote was to be restricted to those who took an oath to oppose "monarchical government in any form in the Hawaiian Islands." This was a classic in Provisional Government phrasing, since it suggested a principled antipathy toward monarchical government when the real antipathy was for Native Hawaiian control. It was not, however, a distinction lost on the Hawaiians, who held a rally condemning the oath as an assault on their traditional form of government "from time immemorial."

The second provision of the loyalty oath was for its taker to "bear true allegiance." This created problems close to where the Provisional Government lived. Americans wanted to know if they were abandoning their American citizenship. Portuguese wanted to know if they would continue to be Portuguese. In response, the Provisional Government insisted that to "bear true allegiance" was not an exclusive thing. White people could be citizens of other countries, America and Portugal in particular, and still vote in Hawai'i. In fact the voter need not even be a dual citizen, which meant that non-citizens were welcomed into voting while the great majority of Native Hawaiians were disenfranchised, along with immigrants from China and Japan and their offspring who had been born in Hawai'i. All the while the issue of fair play was solemnly discussed in public. One of the annexationist newspapers asked how the right to vote was to "be bestowed consistently with fairness and yet retain the power in the hands of those most justly entitled thereto?"

LEAVING NOTHING TO CHANCE and relatively little to discussion, the Provisional Government spent a month going over the draft constitution section by section. In effect this was a rehearsal of its appointed delegates, meaning themselves. A relative handful of voters gathered to elect the eighteen delegates who were to sit with the Provisional Government appointees in the convention. At one of the polling places a Hawaiian wailed, "Kāhāhā," a cry of astonishment and displeasure. Self-righteously, one of the annexationist newspapers said, "Nobody was drunk." As a result of the government's schemes to keep people from voting, participation in the election of 1894 plummeted. The already restricted voting list from the 1890 election was shrunk to less than a third of its original size—this in spite of a Provisional Government voter registration drive.

At the end of May, the thirty-seven delegates gathered at Ali'iolani Hale, across from 'Iolani Palace. The delegates filed in beneath the gilded statue of Kamehameha I that Kalākaua had erected. They alternated seats between the nineteen government appointees and the eighteen who had been voted in by the shrunken electorate. The delegates were given a draft constitution written by the Provisional Government. It is stored today in the archives of Hawai'i—a small, nearly square booklet labeled "Work Draft." Substantive changes were so few that the secretary of the convention produced the second, near-final draft by making pencil notations and by pasting an occasional revision on top of the original.

To Thomas Jefferson's elegant recitation of inalienable rights—life, liberty, and the pursuit of happiness—the delegates added "the Right of acquiring, possessing and protecting Property." The constitution empowered the Legislature to supervise, register, control and identify "all persons, or any class or nationality of persons." It also empowered the Legislature to limit the terms of residence, business, or employment of any class or nationality of persons. It approved freedom of religion so long as this freedom was not "construed as to justify acts of licentiousness." The right to free speech was abridged to allow the Legislature "to restrain and prevent the publication or public utterance of indecent and seditious language." Gratuitously—this was 1894—the constitution made a ringing denunciation of slavery: "Whenever a slave shall enter the Territory of this Republic he shall be free." One might imagine they were trying to make a distinction between the ownership of humans and the Republic's Masters and Servants Act, still perfectly intact, which provided for swift and arbitrary punishment of those immigrant workers who did not fulfill their work contracts.

To be a member of the House of Representatives, a person was required to own $1,000 worth of taxable property or have earned $600 in the preceding year. To merely vote for senators, one had to have $3000 in assets or have earned $600 the preceding year. Given that the dollar was worth about sixteen times what it is worth today, these were not inconsequential amounts of money.[13]

As to citizenship under this new government, those who had taken an active part in forming the Provisional Government were "entitled to all the privileges of citizenship without thereby prejudicing his native citizenship or allegiance." This of course meant that many Americans and Portuguese were granted rights of citizenship in the Republic without their having to deal with the citizenship issues of their native country. The English language barrier to voting—along with the requirement of explaining the constitution (essentials of the Mississippi constitution)—were repeated for citizenship in Hawai'i.

The language of the language provision was: "Be able understandingly to speak, read and write the English or Hawaiian language." If one understood that sentence, it was a step toward being able to read and write in English "any section or sections of this Constitution." Taken together, the citizenship provisions moved the new American minister, Albert Willis, to remark, "It is certainly a novelty in governmental history—a country without a citizenship."

The president was to be chosen not by the voters but by a majority of the House and Senate, both of which were restricted to people of wealth and income. In spite of Dole's concern for "South Americanism," the name Sanford Ballard Dole was penciled into the blank space as the name of the president. The convention retained trial by jury and habeas corpus except under martial law (which soon was to be invoked).

Dole sent a copy of the final draft to Professor Burgess at Columbia, thanking him for his "great help" relative to the science of government. Dole also cited Lorrin Thurston, who "aided me largely." Many years later, a missionary descendant wrote, "Less respect for democracy could hardly have been shown by the leaders of the provisional government."[14]

The delegates were hurried to produce a document in time for the celebration of the 112th anniversary of the signing of America's Declaration of Independence from Britain. The delegates used the Fourth of July deadline as their excuse for not submitting the constitution to the voters for ratification. The reality was that the Provisional Government would not have submitted anything it did to a public referendum, let alone its formation of a government structure designed to perpetuate itself in power.

On July 2, the Hawaiian patriotic leagues staged a rally against annexation. The royalist *Holomua* newspaper said the rally drew over five thousand people. Joseph Nāwahī presided. Nāwahī had a gift for contrasting images. "The House of government belongs to us, just as the Kamehamehas built it," he told the crowd. "But…we were ousted by trespassers who entered our house, and who are now saying to us, to…reside in the lei stand which they have set up and are forcing us all to enter."[15]

Would they live in a lei stand? he asked.

"'A'ole!!" the newspaper reported the crowd as shouting.

People in the crowd were given copies of the anti-annexation resolution, which they endorsed with three cheers. The resolution protested the promulgation of a constitution without the consent of those governed by it. More fundamentally, it protested "changing the form of government from the one under which we have lived peacefully and prosperously for many years.

"And we maintain that the will of the majority of the legitimate voters of Hawai'i should be the supreme power of the land," it went on, "as such power is so recognized and accepted in all civilized countries, and by all of the enlightened governments of the world."

With two rousing cheers, the crowd anointed Nāwahī and two others to present the resolutions to the foreign consuls in Hawai'i. The writer and editor, John Bush, the half-Hawaiian who so prominently had critiqued the queen, along with Robert Wilcox, were among those who spoke for the Hawaiian nationalist point of view at the rally, as was the *haole* J.O. Carter, a consistent royalist.

As a substitute for a ratification vote, the Provisional Government staged a rally two days later, on July 4, 1894, proclaiming the birth of the Republic of Hawaii. Surviving photographs confirm *Holomua*'s contention that there was only a "slim crowd." It said the "Republican cooks" were visibly nervous and eager to get on with the ceremony. "Most of the councillors and delegates carried pistols in their pockets and were feeling unhappy," *Holomua* said. They skipped the prayer and went directly to W.O. Smith, who served as master of ceremonies. Admiral John Walker, the annexationist now in charge of the U.S. navy in Hawai'i, walked about in a fatigue uniform. Sanford B. Dole proclaimed the existence of the Republic and took a new oath of office. In one of the surviving photographs, Will Smith hovers behind Dole as he delivers his statement. Behind Smith is a row of uniformed soldiers of the Republic. The *Holomua* account described the basement of 'Iolani Palace as "filled with armed men." More were stationed on the roof of the nearby opera house and other buildings. The next day the annexationist newspaper, the *Star*, ran a headline that said, "God Save the Republic."

IN ONLY A FEW details did the new government depart from what Thurston had envisioned. One was his proposal to further demoralize the Hawaiians by altering their flag, which had been designed during the reign of Kamehameha I. Thurston had said that while he personally was attached to the flag of Hawai'i, they should pluck the British cross from the field and substitute a "blood red star." It seemed to Thurston that no one act "we can now perform will so thoroughly demonstrate the passing away of royalty as to change the flag." The flag remained as it had been for over eighty years—a Union Jack in the field to affirm the relationship with Britain, and eight stripes (one for each of the inhabited islands) to affirm the relationship with America.

From our vantage a century later, some might be inclined to interpret the Provisional Government and its new constitution as comedy, as a banana republic that temporarily existed within our midst. It was much more than that. It set a tone for the future. In the realm of international diplomacy, the fiction of the Republic did the job for which it was intended. It allowed the various interests and countries to get back to business as usual. The crucial question was the response of the United States government. Cleveland had condemned the Provisional Government. The House of Representatives had condemned Stevens for overstepping his job. Cleveland's representative in Hawai'i had told Dole to his face to step down and restore the queen. But a great deal had changed in the United States in the first six months of 1894. How would the United States react to the formation of a Republic so notoriously grounded in undemocratic practices?

The answer came swiftly. The U.S. government immediately granted recognition to the Republic of Hawaii. Great Britain followed suit, abandoning its long-standing special relationship with the Hawaiians. The other European nations quickly fell in step as well.

What had happened to Cleveland between the time of his speech and his recognition of the Republic of Hawaii? How did he migrate from his morally powerful condemnation of the overthrow, and his insistence that the Provisional Government step down, to washing his hands of the affair and turning it over to Congress? Why did he recognize as legitimate what he had so vigorously condemned as illegitimate? What had happened in America during 1893 and the first half of 1894?

During the centennial observance of the overthrow in 1993, it was widely recalled that Grover Cleveland had held up the first draft treaty of annexation and sent Blount to Hawai'i.[16] In the spring of 1994, during the closing days of the administration of John D. Waihe'e, the first Native Hawaiian governor of the state of Hawai'i, a new courthouse was dedicated to perpetuating the memory of Cleveland. The marker quoted Cleveland's "act of war" statement. This lionizing of Cleveland is a vignette about the difficulty of retrieving history that has been obscured. History comes back incrementally.

Next to the marker that pays tribute to Cleveland, the historian William Williams might be given his say. Cleveland "did not carry through on restoring the queen to power. Instead he recognized the American-dominated Republic of Hawaii that was established on July 4, 1894, and maintained American naval forces in the islands." Williams said that Cleveland, in response to America's deepening economic trouble, turned increasingly to a policy of expansionism. Cleveland had always supported expanding markets and easier access to raw materials, and "he knew he faced a growing revolt within the Democratic Party and he could hardly have missed the appeal of the Republican campaign for market expansion."[17]

Williams quotes Samuel Gompers, labor pioneer, as saying "the great storehouses are glutted." Foreign markets had to be opened. The populist of Kansas, "Sockless" Jerry Simpson, said the "surplus must seek foreign markets." The National Association of Manufacturers soon was to organize, and its first keynote speaker was to be the Republican who would succeed Cleveland as president, William McKinley. Even Robert M. LaFollette, who was to be regarded as the great Progressive, was to launch his career on the expansionist theme of creating a bigger American navy.

Williams's research is especially impressive because he had no interest in Hawai'i per se. He saw it from a national perspective as fundamental to America's further expansion into the Pacific. "The depression," he wrote, "swelled the agricultural chorus for market expansion into a mighty roar."[18] He thought of the overthrow of the native government as being the work of Harrison and Blaine, who served as John Stevens's coaches. Thurston and Dole did not even rate a mention, even though Williams wrote about Hawai'i over and over as one of the most time-and energy-consuming issues of the 1890s. When Cleveland proposed returning Hawai'i to Lili'uokalani, according to Williams, "Agriculturalists marched in the front rank of the angry rebellion ... "[19] The entire spectrum of economic interests, from urban industrialists to prairie Populists, joined in the criticism.

Williams distinguished Hawai'i from all other issues of American imperialism. He contended that while many pro-expansionists opposed the messiness and moral paradox of creating colonies, Hawai'i was "the exception that proved the rule."[20] Under these pressures, Cleveland abandoned his active, moralistic objections to acquiring territory. A clue to Cleveland's thinking lies in the fact that he laid most of the blame on Minister John Stevens, and not on the Harrison Administration—meaning the United States government in its totality. In his message to Congress he said that U.S. forces took possession of Hawai'i without the consent of anyone "except the United States minister." In doing so he fulfilled an apparent need on his part to condemn an unsavory act, but he limited his condemnation in such a way as to maintain a certain amoral flexibility to make up the next steps as he went. In fact, he ended up sending an admiral to Hawai'i who represented expansion of the navy and who nurtured annexation. He then conceded that the sugar industry of Hawai'i was to return to the conduct of its business with the United States as usual.

Cleveland's Democratic Party had won control of both the House and Senate in 1894, but in certain instances—such as the proposed tariff on Hawai'i sugar—a coalition of Republicans and a faction of Democrats actually controlled the Senate. By the next election, the Democratic Party lost control in both houses. In the aftermath, a new tariff bill passed the 1894[21] session of Congress restoring the cane sugar industry of Hawai'i to its privileged position of equal treatment with American growers. In a political climate dominated by economic considerations, Cleveland migrated from his lofty position back to business as usual.

The overthrow "is directly traceable to and dependent for its success on the agency of the United States acting through its diplomatic and naval representatives."

—*President Cleveland*

CHAPTER THIRTEEN

The Hawaiian Revolt

When Cleveland failed to act decisively on his desire to restore the queen, the Native Hawaiians struggled to adjust. Lili'uokalani continued to profess faith in Cleveland. She downplayed the importance of the Republic. "When the U.S. is ready," the queen insisted, "she will undo all that her Minister (Stevens) has done." But four days after Sanford Dole's proclamation of the Republic, she chose three representatives to go to Washington. They arrived on the first of August and spent two weeks getting a better understanding of America's contradictory behavior. The former foreign minister of the Kingdom, Samuel Parker, told the U.S. secretary of state, Walter Gresham, that Admiral Walker obviously was sympathetic to the Provisional Government, and not to the memory of the Hawaiian Kingdom. Parker complained about the frequent presence of American warships as a "constant moral support" to those in power. The American marines who landed to drill were really supporting the Provisional Government, Parker said. One of the Hawaiian delegation said of the oligarchy, "They wear the cloak of religion, but their hearts are as black as tar."

Would or would not Cleveland restore the queen to her position as the lawful ruler of Hawai'i? No, the secretary of state said. "You can hardly expect him to restore the overthrown government." The Hawaiian delegation wanted to see the president and present the petitions from the Hawaiian patriotic leagues that had been generated by the rally of July 2, 1894, against formation of the Republic. The president was said to not be feeling well. His statement was read to them. In it, Cleveland said he had done all he could. Congress had refused to do more, and now there was a government, the Republic, "in full force and operation ... maintaining its authority and discharging all ordinary governmental functions." He said the Republic was "clearly entitled to our recognition without regard to any of the incidents which accompanied or preceded its inauguration."

Cleveland said this led him "to an absolute denial of the least present or future aid or encouragement on my part to an effort to restore any government heretofore existing in the Hawaiian Islands." Even the phrasing was brutal. The Hawaiian Kingdom, and its century of nationhood, became "any government heretofore existing," as if it possibly had never existed.

One of the Hawaiian delegation said that rather than surrender control of their Kingdom to America in 1893, they should have fought. If Cleveland was not going to help them, they wanted to know one more thing. If fighting erupted in Hawai'i, would the United States again land troops from its ships? If so, at whom would their guns be aimed? Secretary of State Gresham said the American battleships existed only to protect Americans who were *not* engaged in the affairs of another country—and the Republic of Hawaii was another country.

The story of the subsequent Native Hawaiian counterrevolt is yet another event that is almost unknown in Hawai'i, yet there is an extensive historic record of the revolt. The members of the oligarchy wrote to one another about it, the press wrote about it, and a resident writer[1] interviewed participants, apparently with an eye toward writing a book that never materialized. The courts, such as they were, also kept a record. More recently Albertine Loomis's book *For Whom Are the Stars?* provided extensive detail. She was initially motivated by reading Lili'uokalani's book, apparently soon after World War II. She said she was "spellbound by the grievous and tragic tale," and she dedicated herself to examining the story from various angles.

The discomfort of seriously examining the American viewpoint, let alone challenging it, is quite real, and obviously it was acute for her in the 1940s and 1950s, when the American story was essentially unquestioned. Ms. Loomis's anxiety probably was heightened by her descent from Henry Loomis, one of the early-day missionaries. She nonetheless made acquaintance with the descendants of Hawaiians whose eyes were on the past. In her prologue she said, "There are many who want to undo history, to roll back events to a time when they feel things were right." She ritually discredited this viewpoint by quoting a Hawaiian chant as follows:

"There is no going back; ways now are different … "

"Look forward with love for the season ahead of us!"

"Let pass the season that is gone!"

History is not altogether useless, she said, but it "can harm us if it is read with anger and bitterness, if it is viewed as a suit for damages." Noting that not much had been written about the Hawaiian revolt, she warned it was such a sad story that "we could scarcely bear to think about it … "

Regrouping inside the comfort of Thurston and Dole's version of events, she wrote that *haole* took up arms more or less spontaneously "to prevent the queen's coup d'etat." She quoted rumors that the queen planned to use force. Casually she said, "Someone said it might be a good idea to bring the United States marines on shore," when in fact this someone was John Stevens, who she described as "an experienced and conscientious" diplomat.

But then, despite her angst, she got into her research and told an interesting, apparently factual story. Cleveland's refusal to use force had convinced not only the queen's delegation to Washington but many in Hawai'i that the Hawaiians had to resort to force.

"At Camarino's fruit store on King Street, at Bush's shop in Printer's Lane, in the saloons along Hotel Street, at the Sans Souci beach resort beyond Waikīkī, in the very shadow of Washington Place where Captain Sam Nowlein's guards held sway at the *Holomua* (newspaper office)," Hawaiians began to talk about taking up arms.[2]

In the early fall, Captain Nowlein inventoried how many guns of varying age and quality might be available. He counted several hundred and concluded they were not nearly enough. He raised money and sent an agent to buy 291 rifles on the West Coast.

All the while, the paid spies who reported to Marshal Edward Hitchcock tracked the general outline of the plan. They filed their reports in bits and pieces and collected their pay of seventy-five dollars a month. The oligarchy beefed up its militia and intensified training. It laid on Gatling guns and built walls of sandbags around 'Iolani Palace.

On the second day of the new year, 1895, a rumor passed among the Hawaiians in Honolulu that their new guns were to land at midnight in the swampy Kaka'ako area between Waikīkī and Honolulu Harbor. "By eight-thirty the trend toward the waterfront was noticeable; by nine o'clock Kaka'ako teemed with natives. When government 'specials' tried to break up the crowds, a group of bold young *hapa haole* royalists fell upon them, took their guns and isolated them under guard on the beach." The police arrived and sent the crowd home. The next night, just short of two years after the overthrow, the shipment was landed at Kāhalawai, in what is now the posh Kāhala area, on the suburban side of Diamond Head Crater, beyond Waikīkī. The guns were buried in the sand and began to rust. The call went out the following Sunday to form up, clean the weapons, and march on Honolulu. Several hundred Hawaiians answered the call, meeting beyond Diamond Head. Many more were prevented from coming by a lack of transportation. Their rendezvous was at the end of the trolley line, and many did not have a dime for fare. Others missed the rallying point for lack of adequate communication.

The forces of the Republic attacked, causing a brief fight at the base of Diamond Head. A person on each side was killed. Thereafter fighting was sporadic above and around Honolulu. Over the course of the next several days the firepower and trained marksmanship of the Republic's soldiers crushed the rebellion. Robert Wilcox embellished his legend by leading the soldiers of the Republic on a chase through the mountains, up through Mānoa, across Nu'uanu, and into Kalihi, before being captured. The participants were jailed, and 190 were charged. Most were Hawaiians, or Hawaiian-*haole* mixtures who were loyal to their Hawaiian heritage. A few were British and American, including a nineteen-year-old American boy.

The constitution of 1894 was rolled into place like a wheeled Gatling. Habeas corpus and trial by jury were suspended. A military court was set up. Those who howled loudest for revenge—the white militia companies, now called the National Guard—were represented on the court, as it was called. One court member was from Company F, one from C, two from D, and two from the judge adjutant. One was a regiment commander. While these designations in themselves have no meaning, they suggest the extent of the oligarchy's military organization.

There was a widespread demand for hangings. Attorney General W.O. Smith said the best strategy was to threaten hanging, frighten as many people as possible, then back off. He proposed giving the death sentence to everyone they convicted, then reducing the sentences as they saw fit. Robert Wilcox, virtually the only trained soldier in the revolt, marched jauntily to the trial in a gray tunic, white shirt, and white tie, with a bandage wrapping an injured hand. Others who had taken up arms wore flowers in their lapels, which the crowd of cheering Hawaiians had pressed upon them.

Only *haole* were inside the courtroom, which once had been the queen's throne room in 'Iolani Palace. Members of the jingoistic American League called aloud for a finding of guilty.

Why do people not know about such history? The best compilation on the revolt and trials, *For Whom Are the Stars?*, paused long enough to explain the high-mindedness of the oligarchy: "To be just but not vindictive, to be safe but not harsh, to draw the fine line between treason and misprision of treason, to distinguish a man's right to hate the government from the crime of plotting against it—this was the task of the republic, lately rescued from overthrow."[3] The military court was an alternative to native juries who "had been known to ignore the evidence and yield to their hearts. Better to have no trials at all, the cabinet had argued, than to run the danger of farce and mockery."

Wilcox was sentenced to hang, along with several others. He was defiant, refusing to give evidence against his comrades in return for leniency. Others crumbled. One man who refused to give information—a close associate of the queen, Joseph Heleluhe—was thrown into solitary confinement in a cell with no light. Many were questioned repeatedly, their stories and confessions used against one another.

The main attorney for the defense was the queen's lawyer, a Caucasian named Paul Neumann. He argued that the entire proceeding was illegal, and that martial law itself was illegal even under the constitution of 1894, since order had been restored almost immediately. The most delicate question was whether to arrest and try the queen. The oligarchy wavered. Petitions from white soldiers demanded her arrest. Whites talked about deportation or hanging. Surely, they argued, with the queen out of the way all the trouble would be over.

On January 16, one day before the second anniversary of the overthrow, the government arrested her. To the soldiers who came for her at Washington Place, she said quietly, "I will go." In search of incriminating evidence, the Republic's chief justice, Albert Francis Judd, entered her home the day after her arrest. He spent four hours rifling through the niches of her desk. He dumped her personal papers into two large grain sacks and took them for further examination to the judiciary building, where the statue of King Kamehameha stood facing 'Iolani Palace.

Her papers disclosed that, a few days earlier, she had named a new cabinet, which amounted to a sort of government in exile. Further investigation found a cache of weapons buried under four feet of soil in her garden. It consisted of thirty-four rusty rifles, twenty-one homemade bombs, eleven pistols, a thousand bullets, and five swords. The few Hawaiian guards of Washington Place were arrested, and white soldiers of the Republic took over the queen's home.

Lili'uokalani was charged with *misprision* of treason. Misprision is one of those words that parochial white historians have used repeatedly without explanation (along with such words as *prorogue* and *abrogate*), as if its meaning were apparent. What does misprision mean? It means knowing something is going to happen but not doing anything to stop it. In other words, the queen was charged with knowing about the revolt but doing nothing to stop it. In court she wore a black dress and responded to all questions in the Hawaiian language. When asked how she pled, she said she was not going to plead. A plea of not guilty was entered for her.

Had she known about the weapons? Had she named the cabinet expecting the uprising to establish a new government?

'A'ole, she said. No. W.A. Kinney, Thurston's law partner, who had given Thurston his book on the French Revolution, led the prosecution. In a furious, rambling outburst, Kinney attacked the queen as having not told the truth to a government that wished her no ill. He closed in a flight of words about annexation. The government, he said, was "looking for peace, with eyes still … turned to the Mother Country… with the belief that ere long … she will take us to herself …"

It is a mark of the immediacy of Hawai'i's history and the extremes of anxiety attached to it, that in Hawai'i to this day there is concern over whether the queen was free of guilt of *misprision* of treason. Loomis quoted the British minister at length to the effect that Lili'uokalani discussed the revolt with him. Then Loomis waffled away from drawing a conclusion. In 1995, a reenactment of the queen's trial suggested her innocence as charged. A subsequent law review article also argued her innocence as charged.

The intensity of this anxiety results from focusing on a small point. Was yet another blow dealt to the Hawaiian people because of a flaw in the queen's person? Did she lie? Was she guilty of *misprision?* First, she had every right to deny the charges and force a burden of proof on her tormentors. Second, the anxiety about guilt or innocence only attaches to the question when some level of legitimacy is given to the proceeding. While people who idealize the queen understandably do not want their heroine to be found guilty of anything, not even misprision, the reality was that even the poor fishermen of Kaka'ako knew about the revolt before it happened—they had clogged the waterfront the night before the actual landing, forcing a postponement of the revolt and a change of landing places. For Hawaiians to hope for the success of the revolt was only human. For a Hawaiian chief to be informed was part of being a Hawaiian chief.

For that chief to be escorted by military guard into her own throne room; to be stripped of rights that had been practiced in Hawai'i for half a century; to be harangued and insulted by William Kinney, partner of Thurston; and to then be proclaimed guilty, fined $5,000, and sentenced to five years at hard labor by the soldiers who had just come from fighting her people—all within the context of a constitution that rivaled the constitution of nineteenth-century Mississippi for its repressiveness—were the most essential features of the story.

Contrary to the benign imagery cultivated by the Republic of Hawaii, The Hawaiian Islands were an armed camp between 1893 and 1898.

Robert Wilcox's popularity came partly from the fact that he was the last to be hunted down.

The environment created by the oligarchy had resulted in her being isolated, spied upon, and threatened with assassination and deportation. Her conviction by a military tribunal under rules of martial law resulted in her being held prisoner on the second floor of 'Iolani Palace, on the side of the palace closest to Waikīkī, behind shuttered windows, a few steps from where she first had heard the marching feet of the American troops.

PRIOR TO THE TRIAL, a statement had been wrung from her abdicating the throne. She said subsequently she was led to believe that if she signed the abdication papers she would save her supporters from being hanged. Attorney General W.O. Smith went to some length, with considerable cruelty, to assure her that no such agreement had been struck, but over the following months the sentences were reduced, and the prisoners were let go. While the queen was in her room, she wrote music, some of which is remembered today. After eight months in isolation, she was paroled to Washington Place.

William Russ, ever faithful to the Republic, wrote that the Hawaiian revolt "was not much of a revolution." Only two or perhaps three people were killed. No one was hanged. People were let out of jail, most of them within months. In this telling, the Republic's ability to restore order gives it further legitimacy, and the failure of the Hawaiian revolt is construed to further belittle the Hawaiians.

Analysis of the event in context of time yields a different picture. The 1895 revolt happened to occur exactly a hundred years after the Battle of Nu'uanu, which had created the Hawaiian Kingdom. In the 1795 battle, Kamehameha led sixteen thousand troops. His opponents on O'ahu, which included the army of Maui, had ten thousand troops. In the Hawaiian revolt a century later, somewhere between several hundred and seven hundred took up arms. The army of Kamehameha was trained and disciplined, and so were the opposing armies. The insurrectionists of 1895 were not trained, nor were they disciplined. As a people trying to survive in a new era of constantly impinging great powers, Hawaiians had not gone to war for five generations. Wilcox, perhaps the only Hawaiian on the scene with a modicum of military training, tried in vain to lead them into formations, much in contrast to the armies of 1795, which fought in a variety of formations—a reflection of their three and a half or so centuries of intermittent interisland warfare.

The armies of 1795 were completely outfitted with clubs, daggers, slings, and spears. Of the twenty-six thousand combatants in the Battle of Nu'uanu, somewhere between a quarter and a half had firearms, in contrast to the fewer than three hundred rifles that the Hawaiians of 1895 struggled to put to use—mostly without success— in their brief revolt. In addition to his musketry, Kamehameha had cannon as well, one of which was famous by its name, "Lopaka." In 1795, warriors died by the hundreds for their cause. One died in 1895. Two years before the Battle of Nu'uanu, the British explorer George Vancouver had remarked pointedly in his diary that a foreign country would invade Hawai'i at considerable cost because of the determination, size, and quality of the Hawaiian fighting force. The total population at that time was still ten to twenty times what it was to be a century later. Kamehameha was militarily strong in part because he provisioned passing ships from his huge upland plantations. The stone terraces of Kona still tell this story, and the renderings of passing artists confirm it—the agricultural terraces that stretch on and on across the terrain. By comparison, many of the Hawaiians who wanted to fight in 1895 were so impoverished they did not have a dime to take the trolley car to the rendezvous point east of Honolulu.

The queen had always understood something of the meaning of firepower. She had yielded to "the superior force" of the United States. In her diary, she often wrote about the danger she and her people were in. *"For we are without arms,"* she had written, *"and they are armed to the teeth."*

If the Hawaiians had seriously challenged the government forces, the U.S. navy would have headed them off—Gresham's assurances notwithstanding. While the Cleveland Administration had adopted a "hands-off" policy in a narrow sense, Cleveland had never really controlled policy in Hawai'i, even when his party was in power. In the 1894 election, the Republicans had regained control of both houses. In December, before the Hawaiian revolt, Senator Henry Cabot Lodge had demanded to know why there was a lapse in the U.S. navy's having a warship stationed in Honolulu. He cited the reports of Admiral Walker, the Republic's friend, who had come and gone. Lodge argued that control of the Hawaiian Islands had become even more important in light of discussion of a bill to construct a canal across the isthmus of the Americas. Thus one piece of the imperial strategy reinforced another, a pattern that recurred throughout the 1890s.

The outline of the American strategy was becoming more explicit. Thurston, in his role as envoy, rushed the story of the revolt to the secretary of state, Gresham. Thurston echoed Lodge. Why was a warship not stationed in Honolulu? Although Gresham had told the Hawaiian delegation that America would not interfere with a revolt, he now told Thurston that an American naval ship was on its way. Given the connotations that Hawaiians, by bitter experience, had come to attach to U.S. warships, the distinction of the navy protecting only noncombatants was a nicety in the extreme. Under John Stevens, the navy had guaranteed that Americans could do whatever they wanted, even overthrow a government. Under these circumstances, the fact that Hawaiians took up arms, however unsuccessfully, is in itself remarkable.

ONE OF THE MANY UNANSWERED QUESTIONS about Hawaiian society at this time was the extent to which it formed a de facto government-in-exile in the years 1893 to 1898, and how well Hawaiians were prepared to deal with events thereafter. Current research into the Hawaiian language press by a new generation of scholars, such as Noenoe Silva and Nancy Morris, suggests far more Hawaiian organization than standard histories have reported. The combination of mass grassroots organizations and Hawaiian language newspapers appears to have been the most vibrant element. If this is so, then the most important Hawaiian leader of this time was Joseph Nāwahī, who has been paid little attention by standard histories. Nāwahī was head of both the Hui Kālai'āina, formed as a political party, and Hui Aloha 'Āina, formed to resist annexation. He presided over the rally protesting the formation of the Republic. He also edited the Hawaiian language newspaper, *Ke Aloha 'Āina*.

He was arrested on December 8, 1895, apparently on the basis of reports by paid spies that he was involved in the planning of the counterrevolt. Two other men were arrested with him, John Bush, the writer, and E.C. Crick, a recently arrived chemist who was perhaps feared by the oligarchy to be an expert in mixing together elements that, on contact, exploded. As the shipment of guns made its way from the West Coast to the royalists, Nāwahī and the others were held in Oʻahu Prison without bail. Nāwahī was bound over to a trial scheduled for February. By the time he was tried he had nearly two hundred co-defendants, and virtually all of them were found guilty. His health declined. He died less than a year after the counterrevolt, in September 1896.

Liliʻuokalani said the people turned out en masse to draw the carriage on which his casket rested. "No private individual in our land," she wrote, "had ever received such a demonstration of love and respect … " A steamer carried Nāwahī's body to Hilo on Hawaiʻi, "where another grand demonstration was made." One of the chants of lament was translated as follows, "The altar of aloha is wrapped with uncontrollable sorrow… The whole race grieves, from the eastern to the western limit of the land."[4] Joseph Nāwahī had told the Hawaiians that the oligarchy had taken their house and was trying to force them into a lei stand. Would they live in a lei stand? he asked. The crowd had roared back, 'Aʻole!!

IN WASHINGTON, THE LEADERS OF THE REPUBLIC tried out different lines to describe their experience with the revolt. They began referring to it as "the late war." While stressing they always had been in control, their alertness had averted "savage butchery." Thurston made his points for keeping a warship in Honolulu. Senator Lodge made his points for the U.S. navy. Lodge and other American annexationists submitted new resolutions to take Hawaiʻi into American custody but there, it appears, the oligarchy wanted to stop. They were waiting for Cleveland to leave office, and they did not want another annexation campaign, believing they again would suffer a defeat.

Francis Hatch in particular was incensed that Americans thought no one had died, when in fact his friend, Charles L. Carter, a member of the Annexation Club, had died. "Carter will be revenged," Hatch wrote. W.O. Smith, who had a remarkable capacity for meanness, blamed President Cleveland for leading Hawaiians into believing they actually should control the government. Cleveland, together with the queen, was the most guilty, he contended. "Sometimes it seems horribly wrong to think of executing Kanaka and not Lili'uokalani & Grover—Damn him!" Smith wrote.

Early on, Foreign Minister Hatch jumped to the conclusion that the United States government had known about the arms shipment but had done nothing to stop it. It was an allegation of misprision at a high level. Specifically Hatch's anger centered on Cleveland's secretary of state, Walter Gresham, who treated the oligarchy with such contempt. Thurston avoided meeting with Gresham any more than he deemed absolutely necessary. Now Hatch began cultivating a theory that Gresham might be brought down. He told Thurston that if they could prove Gresham had knowledge of the arms shipment but did nothing to head it off, a case might be brought against him under international law. W.O. Smith added fuel to Hatch's fire. He said if it could be proved that Gresham had not taken proper steps to stop the ship that carried arms for the Hawaiians, perhaps Hawai'i could force the United States to "pay the whole expense of suppressing the rebellion." It was a case of the foreign minister of the Republic of Hawaii staying up late in conversation with the attorney general. Their thoughts, in turn, agitated their envoy extraordinary and minister plenipotentiary to the United States, Lorrin Thurston. Thurston charged off. He lodged a complaint with Gresham, who referred it to his own attorney general, who said nothing was to be done.

At the same time, Thurston talked to newspaper correspondents from around the country about his allegations. When Thurston returned to Gresham to press his case, Gresham complained vigorously about Thurston maligning the administration by feeding stories to the press. Thurston flared. Gresham, he said, had no right to question him. Gresham bore down. Thurston said he did not *officially* supply letters from Hawai'i to be read by the press. But, yes, he had done so *unofficially*. He backpedaled, apparently impressed by the intensity of Gresham's anger. Thurston said he had · overstepped. Two days later he went back to the secretary of state and offered a verbal apology. Gresham said if he wanted to communicate anything, he could put it in writing. Thurston refused.

Gresham then wrote Thurston a thirteen-page, handwritten letter recounting their exchanges. He told Thurston he had become a persona non grata. He wrote to Hawai'i demanding Thurston's recall. The letter was sent on February 21. Believing he could do no more for the cause of annexation, Thurston returned to Hawai'i only to find that Gresham's letter had never arrived. His comrades initially did not know why he was there. Finally the letter arrived on April 30. It had been to Hong Kong and back.

Thurston said Gresham had been picking on him in a "hostile spirit." He resigned, but the executive council of the Republic let go of him as their envoy reluctantly. He had organized the coup that led to the Bayonet Constitution of 1887, organized the Committee of Annexation, connected the annexationists to America through John Stevens, and made his trip to feel out James Blaine and Benjamin Harrison in 1892, well before the overthrow. He had coordinated the two-layered conspiracy with Stevens, again charged off to Washington, and in his spare time drafted the constitution of 1894. He had his clattering typewriter.

Weeks went by before Foreign Minister Hatch accepted his resignation, and only then after telling the Americans that Thurston had done a good job. Thurston went off to practice law, but those who understood his nature also understood that at the right moment he would be back, because he had an instinct for finding the next crucial step in an unfolding plot. Hatch finally accepted Thurston's resignation on May 31, 1895, in the springtime of the third year after the overthrow, three days after word arrived in Hawai'i that Walter Gresham was dead.

JOHN STEVENS RETURNED to Augusta, Maine, in midsummer 1893, after a rousing sendoff by the American element in Hawai'i. In Augusta he was treated to a reception by his townspeople at the opera house, and he treated them to a talk about Hawai'i. Late in December he lashed back at James Blount's report. His statement was reprinted in *The Kennebec Journal* and reprinted around the country. He was in demand as a speaker, but his movement was restricted by rapidly declining health. He was co-authoring the book *Picturesque Hawai'i*. In it he reported finding intelligent people of

British and American origin in Hawai'i "sharing the good will of many Native Hawaiians, supporting a semi-barbaric monarchy resting on no solid foundation, dead in everything but its vice, coarsely luxuriant in its taste and wishes, spreading social demoralization throughout the islands."[5] He once had been an abolitionist, and in a few short years he had become a crusader against the barbarians. Two years after the overthrow, as he lay dying, Stevens announced proudly to no one in particular that he had raised the flag in Hawai'i.

CHAPTER FOURTEEN

Conjuring the Yellow Peril

Where the story of Hawai'i takes on substance when it is seen in national terms, it takes on a certain additional substance when it is seen in international terms. For those who think of Hawai'i as "picturesque Hawai'i," in Stevens's words, this may seem startling, but from time to time Hawai'i has been a distinctive element in the international picture. In the 1840s, Hawai'i struggled with Britain, France, and America to maintain itself as an independent nation.

It was the beginning of a struggle that was to be paralleled around the world—in the battle of the Indians against the British government, the European takeover of China's port cities, the partition of Africa, and the colonization of the Pacific islands. In the context of the nineteenth century wave of imperialism, Japan stands out for its determined and skillful resistance. Although Japan was in danger of losing control after Matthew Perry's visit, through a process of calculated change, Japan discovered how to run against the tide.

MANJIRO WAS A BRIGHT BOY who initially lacked for opportunity. He was born on the island of Shikoku in southern Japan in 1826, just a few years after the death of the first Kamehameha. Not being favored by Japan's class system, Manjiro went to sea as a fishermen. Most of Japan's boats in those days had no keel. Lacking the deep, centering blade that allows craft to better maintain "way," the Japanese boats were vulnerable to being blown aimlessly before the wind. One of David Kalākaua's legends had to do with a Japanese boat that drifted on the current to Hawai'i—sometime during the period of the original four kingdoms. This same problem of maritime design resulted in ghost ships drifting into Western ports of the United States, their crews transfixed in death. Manjiro was blown before the wind, but he washed up onto an island full of birds located southeast of Japan, along with several of his comrades. He was fourteen years old.

After a half-year of eating seaweed and bird's eggs, he and his friends attracted the attention of an American whaling whip, which took them to Honolulu. Within only a few decades, the attorney general of the oligarchy, W.O. Smith, was to concede that Japanese were intelligent and ambitious, but Manjiro and his friends—and the few shipwrecked sailors who had preceded them—were an unknown entity. The whaling captain, with five Japanese at close range, began to see that one was learning English in the course of the trip, as well as the skills of seamanship. The captain saw in Manjiro not so much his humble status as the brilliant potential of his mind.

The Japanese fishermen were shocked and then delighted to be welcomed by the Hawaiians. Manjiro's companions were spread about the community and became known as cheerful and hardworking *kanaka Nipona*, or Japanese men. One was assigned to work at the Chief's Children's School and became friends with young David Kalākaua. Four settled into niches in Hawai'i, but when the whaling captain sailed for New England, Manjiro sailed with him, and once ashore he was enrolled in Harvard. Manjiro studied diligently, then returned to Hawai'i to see his friends.

On his return to Hawai'i, he attracted the attention of the missionary Samuel Chenery Damon. While the other missionaries were puritans who clung to the land in a grim determination to save the heathens, Damon was a seamen's chaplain. He published a newspaper, *The Friend*, which he distributed around the waterfront to arriving sailors. His thoughts ranged across the expanse of the Pacific.

Damon worked with Manjiro on a plan of return to Japan. One of the Japanese had died and one decided to stay in Hawai'i, but the other two boarded a whaler with Manjiro and were lowered into the water in a rowboat south of Japan near the Ryukyu kingdom, which was later to be taken over by the Japanese and known as Okinawa. The Ryukyu kingdom was a good choice for reentry, because it functioned as a side door to what was nominally a closed country.

For two and a half years, Manjiro sat in various rooms and described his remarkable adventures to Japanese officials. He also shared some of the memorabilia of his trip. One was a book of ABCs. One was a set of drawings of how to build a railroad. The third was something called *Bowditch's Book of Navigation*. It was the American standardization of the revolution in instrument navigation that had allowed James Cook to know where he and his ship's clock were in relation to the clock in Greenwich, England.

Manjiro's debriefing was interrupted by the arrival of large, black ships in Yokohama Harbor. He was rushed north, not to translate the exchanges with Admiral Perry but merely to listen. Had or had not Manjiro been tainted by his exposure to the *gaijin*? After the sages of the Tokugawa shogunate listened to their translators, they would turn to the fisher boy who knew so much. Now tell us Manjiro, the sages commanded, tell us what *you* heard *them* say? Manjiro became their linguistic cross-check. He also came to be trusted again.

He was given the name Manjiro Nakahama, as well as the honor of carrying two swords. He became the first modern navigator of Japan and contributed mightily to the establishment of a navy that was capable of venturing out beyond the Sea of Japan. In 1861, he was part of the delegation that journeyed to Washington, D.C., to establish diplomatic relations with America. On the way, thanks to bad weather, the rest of the delegation stopped off in Hawai'i. They met with Manjiro's old acquaintances and made new ones. By this time David Kalākaua was twenty-four years old, and the idea of being king must have seemed remote. The fourth member of the Kamehameha line ruled Hawai'i with the help of missionaries who had heard the call of new careers in mid-life.

For Manjiro, who first had seen Hawai'i in 1843, the Kingdom was dramatically different than in his youth. But to the other Japanese in the delegation, it probably seemed to be a leisurely paradise suspended idyllically between their own turbulent country and America, which at that very moment was descending into a civil war. The Japanese went home and became embroiled in a civil war of their own, which was won by the forces of modernization—by those who wanted most intensely to know about instrument navigation, trains, and the language of the *gaijin* that was codified in the ABCs. Manjiro not only survived but prospered. He knew the right stuff. The modernizers won and paid ritual respect to the Emperor Meiji.

IN THE ODD CREVICE OF TIME between the authority of the Tokugawa shogunate and the new Meiji Japan, a labor recruiter from Hawai'i named Eugene Van Reed gathered a shipload of Japanese citizens to work alongside the Chinese in the sugar plantations of Hawai'i. The ship included a *samurai* warrior, a lady of poor reputation, gamblers, and a boy so belligerent that he swore at his shipmates indiscriminately. Most were city people. They were transplanted to the primitive conditions of the early plantations and given jobs in the hot sun. Disputes occurred quickly. In response, Japan sent representatives to investigate how its overseas citizens were being treated in this strange, new land. Most went home to Japan. Those who stayed in Hawai'i became known as *Gannen Mono*, or first-year people. From Hawai'i's parochial point of view, *Gannen Mono* were sometimes thought of as Japanese in their first year in Hawai'i, but their name actually resulted from their arrival in the first year of the Meiji era. The new Japan proceeded cautiously with emigration, just as it proceeded cautiously with how to deal with the larger world.

In the third year of the Emperor Meiji, 1871, Japan signed a treaty of commerce and friendship with Hawai'i. It allowed Japanese to live in Hawai'i as long as they had contract work. The signing of this treaty eventually was to have a special impact on history, but for a long time it was as if nothing had happened. Then, in Meiji year thirteen, David Kalākaua, king of Hawai'i, was reported to be en route from San Francisco, California, to Yokohama Harbor. Kalākaua was unannounced. He was unsure what to do. He considered going ashore as an ordinary traveler, looking about, and moving on. To his knowledge, the Japanese did not know he was there.

Kalākaua was surprised when the place went mad. Cannon fired everywhere, including cannon of the foreign ships, which were now welcome in Japan. David broke out his flag and his royal uniform. One can imagine the brilliance of his smile. He had found a venue like the U.S. Congress—a place with scale in which his intellect and charm could shine, where he could put aside the awful problems of his Kingdom. Kalākaua was greeted by the highest levels of Japan's leaders, who paraded him past thousands of Japanese citizens to meet the emperor. David could trace his ancestry back over fifteen hundred or more years in Hawai'i, and the Emperor Meiji could trace his own ancestry back about twenty-five hundred years in Japan. The two hit it off.

Kalākaua Rex was to be remembered in history as the first foreign head of state to visit Japan. He also shook the emperor's hand, which was taboo. The visit was extensively if condescendingly recorded by Kalākaua's traveling companion, William Armstrong, the labor commissioner of the Hawaiian Kingdom. Armstrong's diary, subsequently published, became the standard account of Kalākaua's journey. It also was a reminder that Kalākaua's lifetime of writings did not survive the takeover of the archives by the white oligarchy—or so people thought. Then a distinguished American judge of Japanese ancestry named Masaji Marumoto revised and corrected the history of Kalākaua's visit, based on his find of a forty-eight page diary by Kalākaua in Bishop Museum. He showed that during the better part of his two weeks in Japan, Kalākaua spent most of his time with the most influential people in the country. He dined with the emperor several times. He met the empress. At their farewell dinner, he was presented with Japan's highest award, the Order of Chrysanthemum, not a second-tier award that Armstrong had described.

In the course of this visit, Kalākaua broached what had been thought of in Hawai'i as the purpose of his trip—opening the doors for the immigration of Japanese workers to Hawai'i. Granted, things had not gone well in the immigration experiment of 1868, but with care such problems could be dealt with. Would Japan reconsider?

In truth there was much more to the visit than immigration. When Kalākaua got away from his *haole* adviser, he paid tribute to the sovereignty of Japan by offering to waive extraterritoriality, an arcane diplomatic word that refers to the arrangement wherein foreigners are not dealt with by domestic courts. It is what the French with their warships had forced onto Kamehameha III when they insisted that Frenchmen accused of crimes in Hawai'i could only be tried by their fellow Frenchmen. It is what the Western powers already had forced onto Japan as an erosion of Japan's autonomy. Extraterritoriality perfectly symbolized the threat to Japan's sovereignty, and it is a mark of Kalākaua's cleverness that he offered to waive it.

Next, Kalākaua said, might not the prince of Imperial Japan marry the princess of Hawai'i, Ka'iulani? Finally, would Japan take it upon itself to form a Pacific federation, to which the Kingdom of Hawai'i would ally itself?

Among these proposals, that of an arranged marriage has lived on among individuals who deride, or twitter over, the monarchy. The rest have been forgotten, to the detriment of a more accurate understanding of Hawai'i's history. One of Kalākaua's ancestors was Kaumuali'i of Kaua'i, whose life struggle was keeping Kamehameha at bay. Kalākaua shrewdly assessed the vigor of the Japanese and thought he saw a countervailing force. If he were more closely aligned with Japan, he might keep the Americans at bay. He might keep the Americans at some decent remove from the Hawaiian people, who desperately needed time to adjust to all that had happened to them.

Japan itself was strategizing how to keep its equilibrium while gaining strength. For some of the same reasons that Kalākaua sought an alliance, they politely declined it. As to Kalākaua's proposal of a Pacific federation, the emperor's words seem to have gone beyond ritual courtesy: "... I ardently hope that such Union may be realized at some future day, and keeping it constantly in mind I never fail, wherever time allows me, to discuss the means of bringing about that result ... it cannot only be the fortune of Japan and Hawai'i, but also of whole Asia."[1]

Kalākaua subsequently sent bright young Hawaiians to live and study in Japan. He also sent his diplomatic aide, Curtis Piehu Iaukea, to Japan in 1884 to renew the discussion of immigration. In 1885, the first Japanese immigrants were allowed to go to Hawai'i, anticipating a Labor Convention—a compact of terms—that was signed between Japan and the Kingdom of Hawai'i in 1886. Individual Japanese workers went to Hawai'i for three years. If problems arose, they were resolved by the careful government-to-government relationship that had been worked out. The governing law of the Kingdom was called the Masters and Servants Act, which by its very name conveys the feudal nature of the relationship. The key feature of the Masters and

Servants Act was the right of the Hawaiian Kingdom to enforce the contract by imposing criminal sanctions.

Workers protested in a variety of ways. On occasion the government of Japan was called in. Inspectors representing the government of Japan also made periodic rounds. From Japan's point of view, the national honor was protected. From the Japanese worker's point of view, the inspectors were sometimes regarded with disdain, but in the messy and sometimes inhumane development of sugar plantations, Japan at least provided its emigrants a dignified framework that was otherwise often lacking—such as in the lives of workers from a disintegrating China.

In his study of work in Hawai'i, Dr. Edward Beechert categorized the contract system as indentured labor. His careful definition is instructive: "Indentured labor is a form standing between free labor and unfree labor. It is distinguished from peonage by its definite period of service as compared to an indefinite term of debt; it is distinguished from free labor in that neither employer or employee is free to bargain the terms and withdraw their services whenever conditions are unsuitable. Indenture contracts call for a specific period of service, after which the holder of the contract and the worker are mutually free of further responsibility."[2]

Between 1885 and 1894, twenty-nine thousand Japanese migrated to Hawai'i as *kanyaku imin*, contract immigrants. In 1894, as the Republic was settling in, the contract labor system began to unravel. The role of the Japanese government in recruiting, screening, and overseeing the transportation of workers was replaced by private labor companies. Controls loosened. Laborers who were not under three-year contracts became "free" laborers. The Republic tried to crack down. It became more repressive. Runaways increased, but so did the number of workers arriving in Hawai'i. It was against this background that the immigration of the Japanese became a burning issue in the maneuvering that occurred over annexation.

HOW AND WHY the Japanese contract labor system ended is an important question, because the individuals who were to conjure a Japanese "menace" eventually would say that the dissolution of the contract system was part of a Japanese plot. The limited history of annexation that exists has tended to accept the gist of the loose allegations about Japan's designs on Hawai'i. In this light, Hilary Conroy's small, well-researched book, *The Japanese Frontier in Hawai'i, 1868-1898*, deserves attention. Conroy said the breakdown of the contract system reflected "the vacillation in the minds of the leaders of the Republic of Hawaii on the whole subject of the Japanese."[3] He noted that the oligarchy was anxious about the rising number of Japanese immigrants, but their sugar planter constituents—virtually the only constituents of the oligarchy—were reluctant to give up Japanese labor. "This," said Conroy, "was the basic paradox."

R.G. Irwin, Hawai'i's minister to the Japanese government, was a holdover from the Kalākaua era. He also was the de facto czar of labor immigration, running the recruitment, transportation, and distribution of laborers in Hawai'i as a private business. He negotiated the terms of contracts with the Japanese government on one end and delivered the human product on the other. In the first part of 1894, while the Provisional Government was transforming itself into the Republic of Hawaii, the sugar planters—hard hit by the McKinley tariff—balked at paying the contract rates. Japan already had agreed to cut the wages of male workers from fifteen dollars to $12.50 a month, and now the planters wanted, effectively, a rate of ten dollars a month. They also haggled over transportation costs, as well as the cost of maintaining labor inspectors who were in the employ of the Japanese government.

Sanford Dole was understandably wary of Irwin's dual interests in diplomacy and business, but he told Thurston that Irwin appeared to "be a good American as well as a good P.G. [Provisional Government] man."[4] Despite high-level bargaining involving Japan's foreign minister, the Provisional Government, and the planters, Irwin was frustrated in his attempts to put together a compromise version of the old immigration system. The government-sponsored contract system was dead. Irwin, as the man who had made it work, had lost much of his influence. The point is that the changes that undermined the contract labor convention had originated from the planters in Hawai'i, and Japan in fact had made important concessions aimed at saving the *kanyaku* system.

It was during this same period, 1894, that the Republic enacted a law requiring immigrants to carry fifty dollars at their point of entry into Hawai'i, and to also possess a locally approved work contract. The Republic did not use this legislation until late 1896, but 1894—the year of the adoption of the constitution of the Republic—was the year a new set of controls was put in place.

No sooner had the contract system come undone than a new American tariff bill, Wilson-Gorman, let Hawai'i back inside the lucrative U.S. domestic sugar market. The boom was back on. The cycle of plantation expansion—more capital, more labor, more land, and more water—resumed. Where could the planters get more workers? They looked over the entire globe. They experimented with European immigrants, with enormously costly results. They had tried the Chinese, but the Chinese had fled the plantation as quickly as possible. Where could they turn? They tried China again, and in fact Chinese immigration did increase substantially, but there really was no available labor supply comparable to the temporarily impoverished peasantry of the rapidly industrializing Japan.

Having contradictory goals, the oligarchy of the Republic behaved in contradictory ways. It offended the government of Japan by setting a ratio of two Chinese for each Japanese immigrant, and by then denying they had done so. This makeshift idea was followed by a round of haggling between the planters and the Executive Council, via its Board of Immigration, that allowed a hundred Japanese and Chinese in for every ten white laborers. For practical purposes the white workers were from Portugal. They were so costly that they did not materialize. The sugar market grew, and private companies sprang up in Japan to fill the breach left by the Japanese government. The immigration companies tried as far as possible to contract directly with the plantations. Hilary Conroy counted it a sign of the times that in 1895 the chief inspector of labor conditions for Japan resigned his government post and returned home to start an emigration company. The labor importation business was being privatized. Conroy wrote: "The real effect of this, since Chinese immigration was being fostered as much as possible anyway, was to allow Japanese immigration, now broken loose from the Irwin system, to continue unabated, indeed to give promise of huge expansion as emigration companies mushroomed overnight and vied with each other in giving more labor for less money to the ever eager planters."[5]

A LITTLE MORE THAN TWO MONTHS after the overthrow, in a letter dated March 23, 1893, the Imperial government of Japan raised the issue of voting rights for Japanese immigrants. The Japanese consul in Hawai'i, Saburo Fujii, called Sanford Dole's attention to the 1871 treaty his country had signed with the Kingdom. He went on to discuss the voting rights being exercised by Americans and Europeans, but being withheld from the Japanese. Fujii said his government trusted there would be no further delay in granting rights "enjoyed by the citizens or subjects of the most favored nation." In a subsequent letter he cited the treaty's guarantee that Japanese citizens would enjoy "at all times the same privileges as may have been or may hereafter be granted to the citizens or subjects of other nations." If foreigners were going to vote in Hawai'i, Japan wanted its immigrants to vote, too.

In Tokyo, R.G. Irwin had an audience with Mutsu Munemitsu, Japan's minister of foreign affairs. Irwin was a unique link between Hawai'i and Japan, because he not only had developed the labor system but had been involved in developing an overall friendly relationship. Irwin was married to a Japanese woman. He wrote to Dole that he had known Munemitsu for twenty-two years and believed he was "a most candid, truthful man and ... no other object or wish is entertained excepting that stated by him to me." He quoted Munemitsu as saying Japan was expecting the "same civil rights" as the Americans, English, or Germans. Japan saw no reason the Japanese in Hawai'i "should not have the same privileges as those accorded to other foreigners in Hawai'i." Irwin cited a powerful tide of public and press opinion in Japan to which the Imperial government and Japanese Parliament were responding.

On July 8, 1893, Sanford Dole wrote Irwin a long response explaining why the oligarchy would never let the Japanese vote. "... Japanese like Chinese are always under the order and control of their respective governments," Dole said, "even when they are in foreign lands." He contended that, in contrast, the American and European governments exercised no such control over their citizens in foreign lands. Therefore, Dole said, Japan could not reasonably ask for the vote because "no government can ask for an opportunity of exercising an influence in the local affairs of another government."

ARCHIVES OF HAWAI'I

The Treaty of Reciprocity accelerated the emigration of Asian workers into Hawai'i. The Chinese workers, shown here, were quickly outnumbered by Japanese.

Japanese immigrant plantation workers

Japanese immigrants were ferried into the immigration station, detained, and returned to Japan.

Senator John T. Morgan, an Alabama Democrat, implored the Hawaiians to happily yield to the United States and save themselves from the Yellow Peril. Morgan was the inspiration for Francis Hatch's plot to provoke Japan.

Francis Hatch, Thurston's successor as minister to Washington, was the architect of the scheme to create a show of opposition to Japanese immigration.

Henry Cooper, the Republic's minister of foreign affairs, carried out Hatch's scheme.

It was classic Sanford Dole—an expression of Teutonic supremacy wrapped thinly in the verbiage of reasoning.

It is significant that tension was mounting with Japan during 1893, and yet Japan was not portrayed by the annexationists either in Washington or Honolulu as a reason for annexation—let alone *the* reason for annexation. If anything, Britain was the potential competitor of choice. Britain had been involved with Hawai'i from the beginning of Hawai'i's interaction with the larger world. Kamehameha had an affinity for the British explorer George Vancouver, and Lili'uokalani took pride in her acquaintance with Queen Victoria. The British consul, James Wodehouse, was sympathetic to the Hawaiian royalists, even though the British Foreign Office guided him away from taking sides. After the Provisional Government announced formation of the Republic, Britain quickly recognized the new government. It also replaced Wodehouse. While antagonism toward Britain may have resonated with Americans of the backwoods, Americans who understood the workings of nations realized that Britain was ready to accommodate America's special interest in Hawai'i. Britain was overextended. It had set its sights on forming the Anglo-American alliance that was to become a dominant feature of global diplomacy and warfare throughout the twentieth century.

Just as American and British roles in the world were shifting, so was Japan's. In 1894, Japan undertook a war with China, which extended into 1895. Japan won. Twenty-seven years into the era of Meiji, Japan was emerging as the major power of East Asia.

Throughout this period, Hawai'i's position relative to Japanese immigrant labor was in a state of continuous flux. Demand for labor had lessened with the McKinley tariff, then revived with the new tariff law of 1894. This meant that just as Japan was winning its regional war, and just as the Provisional Government was moving into its holding action, plantation demand for Japanese labor was on the upswing.

The Planters Labor and Supply Company issued a warning in 1894 against the number of "free" laborers aggregating in Hawai'i. It estimated there were seventeen thousand free Japanese laborers and another seventeen thousand Chinese and Portuguese. Although the 1886 labor convention was going by the boards, neither Japan nor Hawai'i wanted to acknowledge it at this early stage. From the Japanese viewpoint, Hawai'i was a source of currency and a safety valve for rural Japanese displaced by the industrialization of the new Japan. The private Japanese immigration companies had taken over where the governments had left off.

It is not altogether clear today how the oligarchy regarded Japan in the transitional year 1894, but some clues occur in its correspondence and legislation. When the Provisional Government of Hawai'i formulated the law requiring each worker to have fifty dollars on arrival from Japan, Thurston wrote from Washington congratulating Dole on a toughness that Thurston had not imagined Dole to possess. At about the same time, publicity of the plan for a new constitution circulated, and the issue of Japanese voting rights came to the fore. In early March 1894, the Hawaiian minister of foreign affairs, Francis Hatch, wrote the Japanese consul that voting rights were to be taken up by the Constitutional Convention to limit the "privilege" of voting in such a way that no discrimination would occur "toward aliens with whom we have treaty relations, except as to those who may have special claim to it from services rendered the government." In other words, Japanese were not going to vote, but neither were other foreigners, other than all the white foreigners who had been involved in the overthrow.

It was the type of thing that had caused Cleveland's minister to Hawai'i, Albert Willis, to say, "Duplicity seems to be the cardinal virtue of their statesmanship." Irwin's valued acquaintance, Munemitsu, wrote Irwin, taking specific issue with Hatch's contorted definition of discrimination. It would, he said, "involve the perpetuation of the specific discrimination against which the Imperial Government have hitherto been reluctantly obliged to remonstrate ... " He said the Japanese could not tolerate it "with a due appreciation of their own dignity."

What Japan sought for its subjects in Hawai'i, Munemitsu said, "... is an actual equality of treatment with the subjects and citizens of other Treaty Powers, unqualified by the discrimination hitherto existing or any other discrimination."

At some point, the question recurs, why is such sensitive history not known? The answer is that it either lies buried altogether or is obscured by half-truths, such as when William Russ wrote that the Japanese pressure for voting rights was so strong that all naturalization was stopped for the time being. While in the narrow sense this statement is true, it fails to tell the reader about the relationship between the odd institution of denizenship and voting rights. It ignores the entries on page after page of the archived minutes of the Executive Council of the Republic. Whenever an American, European, or Portuguese asked for a right of residency— called denizenship—"with voting rights," it was automatically approved. The rare request from a Japanese was deferred indefinitely.

References to new denizens are entered in the minutes of nearly every one of the council's several weekly meetings. For example, on July 16, 1897, a person named W.C. Hallinsead asked to be made a denizen of Hawai'i with voting rights. His application was approved. In the same meeting, a Japanese man named Tamaki Gomi requested denizenship. Although he specified that it be *without* the right to vote, the council decided that a "decision of the matter be suspended," an exercise in Republic doublespeak.

By design, denizenship did not endanger an individual's citizenship in another country, so that white denizens could compete against the voting citizenship of the native-born or the legally naturalized. Henry Cooper, chairman of the Committee of Annexation, soon to be minister of foreign affairs, was a denizen, not a citizen. The secretary of the Republic's legation in Washington, D.C., Frank Hastings, was a denizen. Faced with taking the Republic's oath of allegiance, Frank Hastings had to be reassured by the Republic's foreign minister that it "interferes in no way with your allegiance to your native Country," meaning the United States.

The Republic, then, was systematically granting extraordinary rights to immigrant whites while systematically denying those rights to Japanese and other Asian immigrants. Taking up where the Bayonet Constitution left off, the constitution of 1894 effectively barred Asian immigrants from acquiring the right to vote. Further, the arbitrary requirement that immigrants have fifty dollars at their moment of entry now was on the books, although it had not yet been used.

All of this might have been business as usual except that Japan was engaged in transforming itself into a major regional power determined to be treated with the same dignity as other nations. The same year Sanford Dole rejected Japan's request for the same voting rights as other foreigners, Japan undertook a war with China. By 1895, as the Dole government was putting down the Hawaiian revolt, Japan was winning its war. In this altered context, the expansion of the plantation economy continued, the immigration of the Japanese continued, and the story of a "peaceful invasion" by Japan began to spread like a fire.

The allegation that Japan was engaged in a "peaceful invasion" appears to have developed in conversations between Francis Hatch and U.S. Senator John Tyler Morgan in Washington in early 1896. It took on size as a result of a premeditated provocation of Japan in Honolulu. It then was recirculated in Washington and, finally, accepted as conventional wisdom at the highest levels of the United States government. In simplest outline, it was an allegation that Japan was trying to take over the Hawaiian Islands.

It is perhaps the major reason Francis Hatch deserves to be remembered in history. While overshadowed by Dole, Thurston, and Smith, he was a man of impeccable annexationist credentials. In Lili'uokalani's acidic comments on the oligarchy, she said only, "Of these pseudo-Hawaiians, Mr. Hatch is a lawyer from New Hampshire." Hatch appears in the archives in the early 1880s, negotiating with the attorney general of the Kingdom for a "spirit license" for a Chinese business, Yuen Chong & Co. He also appears on behalf of the sugar baron, Claus Spreckels; for the new telephone company; and then for a succession of sugar, water, and rail companies that, together, helped make a reality of the phrase King Sugar, just when the agricultural commodity began appropriating the word of rank previously reserved to the highest Hawaiian chiefs.

Francis Hatch at one time was president of the Annexation Club. In the Provisional Government, he originally was vice president in the line of succession behind Dole, as well as minister of foreign affairs. It is probably significant that he held this job in Honolulu long enough to get acquainted with the Japanese consul, to correspond with the truly knowledgeable R.G. Irwin in Tokyo, and to grasp the extent of Sanford Dole's wariness of the Japanese. As foreign minister, Hatch handled all the dealings with Thurston in

Washington. He observed, for example, how Thurston launched the campaign for annexation by alluding to the interest of other powers in Hawai'i, Britain being the early favorite.

Thereafter, when Thurston became a persona non grata in the Washington of Grover Cleveland, Francis Hatch took over Thurston's job. He inflated in size. Another second-tier annexationist, Henry E. Cooper (in the queen's words, "another alien"), came into the government in Hatch's original job as minister of foreign affairs. Henry Cooper had served as the subject of Thurston's story of how the Committee of Annexation was formed, and he had read the proclamation of the Provisional Government. As Hatch had deferred to Thurston, now Cooper deferred to Hatch.

With Cooper standing by in Honolulu to execute his ideas, Hatch became the foremost advocate of limiting Japanese immigration. The initial attempts at regulating Japanese immigration had involved talking the planters into using more Chinese and Europeans as plantation workers. In midsummer 1895, the Japanese consul inquired whether Hawai'i was cutting off Japanese immigration altogether. Francis Hatch responded that, far from it, Hawai'i was continuing to honor its 1871 treaty with Japan and its labor agreement of 1885, including assurances given Japan at that time by Walter Murray Gibson that Japanese immigrants would outnumber Chinese. Hatch professed regret at the Japanese consul's "intimation of bad faith" and suggested that it be withdrawn, demonstrating a missionary-like capacity for indignation.

Thereafter the Executive Council made its unsuccessful attempt to require the planters to import one Portuguese worker for every so many Chinese and Japanese. Politically the Portuguese were favorites, because they had lined up for the oligarchy during the overthrow, but economically they were a drag on the plantations' profitability, because they demanded more pay and insisted on bringing their families, which meant higher costs of transportation, housing, and medical care, to say nothing of community infrastructure, such as schools. The economic reality was that planters wanted Japanese labor even if the lawyers who ran the government did not.

For Hatch, the international politics of Japanese labor took on a new level of urgency when he gained access to the intoxicating environment of Washington. He naturally made his way to the door of U.S. Senator John Morgan, Democrat of Alabama, who Thurston would describe as the senator from Hawai'i. Morgan had authored the Senate report attacking Cleveland's plan to restore Queen Lili'uokalani to power. He not only had written the report but led a bipartisan movement in the Senate, in which enough Democratic votes were added to Republican votes to thwart the queen's restoration.

By the time of his private conversations with Francis Hatch, John Tyler Morgan was seventy-one years old. He had established himself as an attorney in Selma, Alabama, before he enlisted in the army of the Confederacy, where he rose from private to brigadier general. After the war, he returned to Selma, and in 1877 was elected to the U.S. Senate, where he began to look at the wider world through the venue of the Foreign Affairs Committee. Ironically, Morgan bore the name of John Tyler, who was president of the United States from 1841 to 1845, during the time the Kingdom of Hawai'i had sought to be recognized as a sovereign nation by the great naval powers. President Tyler had said that America wanted "no exclusive control over the Hawaiian government, but is content with its independent existence ... " Tyler added that if events required, the United States might adopt an opposite policy. In other words, the America of the 1840s had no problem with an independent Hawai'i but might change its mind. John Tyler Morgan was instrumental in America changing its mind.

In his meeting with Francis Hatch, Morgan—as reported by Hatch to the Dole government in Honolulu—said there was "good reason to suppose that Japan has designs upon the country."[6] Morgan quoted a newspaper reporter, Kate Field, as saying there were too many Japanese in the Islands. He wanted to know why Japanese were still being brought in. Further, Morgan told Hatch that a continued immigration of Asians would damage the chances of Hawai'i for annexation. He proposed that the Republic enact laws "looking to the removal" of the entire Asian population. Between Asians, Morgan preferred the immigration of Chinese to Japanese. He urged that the labor agreement with Japan be terminated and that the Friendship Treaty of 1871—both inherited from the monarchy—be modified.

"I went over the whole ground with him [Morgan]," Hatch wrote. "I pointed out to him that that would be a dangerous course in the absence of better support in Washington."

Why was there "good reason to suppose that Japan has designs" on Hawai'i? There was no explanation, but Hatch had developed a new and grander view of the world. "No person," Hatch wrote, "can say such danger does not exist."

He ran on, contending along with Morgan that "the Japs[7] are seeking some excuse to make a quarrel." He contended the Japanese were brooding over "every little incident of real or fancied grievances which had occurred in the last ten years" and they would soon make preposterous demands. He said Morgan feared Japan would interfere in Hawai'i in such a way that it would be hard for America to object— by claiming mistreatment of its citizens, for example, or by claiming Hawai'i's denial of a "promised right."

Hatch said that merely being in Washington had helped him see events better, while "a clear vision is sometimes impossible from being too near the object." He thought Morgan was right. "I think," he wrote, "we should begin to make a record which will appeal to people here."

Hatch boldly outlined a set of instructions: First, try to obtain Japan's consent to modify both the treaty and the labor convention "so that further immigration can be absolutely controlled." Second, if the Japanese did not agree after six months, as Hatch thought they surely would not, then give notice to terminate the labor agreement. Third, raise the fifty-dollar cash requirement for immigrants, "making the discretion of the cabinet perhaps clearer so as not to shut out white settlers."

He returned to his essential point: "There can be no more powerful argument to be used here ... than the claim that we are trying to save the country from the Asiatics, provided we have something to show to base it on."

He suggested the notice to terminate the labor agreement be made after the impending 1896 election, when a new U.S. president was about to be sworn in. Hatch warned that the planters, habituated as they were to low-cost labor, would fight his plan. But it was they, not he, who were reckless. "They are playing with fire," he said. "If their ideas are followed the Republic will be wrecked anyway." He closed by saying how important it was for the time being to keep the Hong Kong authorities happy and to keep the Chinese workers coming. Then the planters would get by with "no real grievance."

Fortified by his new insights, Hatch met two days later with Richard Olney, the deceased Walter Gresham's successor as secretary of state. Olney was more comfortable with expansionism than Gresham and less inclined to moralize. Hatch, in his account to Honolulu, said he again went over the whole story. Olney was a first-time audience. "He said it was all news to him," Hatch said, "that he had had no idea that any but the most friendly relations existed between us." Were it not tragic, Hatch's line would be laughable, because up to that point good relations *had* existed between the nation of Hawai'i and Japan, and the same also was in general true of relations between Japan and the United States.

Olney suggested the possibility of ending the labor agreement, but Hatch said his government "desired to do nothing which could be taken by Japan as an unfriendly act." That was to become one of his most consistent tactics—to create alarm in the American listener about the Japanese, then say Hawai'i by itself could do very little about them, and perhaps nothing. Hatch quoted Olney as saying, "Japan surely can not intend to run against us out there." Olney talked about America's traditional approach of "warning off all other nations." He talked loosely about the Monroe Doctrine, outlining a U.S. sphere of influence in the Americas and also, Hatch said, "a special Hawaiian doctrine in addition."

What Hatch took away from the conversation probably encouraged the oligarchy's subsequent willingness to provoke Japan: "...Olney would not for a moment tolerate any interference in Hawai'i by Japan ... I am confident we can depend on him for prompt assistance in case of any such emergency..."[8]

While a few historians have written about the tension with Japan, they appear to have overlooked Hatch's account of his meeting with Senator Morgan, which clearly describes the impetus behind the Republic of Hawaii provoking Japan. The Japanese often have been described in wary terms for putting pressure on little Hawai'i, but the inner truth appears to be that little Hawai'i intentionally provoked Japan as a tactic to advance the cause of annexation.

The provocation was carried out by Henry Cooper, the new foreign minister, who was so much under the sway of the more experienced Hatch. Cooper seems to have become carried away by the zeal and intensity of Hatch's plan. He proceeded with his task under the cover of Sanford Dole's own suspicions of the Japanese. This climate of suspicion was aggravated by the continued movement of "free" labor, but the immigration of workers resulted from the very real demands of the planters—not for expensive Portuguese workers with families but low-cost, male, Japanese workers.

Cooper assured Hatch, "We are framing a policy which, without rendering us liable to criticism for a violation of the treaty with Japan, will I trust relieve us from the present embarrassment." He said the Republic was telling the planters that further applications for Japanese workers would not be considered. Nonetheless, almost immediately thereafter Cooper met with the Japanese consul and assured him that their agreements were intact, and specifically that Japanese immigration would be favored over Chinese immigration.

Cooper was feeling reassured by Hatch's meeting with the new U.S. secretary of state, saying it was good to "feel that we cannot be buffeted about by all the great powers with impunity." He said the planters were cooperating with their informal ban on Japanese immigration. In the first three months of 1896 they had asked for 987 Chinese and no Japanese.

To further aggravate the situation, the Legislature of the Republic imposed a prohibitive tariff on the importation of wine—not wine made from grapes, but from rice. To the irritation of the Japanese government and thousands of Japanese workers, they placed a one-dollar-a-gallon tariff on Japanese *sake*.

The U.S. presidential election was coming. Excitement was building. If the government of the Republic could create Hatch's "record," perhaps it also could become so powerful in the future as to rewrite its own record of conspiracies. No one would ever know.

CHAPTER FIFTEEN

The Doorway to Imperialism

When William McKinley was elected president, Sanford Dole said, "We are relieved at the election of Mr. McKinley..." Actually he was excited. In late November and early December he dashed off a succession of four handwritten letters to Francis Hatch, probing for information on McKinley. He also reinforced the gambit of provoking Japan without describing it in the calculating terms used by Hatch.

"There is considerable activity in the bringing in of free Japanese immigrants," Dole said. "The several immigration companies are working the business for profits, and are preparing to run it for all it is worth." It is a significant description, because the motive in Dole's words now was profit for private emigration companies—and not, even after the election of McKinley, part of the grand design of Imperial Japan. Dole said the Republic might have to "procure a modification of our Japanese treaty," but not without help from Washington. "It might be helpful to us to ask the good offices of the United States Government in aid of our proposition."

Unmistakably, Dole had signed onto the plan that Senator John Morgan had instigated, and Francis Hatch had refined, ten months earlier in Washington. Challenge Japan on immigration, then run with the results to the United States. Get the United States to shield the little Republic from serious fallout, and then get America to untangle the ensuing diplomatic problems at a later date.

What did Dole actually believe about Japan? No doubt he was genuinely concerned with the volume of Japanese immigration. "The Japanese are still piling in here," he wrote. But did he believe the size of the Japanese immigration really said anything about the intentions of Japan? In the opening days of the McKinley Administration, Dole had pondered how to answer the questions of a New York newspaper. In a summary that he reviewed with Hatch, he led with the importance of Hawai'i "being the western outpost of Anglo Saxon civilization and a vantage ground of American commerce in the Pacific." This was a clear enough appeal to American expansionism and the school of Social Darwinism. Perhaps he imagined Professor John Burgess picking up the newspaper and reading those words. Dole said events were moving quickly in the Pacific and mentioned, in succession, the activities of Russia, Japan, China, and Britain.

Annexation, he contended, could be accomplished without international friction, but it was "impossible to say how long this opportunity will continue." The closest he came to mentioning Japan as a danger was to say that the question of how "to maintain and further develop our civilization in the face of the enterprise of our western neighbors, and our own agricultural dependence upon their labor, is one of difficult solution." The simple answer was annexation. It would "undoubtedly deliver us from this danger."

While Dole's statement was an understated pitch for Anglo-Saxon supremacy in the northern Pacific, it fell short of harking up a menace from Japan. Given the amount of the Republic's political capital that Hatch and Henry Cooper wanted to invest in the anti-Japanese campaign, Dole's statement was odd. It could explain why Hatch did not want Dole to come to Washington to lobby for annexation, and also why there had been so much discussion over the newspaper interview within the white cabinet.

MCKINLEY'S ELECTION was on November 3, 1896, but the news of his election—slowed not only by the speed of a steamship, but also by a new method of counting ballots—was not to reach Hawai'i until November 17. On November 12, the Executive Council met to discuss Cooper's thoughts about the Japanese. Dole presided, and Smith attended, as well as Cooper. In addition there were Marshal Brown and a Japanese language interpreter, Chester A. Doyle. Smith described sixty-six Japanese coming in as "free immigrants" on a Japanese steamship, the *Toyo Maru*. The marshal had received a tip that the fifty dollars of entry money of the workers was not really theirs, but belonged to the steamship company. Doyle had investigated. Doyle said forty-one of the sixty-six "did not own" their fifty dollars but had gotten it from the steamship company.

A list of the forty-one names was turned over to the Customs House, and the forty-one people were forced to return to Japan. It was to be the first of four times that Japanese immigrants were barred from entry into Hawai'i.

THE VICTORY OF MCKINLEY and the Republicans in Congress, along with a show of action against Japanese immigration, together defined the oligarchy's chance to come in from the cold and sit at the great American fireside. It is a mark of the priority of the Hawai'i question in American politics that Henry E. Cooper, minister of foreign affairs of the Republic of Hawaii, held a back-channel meeting with President-elect McKinley on December 9, 1896, barely a month after the election. The meeting was held at McKinley's home in Canton, Ohio. Dole hoped the meeting would be "giving us some light" on how to proceed. Hatch, who was purposely kept out of the meeting because of his visibility in Washington, coached Cooper to lead with the "Japanese question."

There are two historical lines of thought about McKinley. One is that he was a clear-minded and calculating man who moved slowly. The other is that he was a relatively dull man who moved slowly. If the occurrence of the meeting suggested that he might be willing to push ahead quickly on annexation, the actual content of the meeting suggested he would move slowly.

The secretary of the oligarchy's Executive Council, Ben Marx, accompanied Cooper and took verbatim notes. McKinley met them in a general office downstairs and took them upstairs to a private office. The president-elect was referred to as Major McKinley, in keeping with his status as an officer in the Civil War. Cooper opened by saying a mock presidential election had been held in Honolulu and that McKinley had won.

"Yes, I saw that," McKinley said, "and appreciate very much the kind sentiment which necessarily goes with it." McKinley observed there had been "stirring times in the Islands."

One may imagine Cooper sighing as he thought of just how stirring the times had been. "Yes," Cooper said, "we spent many anxious days but feel that now we are masters of the situation so far as local questions are concerned," which meant they had put down the Native Hawaiians but were worried about the Japanese. Cooper explained delicately: "... there is a feeling of unrest that possibly our independence may be disturbed at some future time." His next sentence did not really track, but nonetheless managed to raise a sense of alarm: "We have a treaty with Japan, which is still in force, and under the terms of which the Japanese are coming in, and as they are an ambitious people it is hard to say what the result may be." *They are an ambitious people.* Together he and the major wandered through other issues, such as the solvency of Hawai'i's treasury. It was a question McKinley was to raise more than once, reflecting an apparent concern that the United States not acquire a financially bleeding corpus.

McKinley then asked that nagging, backward-looking question: "How do the Hawaiians feel?" [1]

Cooper blurted out the truth. "More than likely, if the question was submitted to the people, annexation would be defeated." To this Cooper quickly added: "We think that our ability to establish the Government and maintain it for this length of time entitles us to be looked upon as a government *de jure*." If they were not a government backed by men, they were a government of laws of a sort. Yes, the Republic had property qualifications for voting and holding office, but Hawaiians were influential in the House of Representatives—the speaker was a full-blooded Hawaiian—and two Hawaiians also sat in the Senate. Cooper said the Hawaiians had been given every opportunity, but to do what, he did not say.

McKinley said he was exceedingly glad that Cooper had come "and I wish you all prosperity individually and also as a Government, and I hope to see you back again in Washington soon after my inauguration." McKinley might have been noncommittal, but Cooper clung to his parting words—*I hope to see you back again ... soon after my inauguration.*

BY THE PRESIDENTIAL ELECTION of 1896, Theodore Roosevelt had made a mark as both a writer and a reformer, but to influence events directly he needed to sit at the table of real power. As the campaign approached, he looked around for a way to get to the table. In terms of his public identity, would he pursue a position as a proponent of increased naval power, or as an opponent of government corruption? Would he arrive at his destination by land or by sea?

As a young reformer in the New York assembly, he had collaborated with the Democratic regime of none other than Governor Grover Cleveland in cleaning up favoritism in the administration of government. In the milieu of Albany, he wrote, "I rose like a rocket." The famous labor leader, Samuel Gompers, came to see him about outlawing the piecework manufacture of cigars in the tenements of New York City. Gompers told Roosevelt about nightmarish living conditions of the southern and eastern European immigrants who were flooding into New York, and their reduction to work drones behind the closed doors of the tenement houses. Roosevelt went to see for himself. He found two families living in one room, with several children. "Tobacco was stowed about everywhere," he recounted, "alongside foul bedding, and in a corner where there were scraps of food." The families worked day and night making cigars, ate a little, slept, and returned to their work. They spoke no English except for a child, who interpreted.

Roosevelt backed Samuel Gompers's reform bill. When no one else would do so, he pitched the bill to Governor Cleveland, who reluctantly took up the cause. The bill passed but was found to be unconstitutional, causing Roosevelt to say of the judges, "They knew legalism, but not life." He was the kind of domestic politician Americans came to love. He fought Jay Gould, the richest and most notorious robber baron of the age. Grover Cleveland had said of him: "There is great sense in a lot of what he says, but there is such a cocksureness about him that he stirs up doubt in me ... "

Following his journey west, Roosevelt raged on as the young man of certainties, tempered only—if at all—by his grief at the closing of the American frontier. Blocked by James Blaine from becoming assistant secretary of state, he had resumed the role of reformer, serving not only Harrison but subsequently President Cleveland as a U.S. commissioner of civil service. Thereafter Roosevelt had taken an appointment as police commissioner of New York City, roaming the streets at night with the muckraking reporters Lincoln Steffens and Jacob Riis. The idea of great things followed him constantly. In the badlands of Dakota, one of his partners had stopped him in the middle of the prairie to suggest that he become president of the United States. In New York his muckraker friends asked if one day he would run for the presidency. Roosevelt went into a tirade. "Never, never, must either of you remind a man on a political job that he may be president," he said. "It almost always kills him politically. He loses his nerve; he can't do his work; he gives up the very traits that are making him a possibility."

His impact in New York City was immediate, his celebrity value considerable. Where others might have been stuck in a gray appointed job, he flourished, and he naturally was active in the maneuvering that led up to the Republican Party's nomination of its candidate for president in 1896.

Initially Roosevelt and his friend, Senator Lodge of Massachusetts, took up with a losing candidate, but they were ever the pragmatists. They regrouped and campaigned for McKinley, man of the tariffs, pleader for Blaine, and proxy of Marcus Hanna, the industrial baron of Ohio. The Republican Party had become the party of the big financial interests. Hanna supervised the spending of seven million dollars, compared to a half-million for the Democratic Party nominee, the quixotic William Jennings Bryan. The question for Roosevelt became finding a job that would make use of some fraction of his energy and brilliance.

Shortly after McKinley's nomination, Roosevelt took a female friend for a rowboat ride at the family's vacation homestead on Oyster Bay. Her name was Maria Longworth Storer, and she was not only acquainted with Roosevelt but with the next president as well. Roosevelt said there was only one job he wanted, but that it probably was out of his reach.

In 1890 Roosevelt had begun cultivating his relationship with Captain Mahan, whose work on sea power had become increasingly influential. He had stayed in close touch with Henry Cabot Lodge, whose career was evolving in an outwardly more promising way than Roosevelt's. When Lili'uokalani was overthrown in early 1893, Roosevelt had weighed in with a vigorous endorsement for immediate annexation. When there had been trouble in Chile, he immediately had advised war. In response to a problem with Venezuela, he had spoken up for war again.

In other words, while closeted in domestic politics, he had cultivated the essential relationships—and formed the essential lines of thought—that were to lead America into imperialism. During this period, the need to expand overseas markets increasingly had become an article of American faith. While the Hawaiians had organized their revolt against the oligarchy, the manufacturers of America had organized themselves into a more effective lobby as the National Association of Manufacturers. The NAM immediately had embraced expansionism, as had the Populist "Sockless" Jerry Simpson and Roosevelt's acquaintance from the tenements, Samuel Gompers of the American Federation of Labor. To do what such diverse forces as the NAM, Jerry Simpson, and Samuel Gompers were saying, America had to do what Mahan and Theodore Roosevelt all along had been saying. America needed to build a stronger navy.

It was for this that Theodore had been waiting. At Oyster Bay, in the rowboat, he disclosed to Mrs. Storer his ambition. When Mrs. Storer approached McKinley about appointing Roosevelt to be assistant secretary of the navy, McKinley responded by saying he wanted peace. "I am told," McKinley said, "that your friend Theodore—whom I know only slightly—is always getting into rows with everybody."

Gamely seeking to put Theodore in a new light, Mrs. Storer replied, "Give him a chance to prove that he can be peaceful." When Senator Lodge lobbied on Roosevelt's behalf, McKinley said he hoped that Roosevelt had "no preconceived plans" for the navy. Lodge told McKinley not to worry.

While Roosevelt maneuvered to get the appointment, he began work on a revised edition of his calling card, *The Naval War of 1812.* He met with Captain Mahan. He spoke at the Naval War College, which Mahan had headed, and he sought to reassure the skeptics of his reasonableness. After sixteen years of enjoying significant public attention, Roosevelt still was only thirty-nine, and he was so lean and hungry in the photographs of this time as to be almost unrecognizable today.

McKinley chose John D. Long, a former governor of Massachusetts, to be secretary of the navy. Long worried aloud that if Roosevelt were his assistant, he would be brushed aside, but Roosevelt assured him he would be a loyal subordinate. Long was in a position comparable to Blaine's when Blaine had said he might not sleep well if "so brilliant and aggressive a man" were assisting him, but Blaine had possessed the will to make his views stick.

McKinley, after repeatedly reciting all the reasons that Roosevelt should not be appointed, then gave in, confirming Roosevelt's view of him as a man "whose firmness I utterly distrust."

THREE WEEKS AFTER MCKINLEY'S INAUGURATION, W.O. Smith went to Washington, D.C., giving pleasant assurances to Minister Francis Hatch that his role was not being usurped. Together Smith and Hatch went to see the new secretary of state, John Sherman. Sherman was a brother of General William Tecumseh Sherman, who had burned his way through Georgia in the Civil War. Like James Blaine, John Sherman had helped to organize the Republican Party. He had served as a U.S. senator from Ohio and secretary of the treasury and also had been discussed as a candidate for president. Now, at the age of 74, at the end of a long career, he had been named secretary of state, in part to create a vacancy in the U.S. Senate so that the industrialist Marcus Hanna could realize his ambition to be a senator.

Sherman is the clearest indication that at this late date the annexation of Hawai'i was far from being a foregone conclusion. He was wary of annexation and, if the issue had been left to him, would have buried it. Sherman believed Hawai'i had cost the United States a lot of money in lost tariffs, which had gone to a few sugar planters, and it had brought in a large number of Asian workers. Hatch said gamely that "in view of the momentous character of the questions liable at any moment to arrive in Hawai'i," a vague allusion to the Japanese, annexation should proceed quickly. It was clear that Sherman would not lead the effort, but he said he would follow the wishes of the new president.

Next Smith and Hatch went to see McKinley himself, acting on McKinley's invitation to Cooper at Canton, Ohio. "Mr. President," Hatch said, "we come to see you in regard to the annexation of Hawai'i. We are very anxious to see the Stars and Stripes flying over that country."[2] The widely accepted method of annexation in America was for a treaty to be submitted to the U.S. Senate and passed by a two-thirds vote. A fallback was for each of the two houses to pass a joint resolution by majority vote. The Hawai'i delegation told McKinley it was ready to go either way.

Hatch raised the specter of the Japanese. If annexation did not occur, who could say what might happen? He said W.O. Smith was returning to Honolulu and hoped to take some good news to President Dole. McKinley stirred himself to say he wanted to give the idea "early consideration," but in the coming weeks, he took his time. Weeks became months.

FOLLOWING FRANCIS HATCH'S MEETING with Senator Morgan in early 1896, the creation of a Japanese scare played an increasingly central role in the strategy of the oligarchy. The oligarchy created incidents of provocation, and then labored over its stories of those incidents. It honed certain phrases and themes down to shorthand codes. With a nudge or a nod, the "Japan question" became something everyone thought they should know about, and their hard work was picked up readily and put to use by the American expansionists in Washington. The more single-mindedly jingoistic an American was, the more likely that person was to uncritically believe the anti-Japanese line and attempt to sell it to others.

What Hawai'i needed to do, Hatch had said, was to create "a record," not only of words but deeds, in opposition to the continued immigration of the Japanese into Hawai'i. Initially the Republic had placed a high tariff on *sake* and turned back part of one shipload of Japanese immigrants. Then, in the winter of 1897, five days before McKinley's inaugural, on February 27, 1897, the Japanese steamer *Shinshū Maru* arrived in Honolulu with 670 Japanese passengers. Cooper worked frantically for two weeks, running from the ship to the immigration station to the courts and back again, to block a portion of the passengers from gaining residence in Hawai'i. He decided that 470 were trying to enter Hawai'i illegally.[3] Their contracts were not with employers in Hawai'i as specified by the 1894 Hawai'i law, but with Kobe Immigration Company. Worse, he contended, they merely held, but did not really own, their fifty dollars.

Cooper was breathless. "We had a hot fight for two days," he wrote to Hatch, "with the result that we came off victorious on all points." The Supreme Court of Hawai'i denied the motion of the immigration company's attorneys for a writ of habeas corpus—that is, an order to show why people were being held in the immigration station against their will. The court also declared the law to be in accordance with the constitution of 1894, repressive document that it was, creating the sort of paper trail that led historians to write, "The law was declared constitutional." This at least sounded good. The unfortunate immigrants were returned to Japan.

The *Shinshū Maru* incident fell almost exactly on McKinley's inaugural, three and a half months after the first incident. It further aggravated relations between the Republic of Hawaii and Japan. Soon a third Japanese steamer, the *Sakura Maru*, arrived in Honolulu. Of the 314 Japanese on board, 151 were turned back. Thereafter another 549 of the 682 passengers of the *Kinai Maru* were turned back as well.[4]

Of the four incidents in which Japanese immigrants were turned back, the last was the most revealing because of Cooper's surviving explanation to Sanford Dole. Cooper said the laborers had contracts with Japanese immigration companies, not with the Republic's Board of Immigration. But, Cooper conceded, they all seemed to have specific jobs waiting. In other words, they had come as they claimed—as workers on the plantations. As to the fifty dollars of their very own, the test was whether the immigrant had exactly a hundred yen (or fifty dollars) in a separate, original bank pouch. This was deemed unacceptable. To this arbitrary test Cooper alluded to "many other minor details ... sufficient to throw doubt upon the bona fide ownership of the money."

As to legal process, Cooper said, "I maintain that the burden is upon the immigrant to show that he is qualified and not upon the government to show that he is not qualified ... " He said all questions of reasonable doubt "should be given in favor of the government, otherwise the authorities become helpless to see the law properly enforced."[5]

Attorney General W.O. Smith wrote to Hatch in Washington that turning back the immigrants would have a "good effect in the States."[6] Cooper for his part cautioned Hatch against having it appear "that we are forcing the issue for the purpose of annexation." They should not be too obvious. "We should go far enough to show up the matter clearly," Cooper said, "(but) at the same time not overdo it."

The Japanese became increasingly upset. To have over a thousand of their citizens unexpectedly detained far from home, held in cramped quarters, questioned repeatedly, and held to arbitrary standards that never had been employed previously, was not something that happened without a certain amount of friction. On April 9, 1897, a marshal of the Republic pulled up to the pier of the immigration station in Honolulu with the idea of deporting 169 Japanese (apparently from the third ship).

When the interpreters told the Japanese it was time to leave, "there was a murmur, and soon the Japanese were in a rather turbulent state. Rushing here and there in the pens, they informed the deputy marshal, through three or four spokesmen, that they did not intend going back to Japan, and that they would die before going a single step."[7] The Japanese consul general, Hisashi Shimamura, was called out to calm them, "and it was not long before they were quiet and peaceful again," departing for Japan without further conflict. The same day another four hundred-plus would-be plantation workers landed in Kobe. They complained bitterly they had been given only small quantities of rice to eat while penned up in Hawai'i, that they were exhausted by the ordeal, and that a woman among them had gone mad as a result.[8] The investigation of the Republic was reported to be "very unfair and irrational," particularly regarding the fifty dollars. The frustrated travelers at first proposed to go to Tokyo en masse with their grievance, but were talked into sending a delegation.

Count Shigenobu Ōkuma, Japan's minister of foreign affairs, was under pressure from the Japanese press to make a showing for the sake of national pride. Earlier Ōkuma had protested the *sake* tax, saying it was aimed "especially, if not exclusively" at Japan, and that the tax violated the Friendship Treaty of 1871. Ōkuma had appealed to the Republic to not put the dollar-a-gallon tax into effect, but the Republic had done so anyway. The tariff was exactly the type of thing that would rankle a country that was preoccupied, above all, with gaining parity with other world powers. Just as Britain, France, Germany, and the United States were agreeing to discard the "unequal treaties," the smug little foreigners in Hawai'i were flagrantly violating their long-standing most-favored-nation agreement.

The oligarchy had told Japan that foreigners would not be voting, with the exception of those foreigners who ran the government. They had told the Japanese they would honor the ratios of Japanese to Chinese immigrants, then tilted as far as they could to the Chinese side. They further had aggravated the Japanese by ignoring correspondence, stalling situations for many months and sometimes for years. This, too, was an essential feature of Hatch's plans. In this interplay, Cooper seemed to at least believe in the rightness of what he was doing, while Hatch knew from the beginning that Japan would not agree to changing the structure of its relationship with Hawai'i. Hatch explained to Cooper, "Japan has just succeeded for the first time in her history (since the country was opened) in getting treaties which place her on an equal footing with other nations. It is not likely that she will take a step backwards to please us." In 1893 Japan had sent the man-of-war *Naniwa* in response to the overthrow, and now a long series of insults and irritations had built up since the writing of the Republic's constitution in 1894. While Japan badly wanted to maintain its good relationship with the United States, it also wanted its overseas citizens to be treated with respect. The emigration to Hawai'i was crucial to them, because it was the first time that large numbers of Japanese had gone anywhere in the last two hundred and fifty years. From the Japanese viewpoint, the insults of the oligarchy were impossible to ignore because the status and well-being of their overseas citizens were at stake.

Japan was about to react. In their concern with becoming a first-class non-white country, the Japanese quickly had been pushed—or pushed themselves, their critics would say—to a point where they were to be regarded as the sole source of trouble. The historian William Russ rationalized what had happened by saying that while the Republic's attempts to limit immigration might have seemed "unreasonable" in light of the plantations' need for labor, "The policy of limitation is to be explained in this way: Japan appeared to be following a program of peacefully invading the Hawaiian Islands by the method of sending large shipments of 'free' laborers; in other words, those who possessed fifty dollars and who, therefore, need not work under contract."

The fact that the Republic of Hawaii never broached the subject of revoking the Friendship Treaty or the labor convention; the fact that the planters on whom the Republic was politically dependent would not allow it; the fact that the Republic purposely provoked Japan—these are all parts of a picture that has never been examined in the rational light of day.

THE INDUSTRIALISTS OF AMERICA WELCOMED the acquisition of overseas markets, but were divided on the idea of acquiring overseas territories. They were expansionists, but not necessarily imperialists. Although the Republicans had become the party of Manifest Destiny, McKinley himself was wary of making specific acquisitions of overseas lands. He wanted to avoid war. As the writer Nathan Miller points out, McKinley was the last of the presidents who knew about the Civil War first hand. He had seen the bodies piled high at Antietam. War was awful and disruptive, and McKinley was inclined to follow the cues of Marcus Hanna, who had originally believed that America should avoid entangling arrangements beyond its coasts.

Although recognizing that the McKinley Administration approached the subject of Hawai'i with some caution, the annexationists of Honolulu were excited by the possibilities. The door was ajar. With the right dynamics they might wind up as an integral part of America.

In the development of their new annexation campaign, they quickly located their most energetic supporter, Theodore Roosevelt. Nathan Miller describes the Roosevelt who arrived back in Washington as "buzzing with thoughts of nationalism, imperialism, and naval expansion."[9] Roosevelt often wrote to Mahan, who was far and away the country's most prominent naval strategist, and possibly the most prominent American promoter of annexation.

Roosevelt's first letter, after settling into his new desk, is of extraordinary importance to the story of America's adventure into imperialism. It was written on May 3, 1897, two months after McKinley's inauguration, when the direction of the McKinley Administration was far from clear. It began with a declaration of allegiance to Mahan's thinking about Hawai'i. "As regards Hawaii I take your view absolutely," Roosevelt wrote, "as indeed I do on foreign policy generally. If I had my way we would annex those islands tomorrow."[10] If annexation was not possible, Roosevelt said, he would set up a protectorate over Hawai'i.

William McKinley, 25th president of the United States

Marcus Hanna, whose money and political genius boosted McKinley's rise to power

Cleveland appeared almost ill at the sight of McKinley taking the oath to replace him as president.

McKinley, warned repeatedly of young Theodore Roosevelt's craving for power and lust for war, nonetheless appointed him assistant secretary of the navy.

Metropolitan Club, Washington, D.C.

Theodore Roosevelt   Senator Henry Cabot Lodge   Captain Alfred Mahan

He said America needed a dozen new battleships, half for the Pacific Coast, "and these battleships should have large coal capacity and a consequent increased radius of action." Why? "I am fully alive to the danger from Japan," Roosevelt said, "and I know that it is idle to rely on any sentimental good will towards us." He lunged on, describing Cleveland's actions (presumably Cleveland's refusal to annex Hawai'i) as a "colossal" crime. He said they would be as guilty as Cleveland if they failed to reverse Cleveland's policy.

Roosevelt confided to Mahan that on the preceding Saturday evening Senator Lodge had met McKinley and "pressed his views upon him with all his strength." Roosevelt said he had been preparing the navy on the West Coast and hoped to send one additional ship and "if necessary" two to Hawai'i and "hoist our flag over the island. Leaving all details for after action." He vowed to press his own views on his chief, John Long. Roosevelt then rambled through a restatement of his allegiance to Mahan, saying, "I have precisely the same idea of patriotism, and of belief in and love for our country." He said that to no one else other than Lodge "do I talk like this."

Roosevelt at this point apparently took a break from drafting his seven-page letter to talk with Long. When he resumed writing, he returned abruptly to the subject he already had discussed: "As regards Hawai'i, I am delighted to be able to tell you that Secretary Long shares our views. He believes we should take the islands, and I have just been preparing some memoranda for him to use at the Cabinet meeting tomorrow." Roosevelt said that if only someone other than John Sherman had been named secretary of state "there would not be a hitch, and even as it is I hope for favorable action." He said he was telling Long, and through him the president, that an additional American ship should be deployed to Hawai'i without delay, before two new ships were delivered from British shipyards to Japan. "Even a fortnight may make a difference," Roosevelt wrote. "With Hawai'i once in our hands, most of the danger of friction with Japan would disappear."

From one point of view, Roosevelt appears as the shark responding to the bait thrown into the water by such people as Senator Morgan, Francis Hatch, and Henry Cooper, but these people need to be recognized as tacticians of the short term. The voice of strategy was Mahan's, and it was he who was convinced of an Armageddon between East and West. The supposed inevitability of this conflict provided the rationale for an expansionism so aggressive that it would manifest itself as imperialism. On May 1, Mahan wrote a letter to Roosevelt saying "beyond doubt" America would have trouble with Japan unless it took over Hawai'i. He advised Roosevelt, "Do nothing unrighteous; but as regards the problem, take them first and solve afterwards."[11]

Mahan's truncated phasing, "take them first and solve afterwards," is a semi-intelligible code written by one particularly literate man to another. What it meant obviously had something to do with pushing ahead, taking over, and sorting out the ensuing problems later, and it was to become an essential feature of American imperialism in the Pacific. The small cadre of zealots pushed ahead; the formal structure of policymakers lurched along behind, solving afterwards.

As Roosevelt and Mahan were writing one another, the press in Tokyo was awash with indignation over the treatment of the immigrants on the *Shinshū Maru*. Stuart Eldridge, a consul of the Republic of Hawaii and also an immigration inspector, wrote to Henry Cooper saying, "The Japanese have conceived the idea that the refusal of admission to the emigrants in question was dictated by the deliberate intention to stir up trouble with Japan, in the hope that this would, somehow, facilitate annexation to the United States ... They also seem to believe that the Hawaiian government is anxious to discourage Japanese emigration, be it by fair means or foul."[12] Eldridge warned that treatment of the emigrants had put the Japanese press and public in a belligerent mood, and that the Japanese government was under pressure to send two man-of-wars to Honolulu.

The foreign minister, Count Ōkuma, taking pains to say that his aims were diplomatic, not military, dispatched one ship—the man-of-war *Naniwa*. It arrived in Honolulu on May 5, just after Roosevelt had written his letter, and it provided the perfect setting for Roosevelt and his friends to push McKinley toward annexation.

In the maneuvering, Roosevelt was at the center of a group that dreamed of expanding America's sphere of influence. Lodge played a special role, as did Mahan. Another active participant in their circle was Leonard Wood, an army surgeon who craved a return to the field, where he had won a Medal of Honor fighting Indians. Leonard Wood was McKinley's doctor. Roosevelt's group met at the Metropolitan Club in downtown Washington, D.C., and talked about its plans. Virtually every historian who has written about this group has spoken of its members as conspirators, or as members of a cabal. Miller said Roosevelt was the "leader of a coterie of like-minded imperialists: senators, congressmen, ranking military officers (both active and retired), writers, and prominent citizens, who met regularly at the Metropolitan Club and plotted ways to influence American policy."[13]

They were uninhibited in expressing their views, but they were conspiratorial in the advancement of their plan, which could be stated in a few words. America was to become a great global power. It was to have a strong naval presence in both the Atlantic and the Pacific, which were to be joined by a canal that was to be built through Central America. Powerful naval bases were to be anchored on one side in the Caribbean and on the other side in Hawai'i.

The long May 3 letter from Roosevelt to Mahan often has been quoted by diplomatic historians and also Roosevelt's biographers as a means of portraying his aggressiveness and the scope of his plans. It is particularly interesting to the story of Hawai'i, because— while it covers the high points of the global strategy—it grinds away obsessively on the subject of annexation. In this sense, it is a perfect mirror of Mahan's sense of what mattered most.

Up to this point the essential question of the annexation debate had been whether Native Hawaiians should run their own country or, alternatively, whether an oligarchy of white Americans should be supported in their desire to take it over. Now the central issue was insidiously changed. With the Native Hawaiians out of power for four years, with their counterrevolt crushed, they were further marginalized. The issue was no longer America's relationship with indigenous Hawaiians, but keeping Hawai'i out of the hands of another power. Since foreigners were going to control Hawai'i, was it not right that Americans be the chosen foreigners?

IN HONOLULU, FROM THE RANKS of the Republic, Cousin Willie Smith was put in charge of coping with the Japanese and their big ship, just as he had been dispatched to Washington to set up the relationship with McKinley. The surface rationale well might have been that the foreign minister, Henry Cooper, had been so heavily involved in harassing the Japanese that it was a good time to change players. The underlying pattern was that the three who first had met as boys in Kōloa, Kaua'i, Dole, Thurston, and Smith, always found a pretext for taking over at crucial moments. People such as Cooper and Hatch were on permanent standby to do the dirty work, but the triumvirate of missionary descendants held the real power.

The warship *Naniwa* merely sat in the harbor. "Nothing has been heard from her yet," Smith said. Then he announced the Japanese "have behaved very nicely." Over the course of several meetings, Smith and others reported the Japanese were going out of their way to avoid conflict.

Two weeks after the arrival of the *Naniwa*, Hisashi Shimamura appeared before Cooper, insisting on a response to the letter of the minister of foreign affairs, Count Ōkuma, protesting the return of the Japanese immigrants. Cooper said he was just then writing a reply, and the next day he presented one. In keeping with Dole's earlier contention that the Japanese immigration companies were out to make a lot of money, Cooper said the immigration companies had stimulated the labor market "beyond its natural course."

Shimamura, who had seen his fellow citizens penned up on the Honolulu waterfront, lodged a protest. He announced, "Japan asks nothing unreasonable ... If she cannot get it—well, I do not know what will follow." A representative named Masanosuke Akiyama of the Foreign Office was aboard the *Naniwa*. Chatting over drinks with Chester Doyle, who spoke Japanese, Akiyama said the ouster of the queen was wrong. Further, the government of the Republic was made up of people who were "inclined to be foolish and not well acquainted with international law."

Akiyama's party included five reporters from the Japanese press,[14] which had been so actively engaged in wringing its hands over the well-being of Japanese citizens.[15] Perhaps the press expedition reflected an historic division in Japan, in which the *samurai* warrior class was said to have been displaced by modernization, and many of its members had found their way into the nationalistic press. Their presence in Hawai'i reinforced the impression that the outing of the *Naniwa* was to a considerable extent a media event.

The press of Hawai'i threw an enormous party for their visiting counterparts. The Rising Sun of Japan was rendered in red carnations and white asters, and the flag of Hawai'i was rendered in asters of red, white, and blue. Everyone ate mullet from Pearl Harbor and chose from a dozen desserts. The toasts began with a tribute to the emperor, followed by a tribute to Sanford Dole. They progressed through fourteen rounds of toasting, each apparently punctuated by music. An editor, Daniel Logan, traced the growth of freedom of the press from the year 1680. A Mr. Ishikawa announced that the time would come "when the newspapers of the world will be published in one common language," without specifying the language. A business manager said reporters needed business managers. Most of these statements were delivered without reference to the American and Japanese ships in the harbor, but the editor of a local Japanese language newspaper hoped aloud that "the recent little difficulty between Japan and Hawai'i" would be quickly settled "and that the friendly relations existing shall continue." The representative of the five Japanese reporters, an S. Furuya, only twenty-two, announced, "Although far from our native country, we are with friends." It was the first time he had spoken publicly in English outside his university classes in Japan. Around midnight he bowed courteously to his new acquaintances.

BENEATH THE SMILES lay intrigue. Beneath the ambiguities lay duplicity. Cooper was in charge of antagonizing the Japanese, and Will Smith was in charge of mollifying them. While officially the Republic was indignant at the thought of paying an indemnity to Japan, it may be that the Republic paid off the Japanese ship on the side. Much later, a man named Henry Hapai told a story of rowing a skiff out to a Japanese war ship that was anchored in Honolulu Harbor. Hapai was employed by the government of the Republic, and the skiff was loaded with twenty thousand dollars in gold, which was turned over to the Japanese ship. Hapai recalled that Japan was upset because its citizens had been unfairly quarantined. Given the desperado environment of Honolulu—the pattern of duplicity, the reliance on guns, the climate of fear—that seethed beneath the outwardly staid surface of the Dole government, the story seems credible.[16]

In the middle of the maneuvering with Japan, President McKinley's appointee as minister to Hawai'i arrived. His name was Harold M. Sewall, and he quickly became a receptacle for Japanese stories, which he relayed in vivid terms to the State Department. He said Japan and Hawai'i were "at the widest divergence in their views with no probability of reconciliation."[17] For the full story Sewall went to Henry Cooper, who was both the local architect and archivist of the *pilikia* with Japan. Sewall told the State Department that the real reasons for the problem with Japan resulted from the American descendants' desire "to save these Islands from Japanese colonization and ultimate and speedy Japanese domination."

The oligarchy began to gloat privately. Francis Hatch described Japan's behavior as "providential." Cooper wrote, "I am afraid that they are going to back down too soon from their position."[18] Smith said, "I have been urging seeking some way to let the Japs. down easy—let them crawl out." Along with Cooper, he favored portraying the immigration companies as overly greedy. The affair of the *Naniwa*, Smith said, "has doubtless helped us in Washington."

If the sense of conflict was fizzling in Honolulu, the annexationists in Washington did what they could to maintain its momentum. On May 22, Francis Hatch, in a letter to the under secretary of state, William Day, said that if Hawai'i was not annexed, it would be impossible to maintain an independent Republic in Hawai'i. "Yielding to Japan means the complete and final establishment of their power," Hatch wrote, "through the machinery of our own Constitution."[19] Given that Japanese immigrants were completely frozen out of the political process by the constitution of 1894, it was the sort of distortion of which Hatch was so capable.

At the height of the booming trade in Japan stories, William Day empowered the new American minister, Harold Sewall, to create an American protectorate and to use the power of the U.S. navy to make it stick.

SEWALL TURNED OUT TO BE an illuminating player. President McKinley had told the anti-annexation congressman Karl Schurz that he would not appoint an active annexationist to be minister in Hawai'i. Having indulged his habit of telling people what they wanted to hear, McKinley nonetheless turned to Sewall, who was not merely an annexationist but eager to profit both financially and politically from the expansion of American power in the Pacific. On a good day, Sewall's signature was five inches wide, with a line running back from the last "l" nearly to the "H." He had served in the American consul in Sāmoa during the late 1880s, when America's long-term stake in the Samoan Islands was being negotiated with Germany. He also had spent time in Hawai'i and had identified himself with the annexationist cause.

Naturally Sewall was not only from Maine, but from Kennebec River country. His family owned a shipyard and shipping business located in Bath, where the Kennebec flows into the sea. The Sewalls were best known for building enormous wooden ships and then for their transition to the construction of steel ships. Their fleet was involved in transporting coal into the Pacific—no doubt in part to fuel the U.S. navy—and then returning to the West Coast with sugar from Hawai'i. One of their largest ships was named the *William P. Frye* for the Maine senator who by now was an influential member of the Committee on Foreign Relations and an influential promoter of annexation. In fact, according to Francis Hatch, it was Frye whose influence had guaranteed Sewall's appointment.[20]

Originally the Sewalls were Democrats, although Harold had advanced his early career by playing on a family connection with the Republican James Blaine. By 1894, Sewall had come to favor annexation so strongly that he quit the Democratic Party with a highly publicized flourish in protest of Grover Cleveland's attempt to restore the queen. Nonetheless his father, Arthur Sewall, subsequently was nominated to run as the Democratic vice presidential candidate on the ticket of William Jennings Bryan in the fateful election of 1896. In the controversy of a silver-backed currency versus gold, Bryan's candidacy represented a victory for silver within the Democratic Party. Arthur Sewall said the ready availability of silver would free America from "any cornering of money in the money centers by the capitalists and Jews of Europe."[21] Ambitious Harold, faced with campaigning for his father or for his Republican friends, chose his friends, and McKinley in turn chose him to serve as minister to Hawai'i, at the urging of Senator William P. Frye.

While Harold was no longer a Democrat, he was still a part of the shipbuilding Sewall clan. Good titan of shipping that father Arthur Sewall was, he simultaneously advocated American expansion in the Pacific and protection of the American shipbuilding industry. The protectionism among shippers that Arthur so unabashedly represented was one of the many little issues of annexation. Specifically, American shippers were concerned about competition from the ships that were registered under the flag of Hawai'i. How could America annex Hawai'i but avoid annexing ships that might then compete for the lucrative, protected (i.e., Americans-only) coastal trade?

In an early foray to Hawai'i, Harold Sewall had tried to figure out how to buy a foreign vessel at a low cost, register it, and then make a windfall profit at the point of annexation. In his new role as minister, he became a guardian against such disgusting speculative practices.

In his early days in Honolulu, Sewall was the star attraction of the Fourth of July celebration. United States troops from two warships marched in the parade in Honolulu, as did a platoon of the police force and the Mounted Reserve and Mounted Patrol of the Republic. The most popular theme for floats was conflict with Japan. On the side of the American flag was a damsel surrounded by Hawaiian produce, such as mangoes and bananas. On the other side Uncle Sam vigorously waved a board, signifying the bridge the Hawaiian maiden would cross to political union with America. He waved the board menacingly at the Japanese ambassador, who was protesting annexation.

When introduced to speak, Sewall was greeted by a thunderous ovation. He quoted some of Theodore Roosevelt's favorite complaints of the summer regarding the small men who put money before "the self-sacrifice necessary in upholding the honor of the nation and the glory of the flag." Obviously he knew Roosevelt, not Long, was running the navy, because he described the assistant secretary as a representative young American "whom all Americans rejoice to see in authority over the Navy Department."

Sewall said if liberty had not yet reached its fullest development, good Americans should bite their tongues about the possible defects. "It is not for us to proclaim them to strangers," he explained.

Paraphrasing McKinley, he announced that pessimists do not make good citizens. "No, my countrymen!"—His text was filled with exclamations—"The God of our fathers was not a God of despondency or despair, else we had not been here today—nor shall ours be!" American policy, he said, was to "put our flag once more upon the sea as becomes a people with our great ocean frontage and our magnificent maritime traditions," presumably including the ships of his family.

He specifically praised Senators Henry Cabot Lodge, William P. Frye, and John T. Morgan, demonstrating a sure grasp of who was driving the annexation movement in the Senate. Further, he said, the history of Maine would be connected forever to the history of Hawai'i, thanks partly to the now-deceased James G. Blaine of Augusta. He left out the founders of the sugar industry, Ladd and Brimsmade, as well as Luther Severance and John Stevens, but he lavishly praised Sanford Dole, "in whose veins courses a double strain" of Maine's "best bloods," referring of course to Father Dole of the upstream Kennebec River and Mother Dole of downstream. Dole was in the audience, and perhaps he enjoyed Sewall's attention. Perhaps Dole did not yet know that Sewall hoped to take his place as governor of Hawai'i after annexation.

WHEN THE POSSIBILITIES OF MCKINLEY'S VICTORY began to emerge, Lorrin Thurston returned to the fray. In fact, he had never been far away. After his conflict with Cleveland, he had been offered the Republic's Ministry of Foreign Affairs, but he opted instead to practice law. He also revived the Annexation Club, this time as an aboveground organization dedicated to pro-annexation agitation and propaganda. At an early meeting in its revived form, the club passed a resolution inveighing against Hawai'i being "Mongolized." Thurston published a booklet, "Why I Am an Annexationist," which was widely circulated throughout the United States.

"I am doing a good business here now," Thurston wrote, but "I am on tap at all times day or night in the interest of the cause." Judging from his frequent appearances before the Executive Council on behalf of his clients, he was indeed doing a good business. More than any single person other than American Minister John Stevens, he had created the white government, and in his little detour into law he occasionally picked up with the Executive Council more or less where he had left off. For example, on July 5, 1895, Thurston had shared with the cabinet a plan for the laying of a transpacific cable. Thereafter he took a law client who was engaged in competing for that contract to an Executive Council meeting. On a second occasion, Thurston represented a client who had leased fishing rights from the Republic, only to have the water fouled by cholera. Thurston asked for a thousand dollars compensation and got seven hundred fifty. Yet another time he collected an even thousand dollars for himself and his partner, this in regard to legal services for tax assessments. On yet another occasion, the attorney general received a letter from the Japanese Immigration Company regarding immigration. Before taking any action the executive council resolved to speak with the company's attorney, Mr. Thurston. Thurston said he had nothing personal against the Japanese and in fact had appeared before the Supreme Court in forty-seven cases involving the fifty-dollar law—this while developing his own particular twists on the argument that Japan was engaging in a "peaceful invasion" of Hawai'i.[22]

Some of the antecedents to Thurston's law projects went back to the last days of the Hawaiian Kingdom, when he had forced his way into the cabinet as the representative of the Reform Party. For example, as minister of the interior he had helped build a public road to Kīlauea volcano on the Big Island. In his private persona he was part of a company that planned to develop tourism at Kīlauea. What Hawai'i needed, Thurston believed, was more business, and the rest of the oligarchy believed that as well, but the business of companies was modest stuff compared to the business of nations.

Thurston was among the handful of people in the history of Hawai'i who stand out for their ability to venture to far-off Washington and present themselves forcibly. Kalākaua had made a hit in Washington. Lili'uokalani was remarkable for the breadth of her contacts. Thurston had made his crucial visit in 1892, and he had passed up the presidency of the Provisional Government not only in favor of Dole, but in favor of being in Washington. He had been perturbed by Walter Gresham questioning his veracity, and in his memoirs he would go to great lengths to put himself in a good light relative to that incident, but nothing could soothe his hurt feelings like returning to Washington. He began to talk with the Executive Council about going back. He was the de facto minister of agitation and propaganda. He symbolized the overthrow. He could do things no one else could do.

Thurston had to get Dole moving in the right direction and also soften up Hatch, who by now had acquired an identity of his own. His letter to Hatch in early 1897 was pure Thurston: "Our experience has shown in the past that a single day may bring forth radical change." Therefore, what was needed was for Hatch to have a "small working force" at his command to cover anything "which might arise on the spur of the moment." It would be just like the days of January 14 through January 17, 1893. They would get close to Uncle Sam, huddle in an office, and respond to "whatever contingency may present itself." He next wrote his old underling, Frank Hastings, apologizing for not answering Hastings's letter of two months prior. "You know how it is, yourself," said Thurston, "... when business crowds, how personal correspondence goes on the shelf." Thurston congratulated Hastings on the birth of his daughter, chatted about his own daughter, and then launched the pitch he already had given Hatch. If he happened to be the one chosen to represent Hawai'i in the annexation proceedings, he wanted to stay at the Everett House in a three-room suite on the right-hand side of the building. Could Frank please check it out?

Cooper worried about how his old friend Lorrin would behave if he became an annexation commissioner. The problem was, Thurston did indeed symbolize the overthrow. "I hope," he wrote, "Mr. Thurston will not be drawn into a controversy which will give rise to referring (to) the history of 1893." The contention that Hawai'i was a "stolen kingdom" had reverberated across America five years earlier, undermining the plan for instant annexation. The idea now was to avoid the indelicate facts of the overthrow and let the passage of time do its work.

Cooper himself had learned this lesson the hard way. The year before, the Republic had decided to celebrate January 17—the formation of the Provisional Government—as the beginning of its new regime, but Britain had declined to attend the observance, and so had France and Japan. Even Portugal had declined the invitation. The United States minister, Willis, who previously had described the ministers of the oligarchy as duplicitous, explained that since his country had never recognized the Provisional Government (but only the Republic), he would need guidance from Washington on whether to attend a commemoration. Washington had not responded in a timely way.

Cooper had been thrown into a dither of wounded feelings. He proposed to Hatch that they mount a diplomatic protest in Washington on the premise that it was the sovereign right of their country to memorialize whatever dates and events they chose. Hatch at first had been nearly as wounded as Cooper. He raved on about gross discourtesy, but after speaking with his good friend Senator Morgan, he urged Cooper to calm down. He said the incident was not "of sufficient gravity to request the recall of all of the parties concerned." Hatch had spoken subsequently with Secretary of State Olney, who said he had not sanctioned the snub. Cooper was reassured. He determined to persevere. "It seems sometimes as if we were at loggerheads with all the world 'and the rest of mankind,'" he wrote to Hatch, "but I feel confident that we are in the right in all steps we have taken and that final results will prove it to be so."

Cooper's problem was that he tried to create an organized stage for the oligarchy's little theater, where Thurston realized it was all improvisation, and Cooper in fact was one of his props. It was as Thurston was to say in the only surviving account of how the Annexation Club was started. He was walking down the street in Honolulu one day, and a new fellow from America, Henry Cooper, had asked him, what would happen if the queen attempted to subvert the Bayonet Constitution? Thurston replied, why, he would try to do something about it. And that was how it all started, and for all that is known it was Cooper who made the motion nominating Lorrin to go to Washington in 1892 to see if the United States could be counted on. So in 1897 it mattered little what Cooper thought, even though he now was minister of foreign affairs, and in fact it was Cooper who broke the news to Hatch that Thurston was on his way to Washington.

The executive council had decided that Thurston would represent the Annexation Club and hang around in case McKinley picked up the pace of negotiation. Cooper announced it was all right with him, and also that Hatch was not to infer any lack of confidence on anyone's part. Sanford Dole drew up a hand-lettered parchment designating Thurston, along with Hatch, as a commissioner of the Republic, empowered to negotiate a treaty of annexation. Initially W.O. Smith was a commissioner during the course of his meeting with McKinley, but after he returned to Hawai'i he was replaced by his and Thurston's law partner, William A. Kinney. Thurston maintained his stream of correspondence, but now signed off, "Yours for annexation."

WHILE THE ELECTION OF A REPUBLICAN PRESIDENT had caused the government in Hawai'i to rush its annexation commissioners to Washington, annexation was not moving forward. Again the little white group began to worry about being out in the cold, and particularly about being shut out of the American sugar market. When a revision of tariff legislation rose to the top of the agenda of the new Congress in the first months of McKinley's presidency, the oligarchy remembered the McKinley tariff on Island sugar with horror. Since 1894, for three years, Hawai'i growers had been back on an equal footing with American growers, and the sugar industry was thriving. Now, if Republicans looked like good imperialists, with their talk of manifest destiny, were they not also remembered for their tariffs? No less a figure than the secretary of state, John Sherman, had said that all Hawai'i had done was cost America a lot of money, and most of it had gone to the planters.

The 1890s indeed were the age of trusts and cartels, which were organized around products. In an apparently brief time, the American Sugar Growers Society had emerged as a major lobbying force. Petitions—variously against reciprocity for Hawai'i, or against the annexation of Hawai'i—poured into Washington from wherever beet or cane sugar was grown (for example, from California, Nebraska, Iowa, and Louisiana). Editors in Iowa mailed postcards as part of the Sugar Growers campaign. On January 26, 1897, Lou Boydston, editor of the *Montezuma Democrat* in Iowa, filled out a three-by-five-inch card that declared his opposition to the annexation of Hawai'i. Referring to the sugar planters of Hawai'i, Boydston said, in a handwriting cramped for lack of adequate space, "Think it a piece of jingoism to favor a few interested parties." To this he added, "Can't see any benefit to the masses of our people." Asked if his community had demonstrated its ability to grow good sugar beets, he replied: "It has to a certainty." Did his community want a sugar industry? He replied emphatically, "Indeed it does."[23]

The gentlemen from Hawai'i shuddered at the tactics of the sugar trust. William Kinney said, "We are as children alongside of them."[24] Opponents pointed out that Hawai'i sugar still was produced with contract labor, which was illegal in America. The Republic's lobbyists may have been agonizing over the "free" Japanese, but contract labor—and the jailing of the workers for breach of contract—still was the law of Hawai'i. In fact, the Republic's Legislature had taken up a bill to abolish the contract system as a way of laundering the image of the Republic, but the sugar planters had beaten it down, saying they still needed the penal clause to control the work force.

For the most part, the Republic of Hawaii dealt with two committees of the Senate, the Finance Committee and the Foreign Relations Committee. The Finance Committee, which was forever thinking about revenues, threatened to delete reciprocity from the tariff bill. For the Republic of Hawaii, it was a formula for their makeshift house of government to collapse. Without access to the sugar market, Hawai'i would go into another economic depression, the annexation scenario would get sidetracked, and the great majority of Hawai'i's population might have enough time and sufficient reason to rise up against the oligarchy.

The sugar baron Claus Spreckels, who had been friends with Kalākaua, now was the key figure in the American sugar trust. He swung the senator from California, George Perkins, behind the American growers—the same George Perkins who had endeared himself to the queen, and who had been described by Thurston as practically a senator from Hawai'i. Perkins had received a petition from the California State Grange saying reciprocity should be canceled, in part because it had cost the American treasury $72 million in lost duties over twenty-one years. Reciprocity was "only partially and nominally reciprocal," the Grange contended, because for every three dollars' worth of sugar that Hawai'i sold in America, Hawai'i bought only a dollar's worth of goods.

Arguing the opposite point of view, a group of Massachusetts businessmen said that reciprocity was never intended to be a dollar-for-dollar trade-off, "but was meant on the one hand to open a new field for American commerce ... and on the other to make Hawaii dependent financially and therefore politically, upon the United States ... "[25] Hatch and the annexation commissioners worked frantically to maintain reciprocity, and in the end they dredged up enough Republican votes to save it. When viewed at a distance, this was yet another in a long series of instances in which United States policymakers debated—then proved willing to pay for— maintaining their hold over Hawai'i. In terms of power centers within the Senate, it was a matter of the Finance Committee always losing out to the Foreign Relations Committee.

The political scuffle induced by the American sugar growers put into stark outline the most essential features of the deal between the American government and the planter-dominated government of Hawai'i. That is, Hawai'i's sugar never served any real need in America, not in 1876, when the Reciprocity Treaty passed; not in 1887, when the treaty was renewed; not in 1894 when it was propped up by the Wilson-Gorman tariff bill; and not in 1897, when the terms of the treaty were renewed again. On the contrary, Hawai'i sugar was a drag on the development of the continental beet and cane sugar industries, as well as on the U.S. treasury.

Inclusion of Hawai'i sugar in the American market could only be rationalized as a trade-off for America's future expansion into the Pacific—specifically, for control of Pearl Harbor. Hatch, Kinney, and the others knew that to maintain the annexation scenario they had to maintain reciprocity, and ultimately so did the key people who gave final form to the tariff bill. William Kinney punctuated his lobbying effort by telling Sanford Dole that the best thing to do now was to engulf Washington with information "of the desire on the part of the Japs to control Hawaii."[26]

CHAPTER SIXTEEN

Hawaiian Protests

After 1895, the Hawaiians virtually disappear from the extant histories, and they for the most part disappear from the correspondence of the oligarchy as well. Most accounts written in English of the Hawaiian revolt dwelled on the vigilance of the Republic and the disorganization of the Hawaiians. Participants in the revolt had been jailed by a martial-law court, including virtually all the Hawaiian leadership, from the queen to her heir apparent, Jonah Kūhiō, to Joseph Nāwahī, John E. Bush, and Robert Wilcox. Not only were the Hawaiian newspaper editors jailed, but their newspapers were shut down.

What the standard histories do not say is that the Hawaiian resistance reorganized itself in the latter part of 1896, in the wake of McKinley's election. The first order of business was "to select the person to pilot the nation," in the words of a Hawaiian language newspaper story. The new leadership was to take up the work of Nāwahī, who had died in September 1896. Community meetings were held throughout the Islands to select delegates, who gathered in Honolulu in what future petitions would call an *'aha 'elele nui o ka lāhui Hawaii, "a* convention of the Hawaiian nation." What survives of that nationalistic convention are accounts from the Hawaiian language press[1] and petitions resulting from the meeting. The existence of the records of the *hui*, which would be an extraordinarily valuable source, is at this point unknown, but it can be reasonably inferred that thousands of people attended the grassroots meetings around the Islands.

The results of the voting may surprise the student of Hawaiian history today. Robert Wilcox sought the presidency of both organizations. During the trial, he had resisted the pressure to make a deal with the prosecution, and he had been celebrated in poetry and song. A book was published called *Mele Lāhui*, Songs of the Nation, prominently featuring poems such as *Wilikoki Ke Koa Ola Hawai'i* (Wilcox the Warrior Who Is the Life of Hawai'i).[2] Wilcox himself published at least one edition of a newspaper during this period, reporting that he had organized his own *hui*, 'Aha Hui Aloha 'Āina 'Oia'i'o. Through the name he claimed the truest (*'oia'i'o*) aloha for the land.[3] While all figures are gray in contrast to the memory of Wilcox, the today-unknown men who stood as the alternatives to his candidacy did quite well. James K. Kaulia ran for the presidency of Hui Aloha 'Āina, which continued to be the most popular and thriving of the two main *hui*. David K. Kalauokalani, also relatively unknown today, ran for president of Hui Kālai'āina.

Ke Aloha 'Āina newspaper recorded that in the remote community of Kīpahulu, Maui, beyond Hāna, twenty-seven Hawaiians voted at the grassroots meeting.[4] Since Kīpahulu is a small area, the size of the voting populace is an indication of extensive grassroots participation. The result was twenty-four votes for James Kaulia, three for Wilcox. A man known for his writings, Moses Manu, was elected to go to Honolulu as a delegate, bound to the support of Kaulia.

The subsequent meetings in Honolulu were held across from 'Iolani Palace, almost exactly where the American soldiers had camped with such crushing effect in 1893. Hui Kālai'āina met on November 27, 1896, and Hui Aloha 'Āina met on November 28, which had been celebrated for over half a century as *Lā Kū'oko'a*, or Independence Day, to mark Britain and France's joint agreement to recognize the sovereignty of the Hawaiian Kingdom.

The Hui Kālai'āina meeting was held at a favorite Hawaiian rallying point, Palace Square, apparently a niche southwest of 'Iolani Palace. Robert Wilcox delivered a speech, and David Kalauokalani was elected president.

The Aloha 'Āina meeting was held at Arion Hall, which stood across the street from the palace, and next door to Ali'iolani Hale, where Henry Cooper had read the proclamation of the Provisional

Government. The Aloha 'Āina meeting opened with half an hour of prayer. Although the political societies were divided by gender, at least one of the delegates was a woman from Hilo, which was interpreted as "a sign of unity" in the work that lay ahead. There was a solemn discussion of choosing new leadership. James Kaulia said that one of the duties of the new president was to lead the people spiritually. Kaulia had been a sheriff on the island of Hawai'i before becoming a lawyer. He had served as secretary to Aloha 'Āina while Nāwahī was president, and he had spent fifty days in jail in the aftermath of the Hawaiian revolt. He apparently was elected to the presidency without serious opposition.

The fact that Kaulia and Kalauokalani emerged as the successors to Nāwahī has something significant to do with the vitality of Hawaiian tradition, because the vote was for consensus and effective organization. While Wilcox undoubtedly *was* popular, the vastly more popular figure did not need to be seen or heard. It was the traditional *mō'ī* and monarch, Lili'uokalani. As one of the poems in the *Mele Lāhui* said:

O Lili'uokalani i ke kapu
Mōi'wahine o Hawai'i
Lili'uokalani, the sacred person
Queen of Hawai'i,
You are crowned by the firmament,
By the most sacred and powerful Lord

It said to her, "For you, the seas; for you, the uplands," and concluded:

May Hawai'i's land live
May Hawai'i's nation live,
May Lili'uokalani live,
And sit again in the throne.[5]

There was a concerted movement among Hawaiians during this period to refocus the central role of Lili'uokalani.[6] The Hawaiian press was filled with letters, poems, and songs written in adoration of her.

Long articles detailed the forced nature of the abdication papers she had signed. She was referred to by traditional leadership titles, such as Ke Ali'i 'Aimoku (loosely, the *ali'i* who rules over the islands) and Kalani, the heavenly one. She was still the exalted person, the person of high birth and rank. While not only Wilcox and Bush but Nāwahī had challenged the concept of the monarchy, it was Wilcox who so repeatedly had tested the limits of his power and popularity. In the convention of the nation, he had found those limits. The active supporters of the queen apparently won the elections in overwhelming fashion. Robert Wilcox had criticized her excessively. Although following the overthrow he had fallen in step with the movement to restore the monarchy, he obviously was not regarded as a good choice for the tasks at hand in 1896. While there is no evidence that she swayed the grassroots vote that determined the composition of the convention, her continued prestige and *mana* in alignment with the stalwart service of such persons as Kaulia and Kalauokalani seem—in the absence of additional new information—the most likely explanation of the vote.

If this perception is accurate, it follows that the Hawaiian leadership system—far from being shattered as it has been portrayed historically—had renewed itself in an essentially familiar form. The supreme chief was at the center, supported by chiefs of lesser rank, who were supported in turn by the Hawaiian populace. The queen's brief reference to the convention said, "Perfect harmony prevailed."[7] She said she was pleased because the missionary party thought that with Nāwahī's death the patriotic societies would dissolve, but to the Republic's "great astonishment" they forged ahead and in fact hit a new level of activity. The likelihood of the queen's central role in the convention is enhanced by the fact that she departed for America eight days later.

SANFORD DOLE WAS SURPRISED when the queen rode up in a carriage to his residence, in the company of a female companion, early on the morning of December 5, 1896. He responded in a gentlemanly way, as befit his understanding of himself. Lili'uokalani wrote, "As I entered, he rose from his seat, approached me at once, and extended his hand, which I took."[8] Two months previously, Dole had issued a pardon to the queen and restored her civil rights. Now Lili'uokalani came to say good-bye, and to say that she needed to go to America and visit her late husband's relative, who was ill. She also left Dole with an impression that she would spend a week in San Francisco, and that she would see her niece Ka'iulani somewhere—perhaps in Europe. In response to a discussion of cold weather, Sanford Dole brought out Mrs. Dole, who was an expert on low temperatures as a result of growing up in Maine. She cautioned the queen against the cold. The queen thanked her and Sanford for their kind interest. Dole "very gallantly" escorted her to her waiting carriage. He announced he would have passports drawn up immediately for her and her party. As the carriage pulled away, she said, he politely bowed. *Adieu.*

The timing of her visit was peremptory. She left Dole no time to think or to confer with his cabinet. She then boarded her ship. After she was on board, Dole sent an aide with the passport, signed by W.O. Smith, made out to Lili'uokalani of Hawai'i. He also sent passports for the Hawaiian man and woman who attended her, Joseph Heleluhe and Mrs. Kia Nahaolelua. The queen sailed at ten that morning. She said that in Hawai'i she no longer knew whether every look, word, and act, were being spied upon and reported. "For the first time in years," she wrote, "I drew a long breath of freedom."

Dole was puzzled that he had not heard rumors of her trip before she appeared in front of him. To Hatch he said, "I do not know that her trip has any political significance whatever." A second time he reassured himself that if her trip was politically motivated, he would have heard about it in advance. Smith's thoughts echoed Dole's. He said he didn't know why Lili'uokalani had left Hawai'i, but that possibly she was going to meet her niece Ka'iulani.

Hawaiian correspondence to and from Hawai'i, as well as Hawaiian language newspaper stories, followed the queen on her journey. In the meantime, the native societies continued their organizational drive. The women's organization appears to have led the way. From the original Aloha 'Āina protests of 1893, a woman named Abigail Kuaihelani Campbell had emerged as the leader of the Women's Patriotic League. Mrs. Campbell was a high-born woman married to James Campbell, who had left Ireland at age thirteen and eventually made his way to Hawai'i. By the mid-1890s

Campbell had become an extraordinarily wealthy landowner and, probably much to the discomfort of the oligarchy, a royalist. Mrs. Campbell was originally from Lāhainā, Maui, but she and James Campbell had migrated to Honolulu, where they lived in relative splendor, surrounded by Hawaiians, as chiefs had been surrounded by their retainers in the time of Lili'uokalani's father.

During December, the Hawaiian Women's Patriotic League developed three documents in the name of "the great majority of the Hawaiian women of the Hawaiian Nation." Two were expressed as resolutions, reaffirming the legitimacy and central role of the queen. One asserted the women's trust in the queen's "wisdom and integrity" and informed the people of America "that the large majority of the Hawaiian people have in the past and now in the present time recognize Her Majesty Queen Lili'uokalani as our lawful and Constitutional sovereign." They dismissed her forced signature of the abdication papers before the trials as "made for the sole object of saving her life and the lives of a number of her loyal subjects."

The more general message was a petition to William McKinley as the new president of the United States. It set the tone for the petitions of the men's organizations that were to follow. Together the letter of the Women's Patriotic League (the women's Aloha 'Āina), and the subsequent letters of Hui Aloha 'Āina and Hui Kālai'āina were so similar in content as to be one and the same. All were in the same beautiful handwriting. Each was worded similarly and made the same essential points. Aloha 'Āina portrayed itself as "an organization in which the great majority of the Hawaiian people are associated," while Hui Kālai'āina made a lesser claim to being "an organization in which a number of the Hawaiian people are associated." Both referred to the *'aha 'elele nui o ka lāhui* in Honolulu as the source of the leaders' authority to address the United States. In other words, they represented the convention of the nation.

While the statements largely repeat one another, and also previous statements, the redundancy seems inherently important, since Hawaiians so frequently have been described as disorganized, leaderless, and lacking in unity. Four years after the overthrow, on the eve of a change of governments in the United States, the statements reaffirmed the Hawaiians' "hope and trust" in the U.S.

government in general and now McKinley in particular. They said this trust was strengthened by the memory of the U.S. government's support of the sovereignty of Hawai'i in 1843, when international recognition was being negotiated with the great naval powers.

The most important point was the third: "…no cause whatever can arise that will alter or change the mind of the Hawaiian people, and their desire to see the monarchy restored, and the throne occupied by the queen, who would never have been deposed by a handful of foreigners but for the support rendered them by the U.S. Ship Boston." To this they added that the queen and her people were "of one mind" that if she were returned to power she would grant amnesty to those who had overthrown the monarchy—reiterating in essence the guarantees that Cleveland had sought when he had talked about restoring the queen to power. The petition closed by restating the Hawaiians' confidence that "a nation so great and powerful would never allow so great a wrong to remain unredressed." The petitions were sent to Lili'uokalani and eventually were placed in the hands of U.S. government officials. This is attested to by the fact that these petitions today are in the State Department files of the National Archives of the United States.

ALL THE WHILE, QUERIES FOR INFORMATION and assistance arrived at the Republic's legation in Washington, reflecting ordinary Americans' excitement about the acquisition of faraway islands. "I desire to find out what I can regarding the lands which your government is trying to colonize with American settlers," wrote Herbert Hunter, who identified himself as a dealer in general merchandise. "I am anxious to move to a milder climate … I have friends who have visited the islands and are in love with the place." One letter arrived on a letterhead showing school children. "I should like to get into the schools there," said a school administrator in Johnson City, Tennessee. "What are the requirements, salaries paid, and length of the school year?"

D.C. Hoyt of Orvosso, Michigan, announced himself as one of a contingent "talking strongly of going to the Sandwich Islands to settle." Was it too much to ask about the price of land? Lyon Brothers of Baltimore asked for a list of merchant vessels sailing under the Hawaiian flag, while the Parker Shoe Company of Jefferson City,

Missouri, said, "We would like if possible to have a few names of the principal dealers there handling shoes."

To bring settlers to Hawai'i in large numbers, Sanford Dole wanted to start an American-style homesteading program using lands the Republic had taken over from the Kingdom. But such a program would have required tedious development of crops and infrastructure. Only a few homesteads were subsequently developed, although a homesteader on the central plain of O'ahu was to become famous for his innovations in the growing, canning, and marketing of pineapple—James Drummond Dole, Sanford Dole's second cousin. In Sanford Dole's view, the goal of homesteading was to create a substantially larger white population, which would offset the ever-growing Asian population.

As early as 1892, the idea of encouraging visitor travel to Hawai'i had been couched in distinctly similar terms. During the lull between the Bayonet Constitution and the overthrow, while Lorrin Thurston was out of the government, he had helped form the Hawaiian Bureau of Information. Its statement of purpose included not only the encouragement of tourist travel but "the immigration of desirable population; the settlement of the country; the creation of new industries, " etc.[9]

When Albert Willis, Cleveland's minister, had watched the oligarchy install itself in the government, he had wondered if its members might not forget about annexation and try to maintain their elite position in Hawai'i forever. While Willis's question was grounded in a certain logic, it did not take into account that beneath the oligarchy's methodical pursuit, there was a current of insecurity that sometimes must have felt like anxiety, and sometimes like active fear. Under the tutelage of John Stevens, the conspirators had helped set in motion a situation that subsequently dwarfed them. Although they had gone to extraordinary lengths to control the government, they were never more than a tiny minority without real legitimacy.

As a result, they kept one eye on their military arsenal, and on the fighting trim of their little army. As late as January 6, 1896, Dole was writing to Francis Hatch about the U.S. government's experiments with Maxim guns. He asked again for a Krag Jorgensen rifle with sample ammunition. "Having the best weapons counts in our favor," Dole said, "and they are cheaper than men." Cooper for his part felt insecure in the presence of the Japanese consul, Hisashi Shimamura. He described one of Shimamura's visits as courteous but nonetheless sounding like an ultimatum. Cooper said, "We cannot consider ourselves safe" until annexation was achieved and the labor agreement with Japan canceled. Smith wrote, "Not until we come under the direct protection of the United States will there be permanent stability and abiding confidence." Similarly on another occasion he wrote, "There will be no peace here, or freedom from revolutionary schemes till we come under the U.S." As Christmas of 1896 approached, W.O. Smith said, "Alone, we are in a great degree helpless. We cannot prevent the tide of Japanese immigration. Japanese property, trade and interests are gaining ground all of the time." On hot nights when the trade winds ceased to blow, when the air was deathly calm, they did not lack for worries.

While their darkest fears led them to a preoccupation with guns, their everyday fears led them to work constantly at warding off the possibility of Hawai'i's citizens actually voting on annexation. The files they so carefully left behind are littered with the theme of preventing a free and open vote. Henry Cooper worried that Lorrin Thurston and the Annexation Club, by creating a campaign atmosphere, would cause the opposition to revive and bring on "the undesirable plebiscite." He was certain it could only result in a restoration of native government and the continuation of a Hawaiian nation. "I believe that there is very little enthusiasm so far as annexation is concerned," Cooper wrote, "except within the very small circle of our original yeomen." He had checked with several of the members of the Committee of Annexation, and they agreed. What had begun as a coup d'etat government years earlier remained a coup d'etat government in 1897. Cooper was further distressed that, to get signatures on their petitions for annexation, the Annexation Club was making the rounds of government workers' offices. They were getting signatures of people who could be pressured, but not the signatures of everyday citizens.

Even their most expansionist friends in America often asked them, could they not let Hawai'i's people vote on the question of annexation? Surely, this line of reasoning went, the majority of people in Hawai'i wanted to be part of America. Smith and Thurston had researched ways to give the appearance of a democracy while functioning as an oligarchy, and yet the idea of native citizens voting never obligingly went away. To James Blaine, Lorrin Thurston had made what in retrospect became a preposterous claim—that Hawaiians could be induced to vote for annexation. Henry Cooper, by way of contrast, had exercised a certain grim commitment to fact at his meeting in Canton, Ohio. "If the question was submitted to the people," he had told McKinley, "annexation would be defeated."

Smith said that if a vote could be taken from the greatly shrunken voter list of the Republic, a majority of their short voter list initially would support annexation, "but as soon as it is decided to ask for a vote, large numbers of royalists and others opposed to annexation would register, and an adverse vote would be certain." Cooper was to be shaken by language in a draft treaty of annexation that called for native-born or naturalized citizens to vote. "It will, as I read it, practically disfranchise three fourths of our present electorate," Cooper said. By midsummer of 1897, Cooper was certain that so many sugar planters had deserted them that they could not get a majority vote for annexation *even from the existing voter list.*

CHAPTER SEVENTEEN
The Treaty of Annexation

When Lorrin Thurston returned to the mainland in early 1897, most of his energy went into agitating for annexation. He spoke widely. "Why I Am an Annexationist" circulated around the country as a handbook of pithy arguments for those who shared his views. Apparently sensing that the military arguments were working best, he sharpened his lines regarding Hawai'i's strategic importance.

Thurston also needs to be credited with taking the Japanese scare to a more intense level. Citing public immigration statistics, he said immigrants were pouring in at a rate that would result in the Japanese becoming a majority within five years. "It is the well nigh universal belief in Hawai'i that the present extraordinary movement from Japan to Hawai'i is part of a systematic plan," said Thurston, "with the full approval of the Japanese government, to gain control of the islands. Whether this is so or not I cannot say. Certainly no more certain method of accomplishing that result can be followed than that which is now going on."[1]

His statement was an extension of the campaign started by Senator Morgan and Francis Hatch, and it was to reverberate throughout the country in the months ahead. It was a variation on his warning in 1893 that if Hawai'i was not annexed, it would go to Great Britain, except now the demon in the devil theory was, in the lexicon of the Annexation Club, a Mongol.

Thurston argued that with Hawai'i as a base, ships at sea could be supported from Panama to Hong Kong, and from Alaska to Tahiti. "In all that Pacific area of 9,500 miles by 4,500, Hawai'i was the only spot where a ton of fuel or a loaf of bread could be had," wrote

Thurston. "A nation controlling Hawai'i would virtually control naval operations in the Pacific ... "[2] He devised an image of this area being equivalent to the distance from San Francisco across the United States, the Atlantic, and Europe to the Middle East, and from Greenland to Rio de Janeiro. Thurston tried to pry a specially rendered map out of the navy's map office to depict this idea, as part of his annexation presentation. When the mapmaker stalled over details of accuracy, Thurston went to Theodore Roosevelt.

Roosevelt was at a desk at the navy office. The desk itself must have impressed Thurston, to say nothing of the man. It had originally belonged to the first assistant secretary of the navy during the Civil War, and Roosevelt had pulled it from storage. The American flag was carved into the front of the desk, and cannon belligerently stuck out from both sides.

"Do you think the map would be helpful to annexation?" Roosevelt asked.

Thurston said it would. Roosevelt immediately wrote orders for Thurston's map piece, which Thurston in turn used "in and about Congress."

Thurston's lobbying stories reinforce William Appleman Williams's argument that virtually the entire political spectrum of America favored a substantial expansion into the Pacific, and the only real argument was over taking and administering colonies. Up to the time of McKinley's election, one of the most divisive issues in American politics had been gold versus silver guarantees of the currency. With McKinley's victory, a lobbyist for the silver standard named George P. Keeney found himself unemployed. "As the Republicans were committed to annexation," Thurston wrote, "our hunting ground was among the Democrats and Populists, who had considerable strength in Congress." Night after night Thurston and Keeney invited Keeney's friends from the old silver crowd to a hotel where both were staying and pitched them on annexation. "Our visitors usually became converts," Thurston said.

Thurston even made friends with the socialist Eugene V. Debs, who he claimed as a convert to the cause of the Republic. "I never shared his socialistic view," said Thurston, "but I believed in his absolute sincerity."

Lorrin Thurston was with Theodore Roosevelt one day when they received word that a Japanese prisoner had escaped from jail in Honolulu. The prisoner swam out to the Japanese ship, *Naniwa*. The commander of the cruiser, Heihachiro Togo, initially refused to return him. Hearing this story, Roosevelt said to Thurston, "Do you think, Thurston, the Japanese really intend to fight in Honolulu? If they do, I hope they will do so now, and we certainly will given them a bellyful."

"And he smiled characteristically," Thurston said, "with a show of all his teeth."[3]

In one of Long's numerous absences, Roosevelt briefed President McKinley on the availability of U.S. warships on the West Coast. On May 26, as W.O. Smith busied himself with mollifying the Japanese in Honolulu, Roosevelt laid out a war game for the Naval War College: "Japan makes demands on Hawaiian Islands. This country intervenes. What force will be necessary to uphold the intervention, and how shall it be employed? Keeping in mind possible complications with another Power on the Atlantic Coast." To which he added the word, "Cuba." Roosevelt had located a war game for the projection of sea power in the two-oceans naval strategy that expansionists had been working on, and which specifically preoccupied the group that had formed around him in the early moments of the McKinley Administration. America must be ready to fight in both the Atlantic and the Pacific on short notice.

In his impatience, Roosevelt was a study in indiscretion. On June 2, he delivered a speech to the Naval War College that attracted wide attention in the press. "Peace," he said, "is a goddess only when she comes with sword girt on thigh." He said peace resulted from having first-class battleships, and that diplomacy was "utterly useless" when it was not backed by force. Had Roosevelt stopped there his remarks might simply have been a call for preparedness, but there was a part of Roosevelt that reveled in the idea of war. "No triumph of peace," he said, "is quite so great as the supreme triumphs of war."

On June 7 Roosevelt wrote to an annexationist in Hawai'i, A.S. Hartwell, confiding that Secretary Long agreed with him on taking possession of Hawai'i "in some shape or other." Of course, he went on, "I absolutely agree with you that it should be done at once; but this must be kept as confidential, for . . . I haven't any authority to commit the administration." In a second letter written the same day, he blurted out to a man in New York that he was "hot with indignation at the seeming utter decadence of national spirit among us, and the craven policy which actuates the dilettante and the man to whom making money is all that there is in life."

On the day of these letters, June 7, 1897, a dispatch arrived at the State Department in Washington from the American consul in Honolulu, reporting on the letter of Count Ōkuma, the Japanese minister of foreign affairs, to the Republic of Hawaii. It demanded that the Republic of Hawaii pay Japan an indemnity for the suffering caused to the Japanese immigrants who were held in Honolulu and then returned to Japan. Otherwise Ōkuma insisted that the Republic live by the terms of its 1871 treaty of friendship with Japan, allowing Japanese the right to reside in Hawai'i, to participate in the economy however they wished, and to be treated as citizens of other nations were treated. With the addition of a demand for an indemnity, it was a reiteration of Japan's position, but in context of the friction with Japan the dispatch created an alarm. Secretary of State Sherman quickly forwarded it to McKinley with a note underscoring its "extreme importance."

The next day, June 8, McKinley turned to Roosevelt, who was his most bellicose adviser. To Roosevelt's surprise, McKinley praised his War College speech. Roosevelt in turn urged "immediate action by the President as regards Hawai'i."[4] In describing the meeting to Alfred Mahan, Roosevelt reiterated Mahan's opinion that taking Hawai'i immediately would end the possibility of trouble with Japan. Roosevelt then predicted, "I believe he will act very shortly."

A succession of people—John Morgan, Francis Hatch, Sanford Dole, Henry Cooper, and now, most prominently, Theodore Roosevelt and Alfred Mahan—had been involved in conjuring the idea of a Japanese menace. Hatch was telling William Day that without annexation, the oligarchy would lose control. Even John Long, who Roosevelt derided for his lack of fight, was moved by a plea from his niece Julia, who had married the brother of Bill Castle, the prominent missionary descendant and annexationist. The ultimate audience for all this was, of course, the president, McKinley. The arrival of Ōkuma's letter and Roosevelt's ensuing meeting seemed to confirm for him that Hawai'i must be annexed.[5] He told his under secretary of state, William Day, who was in charge of the annexation question (and not Sherman),[6] to move ahead with a treaty.

Why should Hawai'i be annexed? Subsequently McKinley was to tell a wavering United States senator he had become convinced that if America did not take Hawai'i over, Japan would. Otherwise he relied on reasons that floated through the air. He said it was America's manifest destiny.

The Republic of Hawaii had provoked Japan by arbitrarily turning back its immigrants. Japan had responded by sending a warship, demanding an indemnity, and reiterating its position on the extant treaty of friendship between Hawai'i and Japan. The American president had responded by moving ahead with a treaty of annexation. Did McKinley, or for that matter Roosevelt, understand that the Republic had consciously provoked Japan? Apparently not. Did subsequent historians who wrote about the history of deteriorating relations between Japan and America in the Pacific know the provocation was intentional? Apparently not. William Russ, on whom historians of American imperialism seem to rely for a reading of the Archives of Hawai'i, either missed or did not report Francis Hatch's letter of February 17, 1896, to Henry Cooper, the letter that is the clue to Cooper's subsequent development of the provocation. ("I think," Hatch wrote, "we should begin to make a record which will appeal to people here.") Written history has been left with the end result of the Republic's provocation—that is, America's indignant response to Japan's position.

Four days after McKinley's meeting with Roosevelt, William Day called in Francis Hatch. Day asked, "Are you prepared to enter into negotiations looking toward turning Hawai'i over to the United States?" When Hatch said he was, Day handed him a draft treaty representing the McKinley Administration's views. Hatch read it, then said he would like to talk with Thurston and the other Hawai'i commissioners before responding.

"Very well," Day said, "but I advise that you act speedily."

"At what hour later in the day can we meet you?" Hatch asked.

Day set the time at three o'clock that afternoon, a Saturday. Hatch, Thurston, and William Kinney presented their elaborate parchments identifying themselves as representatives of the Republic of Hawaii. They raised only one question, which concerned the treaty's terms of citizenship. Day said they were raising an issue that was not in the draft of 1893.

"No," Hatch said, "but we thought it would be an improvement of that treaty if the subject were settled."

Day said McKinley feared the question of citizenship would provoke debate and slow down ratification. Hawai'i's commissioners agreed. Day told them to stand by. On Tuesday, at four o'clock in the afternoon, they received a note to report to the State Department at three-thirty. Although they had missed the meeting, they ran over anyway. There they found the secretary of state, John Sherman, just as he was leaving the State Department. Sherman was taking a hand in ceremony, if not in policy. Perhaps to remind them that he personally was not enthusiastic, he told the commissioners from Hawai'i to come back at nine o'clock the next morning. Four days after being presented with a treaty, everyone signed. If Sherman had been present, they probably could have signed on the first day.

The Grand Army of the Republic wanted to photograph the signing of the treaty. When all were in their places in the reception room of the State Department, someone noticed that Walter Gresham's portrait was looking down from the wall of the chamber onto the ceremony. They took it down and replaced it with the portrait of James G. Blaine.[7]

As they were signing, Sherman said, "I suppose you know that Japan protests against this?"

"No, we had not heard of that," Hatch said.

Sherman said Tōru Hoshi, Japan's ambassador to America, had delivered a protest. Hatch asked, a protest on what grounds?

Sherman said, "Well, Mr. Hoshi does not talk very good English, and I knew that it would not amount to anything anyway, so I did not pay very much attention to what he said."

WHEN CLEVELAND HAD ALLUDED to "a familiar and unpleasant name" for the control of both sides of a bargain, he did not say what the name was, and as a result some colorful bit of nineteenth century vernacular was lost, but not the idea. The negotiation of a treaty between the annexationists of Hawai'i and the American government was not really a negotiation. It had not been a negotiation in the rush to annexation of 1893, nor was it in 1897. The complete dominance of the American secretary of state and the complete acquiescence of the Hawai'i commissioners seems to be, in itself, of historical significance. The circumstances accentuate the extent to which annexation was an American event. America had chosen the time and place and announced the terms. The terms were agreed to by Lorrin Thurston, the founder of the Committee of Annexation; the committee's vice chairman, Francis Hatch; and William A. Kinney, Thurston's law partner.

Along with the several men who managed the government in Hawai'i—particularly Sanford Dole, Henry Cooper, and W.O. Smith—these men were the inner sanctum of the conspiracy. They had been coached into first the overthrow and then the formation of a government by the American minister to the Kingdom of Hawai'i, John L. Stevens, a close associate of then American Secretary of State Blaine. They had been protected by American marines and thereafter sheltered by the frequent presence of American warships. And now all present had agreed for the second time to the extinction of a nation that previously had an unbroken tradition of nearly two millennia, and which had functioned as a nation among nations since 1795, only eighteen years after America itself began to function as a nation.

The treaty of annexation began with these words: "The Republic of Hawaii hereby cedes absolutely and without reserve to the United States of America all rights of sovereignty of whatsoever kind in and over the Hawaiian islands ... " What had been a nation became, semantically, only land space. Soon these places would be, in the American vernacular, "the Islands," suggesting nice places to visit across the water.

Within the oligarchy, there had been a modest division of opinion about the terms of annexation which is instructive. Hatch, Smith, and Thurston favored keeping it simple, by taking whatever deal they could get. Smith frequently counseled people to get inside among friends, and then work out the details. In contrast, Dole and

Cooper worried over terms. Cooper had argued, "I do not think we should proclaim to the world that we are in for annexation without terms."[8] Dole wanted the future government of Hawai'i to have ownership of all the lands that had once belonged to the Hawaiian monarchy and to the Kingdom. He had wanted to throw these lands open to homesteading by white settlers, so that Hawai'i would become what he had described—the westernmost outpost of Anglo-Saxon civilization, but Dole's idea of maintaining local ownership of crown, public, and government lands evaporated like mist in the sun.

The U.S. government took ownership of all these lands for what was to become an obvious reason—the desire to sort out the lands that most readily facilitated turning Hawai'i into an elaborate system of military bases and training camps. In the words of the treaty, the Republic ceded the land, which amounted to 1,800,000 acres, or 45 percent of the entire acreage of the Hawaiian archipelago. They were the lands that had been retained by the monarchy and government in the 1848 land division as an institutionalization of the ancient land-holding prerogatives of the paramount chiefs. These lands had constituted most of the remaining wealth of the once-vibrant and populous Hawaiian nation. Significantly, the treaty provided for maintaining Hawai'i's lands in a status separate from other federal lands. All revenue from these lands—other than lands taken by the federal government for civil, military, or naval purposes—was to be used solely for the benefit of the inhabitants of Hawai'i "for educational and other purposes." Further, Congress at some future time was to enact "special laws for their management and disposition."

The annexation treaty was silent on how Hawai'i was to be governed. When Kamehameha III had talked about annexation, he had asked for statehood. When the first commissioners of the Provisional Government, including Thurston, met with then Secretary of State John Foster in 1893, they too had asked for statehood. Foster had advised them to let go of the statehood idea for the time being.

Now the oligarchy had let go of any provision regarding the mode of governance, other than the treaty's description of Hawai'i as a territory. The treaty provided only that the president of the United States would appoint five commissioners, at least two of them from

Hawai'i, to recommend legislation "they shall deem necessary and proper." From the point of view of expansionist America, perhaps such an arrangement reflected the making up of imperialism as it went along. From the point of view of the oligarchy, this proviso was faithful to the advice of W.O. Smith, who had said they "must not haggle over details." For the Hawai'i of future generations, it is a clue to the question people puzzled over for decades—why was Hawai'i not granted statehood? Why was Hawai'i held in a territorial status for sixty-one years, and its citizens held in a second-class status far longer than any other territory that subsequently achieved statehood? One answer is that statehood was never implied and never intended. In fact, Sanford Dole was to offer the opinion that Hawai'i would never become a state for a simple reason. If it did, it would elect a Japanese governor.[9]

As for the Chinese, the annexation treaty said no further immigration into Hawai'i was to be allowed, "and no Chinese by reason of anything herein contained" was to be allowed entrance into the United States from Hawai'i. It was a phrasing that did not bother to clarify that Hawai'i, by virtue of the treaty, was to become part of the United States. (It did not say, for example, that no Chinese was to be allowed to go anywhere else in, or to the rest of, the United States.) The meaning was apparent that the Chinese Exclusion Act of 1882 was to apply to Hawai'i, and that persons of Chinese ancestry already in Hawai'i were to be kept there, their new rights as Americans notwithstanding.

As for Japan, and for the guarantees given by the Kingdom and affirmed by the Provisional Government and the Republic to the Japanese in Hawai'i: "The existing treaties of the Hawaiian Islands with foreign nations shall forthwith cease." The Treaty of Friendship of 1871 that so strangely had endured the life of the Republic was to be nullified.

AFTER JOHN SHERMAN TOLD Francis Hatch that Japan had protested the annexation treaty, allegations concerning Japan's motives hit a new level of intensity. Where originally the uncontrolled immigration of Japanese workers into Hawai'i had been interpreted as a change from the government-supervised contract system to "free" immigration, and subsequently as a function of the greed of the

Japanese immigration companies, Henry Cooper migrated to Thurston's line of argument, saying the "peaceful invasion must have been stimulated by the Japanese government."[10]

As lobbying for Senate passage of the treaty intensified, McKinley himself was to echo the "peaceful invasion" theory almost word for word.

Smith heard rumors that Japan planned to recall all its immigrants in Hawai'i, or at least those not under labor contract. This "would cripple the whole agricultural industry of the islands," Smith said.[11] Smith was both excited and frightened. Japan's protest of the treaty was "a surprise—a showing that must help our cause." But he said the news from Japan reflected strong feelings, and he feared that "Japan may attempt a 'master stroke' and take possession here." For the anxieties of the oligarchy, there could be only one solution. Smith said, "The U.S. had better annex and settle matters."

AS WITH THE LARGER ANNEXATION STORY, the story of the "Japan question" came to be virtually unknown among the general publics of Hawai'i and the United States.[12] Today we make inquiry across a chasm to retrieve some understanding of those times. When W.O. Smith glanced around nervously at the Japanese immigrants, when Thurston talked about a "peaceful invasion," when Julia Castle wrote plaintively to her uncle John Long, what *was* going on? In fairness to those who today might be perceived as merely fabricating a racist scare story, it is true that *something* was going on. That something was a process of continuous and rapid change in an era of runaway expansionism by nations, in which expansionism gave way to imperialism.

The nation of Hawai'i had struggled most of its national life with this accelerating imperialism and in 1897, as a result of it, was on the brink of national extinction. The European powers were devouring whole portions of the globe, and American expansionists were tempted to follow their example. Previously insular Japan likewise was evolving from resisting Western expansion to imitating it. The expansionist faction in America was inspiring an expansionist faction in Japan, and vice versa, and these two forces were beginning to play off one another for rationalizations of their behavior.

This process of interaction was penetratingly described by Dr. Akira Iriye, professor of history at Harvard University, in a 1972 study entitled *Pacific Estrangement*. Iriye quotes at length from Mahan's contention that the real issue was "whether Eastern or Western civilization is to dominate throughout the earth and to control its future." He describes America's passage from expansionism to imperialism as follows: "What seems to have happened is that imperialism came to be justified in the framework of an emerging perception of the West's struggle to maintain its strength and superiority. America's expansion could be seen as a necessary chapter in the West's effort to preserve its civilization. Imperialism became more comprehensible and defensible ... "[13]

By Iriye's careful definition, Japan crossed the threshold from expansionism to imperialism in its war with China in 1894—an historic watershed that was on the minds of white annexationists in both Honolulu and Washington. "As the Japanese people drank the sweet cup of military victory, they began entertaining dreams of empire... There is no question that the war made Japan imperialist... "[14] The question then becomes, how far did Japan's ambitions reach?

Another study[15] searched for evidence that Japan planned to invade Hawai'i in 1897. The closest it came to evidence was a dispatch from Japan's ambassador to Washington, Tōru Hoshi, to the Japanese foreign minister, Count Ōkuma, in which a frustrated Hoshi was quoted as saying there was only one way to stop America's annexation of Hawai'i—namely, "our occupation of that Island by dispatching, without any delay some powerful ships under the name of reprisal."[16] First, Hoshi is known in Japanese history as hotheaded. Second, and much to the point, Iriye puts Hoshi in perspective by quoting Count Ōkuma's reply: "Continuation without interruption or disturbance of our intercourse with the United States is of vastly more importance to Japan than interests that will be menaced by annexation." Consequently, Ōkuma told Hoshi, Japan's "opposition to annexation should be within limits of diplomacy."[17]

Within these bounds, Japan's interests lay in the well-being of its immigrant colony in Hawai'i, which during the years 1893-1898 was the largest of Japan's overseas populations. One can imagine that Japanese workers in Hawai'i shared in the national pride that resulted from the victory over China in 1894. Japanese merchants were starting to sell Japanese goods in Hawai'i, and Japan itself was beginning to strategize how to gain greater control over—and profit more from—overseas trading. A "Colonization Society" was organized in Japan in 1893 that included prominent politicians, writers, and intellectuals. Thomas Malthus's theories of exponential population growth were being read in Japan, and emigration—the act of going out—was becoming a part of Japan's national strategy.[18] How these emigrants were treated was fundamental to how Japan was regarded, and it is in this light that the *Shinshū Maru* and other such incidents became especially loaded.

Hilary Conroy said the Japanese government was "profoundly irritated" by the situation in Hawai'i, particularly the rejection of its immigrants. "But even so it was exceedingly careful to deny categorically that the protest implied that Japan had any idea whatsoever of herself menacing the independence of Hawai'i or a desire to 'embarrass the United States.'"[19]

Two successive American ministers to Japan advised the U.S. State Department that Japan's concern for its emigrants was sincere and paramount, and that Japan had no military or territorial ambitions in Hawai'i. A highly regarded career diplomat, Edwin Dun, said Japan sent a warship only to meet "the popular clamor" resulting from Hawai'i's treatment of Japanese emigrants. Further, he ventured the opinion that the Japanese government would be willing to amend its immigration convention with Hawai'i to avoid such problems in the future—something that the Republic, for all its posturing, never asked for, almost certainly because of the planters' dependence on Japanese immigrant workers.

Dun's successor, A.E. Buck, the American minister in Tokyo in late 1897, said Japan was genuinely concerned for the Japanese in Hawai'i and would continue to exert pressure on their behalf, but that all else was a show to placate an unhappy Japanese public and press. Buck said Japan sincerely believed it had "just cause for complaint" over the Republic's behavior, and further that the Republic's minister to Japan (Irwin) agreed not with his own country but with Japan.[20] A worried Francis Hatch wrote to Cooper on May 11, 1897 (before the arrival of the *Naniwa* in Honolulu), that Japan's version of events was "gaining credence" in Washington. Originally the perpetrator of the plan to create a "record" with which to impress Washington, Hatch wrote at this juncture, "I am particularly anxious that they should not succeed in persuading anyone here that we have recklessly sought the difficulty. They have nothing to back up their assertions at present. *I hope nothing foolish will be done by any of our hotheaded supporters which could be relied upon as supplying the missing evidence.*" Among the hotheads, Hatch perhaps worried most about his correspondent, Henry Cooper. While the United States government never explicitly agreed with Japan's contention that Japan had been wronged, the U.S. State Department exerted pressure on the Republic to take seriously—and resolve—Japan's demand for the payment of an indemnity.

Nonetheless, while Ambassador Buck was reporting his views to the State Department, the new American minister in Hawai'i, Harold Sewall, was nearly as busy strategizing for annexation as John Stevens once had been. Even though the *Naniwa* had gone home, and fear had dissipated, "There is good reason to believe that the Japanese government is at work by means I have not hitherto suspected." It was around this time that Roosevelt wrote orders to send additional American warships to Honolulu, and William Day empowered Sewall to use his discretion in directing the use of the U.S. navy.

Subsequently, Day rescinded his order, perhaps recalling what had happened when John Stevens once exercised such power, or perhaps having heard that Harold Sewall had a reputation for exaggeration. Sewall's dispatches toned down. The Japanese reporters went home. By July, a high-level American naval officer in Honolulu gave an interview, under a cloak of anonymity, ridiculing the possibility of war with Japan. He said America had many more men under arms and a better navy. While Japan had defeated China in 1894, "they went up against a lot of coolies, who ran away directly (when they saw an armored cruiser coming toward them)."[21] That Hawai'i would be annexed, he thought, "is as certain as the sun rises in the East, but I hardly think it will be during this year."

On December 22, 1897, even though no settlement had yet been made of Japan's claim to an indemnity, the Japanese withdrew their objection to the treaty of annexation.

Throughout, the Republic of Hawaii persisted in irritating Japan, perpetually stalling on issues Japan regarded as important. At one point, the United Guild of Sake Brewers of Japan sent a petition to Sanford Dole. With Japanese politeness, the petition said the greatest pleasure of the overseas Japanese laborer was "to indulge in occasional cups of *sake* of their native country." In response to the fourteen thousand brewers of the guild, would the Republic please lift its prohibitive tax? When Honolulu attorney Paul Neumann pleaded to the Executive Council on their behalf, the Council deferred action on his request indefinitely.

Consul Hisashi Shimamura, on behalf of his government, pursued the issue of indemnity payments for the losses suffered when immigrants were returned to Japan. When the U.S. government cued Hawai'i to wrap up its loose ends with Japan, the Republic asked Japan what it wanted to talk about. Japan had a five-point agenda, which Hawai'i wanted to edit to a four-point agenda. Discussion of the agenda alone went on for months. The idea of arbitrating the indemnity arose. The Republic asked, if an arbitrator found in Japan's favor, how much money would Japan want? Not much, was essentially the answer. From Tokyo, A.E. Buck wrote John Sherman in Washington that Japan was "becoming somewhat impatient" with the way the Republic of Hawaii would take exception to its position but not give it timely counterproposals. Buck said the Japanese were becoming suspicious that Hawai'i was perpetually stalling, while in his view the Japanese earnestly sought a speedy solution to their problems with Hawai'i.

MANY QUESTIONS REMAIN as to what went on in this murky water. The relatively clear answers seem to be that American expansionism focused first and foremost on Hawai'i, while Japan's ambitions were focused elsewhere—namely, on China, Korea, and islands in the western and southern Pacific. America's interest in Hawai'i was paramount, while Japan's was peripheral. America sought military and commercial advantage, while Japan sought a population base through which it might extend its trade and interaction with the wider world. America was looking for a semi-respectable way to take over Hawai'i, while Japan was looking—none too seriously or coherently—for a way of maintaining Hawai'i's independence.

Hilary Conroy wrote that until 1897 U.S.-Japanese relations "had been marked by great cordiality." Iriye should be quoted in this regard at some length: "Among the events that held the interest of the American public and predisposed it in favor of expansionism, the rise of Japan as a power was one of the most significant. It was no accident that Hawai'i provided the first serious crisis between the two countries. It had all the factors—racial antagonism, jingoism, struggle for influence and power away from the home-base—that were to characterize the subsequent decades of Japanese-American antagonism."[22] Insofar as the oligarchy influenced events with its calculated provocation of Japan, the first steps in the deterioration of U.S.-Japan relations must be counted as part of its legacy.

Yet for Americans who to this day are suspicious of Japan, or despise Japan, for its attack of December 7, 1941, the oligarchy's arguments will continue to resonate. Those who perpetually distrust Japan might ask, what would have happened if Hawai'i had tried to remain independent? The answers lie in what the Japanese settlers would have faced if they had tried to take control. First, they would have had to deal with the remaining three-fourths of the population who were not Japanese. Over half were Hawaiians who still possessed a strong sense of their indigenous claim and nationhood. Economically, four-fifths of the land and virtually the entire cash economy was controlled by whites. Reciprocity was still in place, and America was starting to build its first facility on its strategically located piece of turf at the mouth of the Pearl River. Finally, the main Hawaiian Islands lay more than half-way across the Pacific, toward America.

THE SENSE OF VULNERABILITY OF THE AMERICAN colony, which seems to have eaten at it like a cancer, lay in the startling demographic statistic: Only 2 percent of Hawai'i's population was made up of Americans and American descendants. Beneath the missionary descendants' cool logic and recurring self-righteousness, fear lurked. Although written histories reflect so much American influence as to completely obscure the fact, Japanese outnumbered Americans in 1897 in Hawai'i by roughly twelve to one. The number of Japanese men arriving in a single year often far outnumbered the entire colony of white males. In the overall population, Americans were outnumbered roughly fifty to one. Yet American influence was so omnipresent that few people seem to have known exactly how small the American colony really was. Ambassador Tōru Hoshi alluded to the situation by telling the U.S. State Department that "only a small fraction" of Hawai'i's people wanted annexation.

Secretary of State John Sherman replied that by well-established practice, it was the government and not the people that determined the will of a nation. The Republic of Hawaii, Sherman said, had maintained peace and added to Hawai'i's prosperity. "The Government of the United States," he said, "sees no reason to question its complete sovereignty, or its right to express the national will."

ALMOST SIMULTANEOUSLY WITH the signing of the Hawaiian annexation treaty, Theodore Roosevelt was establishing himself as the leading voice for a stronger military posture in general and a bigger navy in particular. He would describe how he and his cohorts set out to build battleships but had to start by building cruisers that were promoted as shields of commerce. Then, in the further pursuit of battleships, they built ever more powerful ships that were called, progressively, "armored cruisers," "coast defense battleships," and "sea-going coast defense battleships." He said the fact that the names had become contradictions in terms was "of very small consequence compared to the fact we did thereby get real battleships."[23]

When Japan protested the annexation treaty, he bristled. "The United States is not in a position which requires her to ask Japan, or any other foreign power, what territory it shall or shall not acquire." Long was angered by the aggressiveness of Roosevelt's public remarks, but Roosevelt mollified Long with elaborate apologies and proceeded on. A week after Japan's protest, he told Long darkly, "We have information that the Japs are feeling decidedly ugly about Hawai'i."[24] But, he added, "I am very sure their feelings will not take any tangible form."

WHEN THE ANNEXATION TREATY went before Congress, Roosevelt, Mahan, and Lodge went to work in search of a vote for ratification. Roosevelt was aghast that many members of Congress, along with a large element of the American public, did not share their eagerness to take over Hawai'i. If America missed this opportunity, he wrote Mahan, "It will show that we either have lost, or else wholly lack, the masterful instinct which alone can make a race great." It was a raw expression of Social Darwinism that John Burgess of his alma mater, Columbia University, would have liked. "The terrible part," Roosevelt said, "is to see that it is the men of education who take the lead in trying to make us prove traitors to our race."

By September of 1897 he was writing to Lord James Bryce of Britain that America "ought to take Hawai'i in the interests of the white race."[25]

Months went by, and Congress failed to do its job despite the benefit of Roosevelt's prompting. He complained that his countrymen had a "queer lack of imperial instinct," but all was not lost. While Hawai'i was a conveniently available step, and logically the first step, Roosevelt had larger plans. He wrote, "I have been hoping and working to bring about our interference in Cuba."

To His Excellency

William McKinley,
President of the United States of America.

The Humble Petition of the undersigned.
President of the Hui Kalaiaina of t
Hawaiian Islands.

Showeth:

That at a Convention of the Hawaiia
tation held in the City of Honolulu on
day of November, A.D. 1896, Your Petition
David Kalauokalani was du
ected President of the Hui Kalaiaina
he Hawaiian Islands in room of the late
J. A. Kahooneii

he said Hui
ian Islands
mber of the

CHAPTER EIGHTEEN

The Queen in Winter

When Queen Lili'uokalani visited Sanford Dole unannounced, obtained a passport, and departed from Hawai'i, she went first to San Francisco. In her book, she ponderously explains that she had no sooner arrived in San Francisco than she was contacted by the native patriotic societies. And, she said, "these representative bodies of my own nation prayed me to undertake certain measures for the general good of Hawai'i." It would appear from her subsequent activities that she had gotten safely out of Hawai'i, where she had been a prisoner, then a parolee, and had resumed active communication with the nationalist organizations, Hui Aloha 'Āina and Hui Kālai'āina. She said the native societies wanted her to make one last appeal to Grover Cleveland before he left office, and that they had sent petitions for her to give to him.

From San Francisco the queen went to Boston and visited relatives, as she had told Dole she would. In Boston, she received a second packet from the native societies addressed to the president-elect, McKinley. While in Boston she renewed her acquaintance with a man named Julius Palmer, a reporter for the *Boston Globe*, who had been to Hawai'i and listened carefully to the oligarchy's story. Palmer had written that in the Republic of Hawaii he could find no republic at all, and as a result he was high on the list of people the oligarchy particularly disliked. Palmer signed onto the queen's staff without pay. He was described as a secretary, but his main job was to help her finish her book.

On January 23, 1897, the queen arrived in Washington, D.C., by train with Palmer and her entourage. Cleveland had lost the election but was still in office, and the queen was greeted by his secretary of the treasury, Daniel N. Morgan, who Lili'uokalani described as a high-ranking member of the Masonic Lodge. January 23 was a Saturday. As she was leaving Boston, the White House had advised her that the president was going hunting, and she arrived to gossip that Cleveland was avoiding her. On Monday, January 25, she sent him a brief note, "advising him of my presence in the city, and offering to express to him my friendly feeling by a personal call, if it would be convenient to receive me." He immediately invited her to the White House at three p.m. that same day.

The queen does not say that Cleveland felt badly about failing to restore the native government, but she dwells on the lengths to which he went to treat her with courtesy and respect. The queen gave him "the documents" of the Hawaiian patriotic leagues. She told him his name was dear to the Hawaiian people because of his effort to restore Hawai'i's lost independence. She assures her readers that Cleveland was sincere, and that as she came to better understand "the obstructions placed in his way by the supporters of Minister John L. Stevens, I understand far better than formerly that he failed through no fault of his own."[1]

The queen inquired about Mrs. Cleveland. The president had just arrived from his business office. He asked around the White House for his wife, but was told she was out for a walk. Thereafter the press said Mrs. Cleveland had snubbed the queen. Several days afterward, Mrs. Cleveland sent a note saying she had arranged a reception in Lili'uokalani's honor, and would she be so kind as to come early, so they could chat in private?

When Lili'uokalani had been allowed by Dole to leave Hawai'i, neither Francis Hatch nor Henry Cooper had been consulted. Not long after her arrival in Washington, Hatch wrote Cooper, "Lili'uokalani has thrown off the mask and poses as Queen."[2] Cooper said he had known all along she would cause trouble.

The queen says during this period she gave a reception every two weeks, and that she received "callers at eight to nine any evening, and often at other times." Congressmen, or their wives and daughters, were well-represented at these receptions. She said there were seldom fewer than two hundred visitors and once there were five hundred. Guests presented themselves to Julius Palmer with cards and were then presented to her.

The queen decided at the last moment, six days before McKinley's inauguration, that she wished to see the new president sworn into office. Julius Palmer went the same day to see George C. Perkins, the

California senator who had previously helped Lorrin Thurston clean up the Provisional Government's problems with the sugar tariff. Perkins quickly got an agreement from both the outgoing and incoming secretaries of state that the queen and her escort, Joseph Heleluhe, would sit in the diplomatic gallery.

"The storm which burst from the reporters' gallery when they saw me there," she wrote, "will be remembered by those who read any of the newspapers on the day following." It was a beautiful day, and her friends teased her that she had brought the weather from Hawai'i. That night she saw the navy admiral, George Brown, riding with the new president, the same Admiral Brown who had been with Kalākaua in San Francisco and transported his body back to Honolulu. Perhaps her hopes rose that she would have a navy friend in high places. Brown had visited her hotel to show her a medal that Kalākaua had given him. When he met her "under the changed circumstances which had befallen," Brown wept.

One day a girl's college held a reception for her at the Shoreham Hotel. They gave her their college colors. She gave them a copy of *Aloha Oe*, written in her own hand. They insisted that she speak. She saluted their desire as young women to advance themselves intellectually. "It shows the progress of the world," she said. "The world cannot stand still. We must either advance or recede." Her list of visitors went on and on—delegates to the International Postal Congress, representatives of the Chinese embassy, delegations from Missouri and Minnesota, Catholics, Methodists, Episcopalians, and Masons—her story is densely populated with Masons.

The agonizing ambiguity of the relationship between Americans and Hawaiians seemed to be fully in motion. Somewhere beneath America's relentless push to expand, beneath the extant theories of Anglo-Saxon supremacy, beneath newspaper cartoons of the day depicting the queen as a "black savage," Lili'uokalani engaged in seemingly endless rounds of warm, cordial, and dignified discourse. From the time the first Westerners had arrived in Hawai'i with their great ships and their guns, the Hawaiians had sought parity. While they had not succeeded, neither had they failed. Many Americans seemed to have been stunned by the verve, brilliance, and aloha of the Hawaiians, and their resulting feelings seemed to do battle with the theories sequestered in their brains.

The queen spoke with particular regard for Senator Perkins, who had arranged her inaugural seats, and Representative Samuel G. Hilborn, also of California. Both had visited Hawai'i. Hilborn introduced his wife, Grace, who sang the queen's songs. Lili'uokalani said her singing "gave to me that joy, so sadly sweet, of listening to the sounds of home in foreign lands."

All the while she was writing her book, which would be titled, *Hawaii's Story, by Hawaii's Queen*. She also released, through a publisher in Boston, her translation of the creation chant, *Kumulipo*, which she had worked on during her imprisonment in 'Iolani Palace. She also copyrighted many of her songs and turned them over for what would become widespread publication.

Although her book makes no mention of ill health, her diary is checkered with references to seeing a doctor during this period. She found lumps around her neck and shoulders. The doctor lanced them, apparently without anesthetic. At one point she made a notation that she had cancer, which would seem certainly to not have been so, given how much longer she was to live.

She takes care to portray herself as being in frequent touch with representatives of the large majority of people in Hawai'i, and to be sustained by them. She describes her Hawaiian male secretary, Joseph Heleluhe, as a special envoy who represented the disenfranchised citizenry. Nonetheless there were times when she felt horribly alone—"one woman, without legal adviser, without a dollar to spend in subsidies, supported and encouraged in her mission only by three faithful adherents, and such friends as from time to time expressed to her their sympathy."[3]

While she tracked the possibility of annexation, she also tracked the possibility that she would be paid a settlement by the U.S. government.[4] She was going deeply into debt. How much she and others spent on the Hawaiian resistance movement is as yet unfathomable, but a tantalizing fragment of information exists in a ledger of the estate of James Campbell, the husband of the devoted royalist Abigail Kuaihelani Campbell. A compilation made in 1900 of outstanding loans shows two lines for Lili'uokalani, one a mortgage for $16,000, a second for $10,000. An entry for Joseph Nāwahī's widow shows a loan of $5,630. Another staunch Hawaiian royalist, Lucy Peabody, a leader of the Women's Patriotic

League, had borrowed $40,000. Samuel Parker, formerly the queen's foreign minister, carried staggering debts—$128,000. Although Parker had financial problems prior to the resistance movement, his problems no doubt worsened with the events of 1893 to 1898. If his debts are included, the total rounds off to $200,000 in the currency of the 1890s. Some idea of the value can be derived from the fact that the Republic of Hawaii required an annual income of six hundred dollars for a person to vote. In these terms, James Campbell had loaned to the royalist camp the equivalent of several hundred annual incomes, which in today's currency amounts to several million dollars.

The queen's anxiety over money was coupled to the queen's anxiety over being displaced by the foreigners. Just as Lili'uokalani had once been haunted by spies who roamed the streets of Honolulu, now she was acutely aware of the commissioners of the Republic roaming the streets of Washington. She said they had tried in vain to excite Americans against Great Britain, then had "willfully violated treaty obligations with the friendly power of Japan." Although Congress had been in session (the 1897 session), it had "shown no interest whatever in the troubles of a few adventurers two thousand miles from California, claiming to be both Americans and Hawaiians."[5]

She particularly resented *haole* describing themselves as Hawaiian. It was here that she described Hatch as a "pseudo-Hawaiian" from New Hampshire, Cooper as an "alien," and William Kinney as being better acquainted in Salt Lake City than in Honolulu. Lorrin Thurston's political methods, she said, needed no mention. He had been sent home in disgrace by the Cleveland Administration, but now he was back at it in Washington. She wrote, "He is again attempting to negotiate a treaty bartering away his adopted country."

When the treaty was hurriedly signed in mid-1897, she sent Julius Palmer and Joseph Heleluhe to Secretary of State John Sherman with a protest, which she had written previously. "I declare such a treaty to be an act of wrong toward the native and part-native people of Hawai'i," she said, "an invasion of the rights of the ruling chiefs, in violation of international rights both toward my people and toward friendly nations with whom they have made treaties, the perpetuation of the fraud whereby the constitutional government was overthrown, and, finally, an act of gross injustice to me."

She recited her yielding only to the superior power of the United States; Cleveland's reaction; Blount's condemnation of the overthrow; Willis's demand that Dole step down; and the fact that Hawaiians had never been allowed to vote on annexation. The Republic, she noted, was trying to give away the combined government and crown lands that made up a major portion of the land mass of the archipelago. She claimed much of this land had belonged directly to her in the form of crown lands, referring to lands that had been set aside for the ruling monarch, and the rest of the lands were dedicated to support of the Hawaiian government. It was the cession that Cleveland originally had described so pungently in his message to Congress, and which Lili'uokalani now described as a transfer of power "from the hands of those whom its own magistrates ... pronounced fraudulently in power and unconstitutionally ruling Hawai'i."

In her protest of the draft annexation treaty, she was describing, clearly enough, America's two-handed game, in which Hawai'i was being passed from an illegitimate government that had been created with American support into direct American control. Yet in her more visceral expressions she continued to focus on the missionaries, while looking hopefully toward American ideals. The missionaries had betrayed her, but the American people were good and, other than John L. Stevens, Americans were gentlemen. In the closing words of her protest, she implored Americans, from whom her ancestors had learned Christianity, to practice fair play in accordance with the principles of their fathers.

She maintained she had not seen McKinley in the four months since the inaugural only because she was sensitive to how busy he was. She thanked those who had socialized with her in such a kindly way, then left Washington after the Fourth of July for New York. There she heard from the patriotic leagues again. They voiced their regret that she had not presented their petitions to McKinley. Almost certainly these are the petitions that were written by the *hui* between the end of 1896 and early February 1897. She, or Joseph Heleluhe, had been carrying them for four to six months, unable to deliver them directly to McKinley. She returned to Washington on Saturday, July 24.

The following Monday she sent Heleluhe and Julius Palmer to give the documents to McKinley. Both she and Heleluhe wrote cover letters.

The queen said Hawaiians were in an unhappy condition, "as that of the weak in the grasp of the strong." She said it would have been a pleasure to have met with him in person, and that the Hawaiian patriotic societies had expected her to deliver their petitions in person, even though they were not officially represented in Washington. Heleluhe made a point of transmitting the documents as a member of Hui Kālai'āina, and also on behalf of Hui Aloha 'Āina and the Women's Patriotic League. He complained that he had been trying to deliver the letters since the week of the inauguration. All he had gotten back was a note from McKinley's secretary saying that the matter was being considered. In fact, this secretary wrote thousands of such notes, eighty on one particular day during this period, while McKinley wrote virtually nothing.

At the White House, Heleluhe and Palmer were told it was a "reception day" in which McKinley apparently received a variety of people in an informal social setting. Hearing this, the queen went to the White House with Palmer, presented her card, and was ushered into the East Room. There McKinley mingled in the company of a hundred or so people. Lili'uokalani sat. He approached her. She rose and advanced to meet him. She thought he was gentlemanly.

The oligarchy had engaged in a consistent tactic of isolating the queen, and in such moments as her meeting with McKinley she indeed seemed isolated—a brown-skinned woman approaching sixty years of age, in the mansion of the American president, where the only other persons of color almost certainly were servants. In the oligarchy's correspondence, they discounted the importance of other Hawaiians, as well as the Hawaiian people in general. In written histories that ensued, the characters of the queen and her brother were attacked, and Hawaiians other than the queen virtually disappeared from sight. William Russ, for example, describes the Hawaiians as "leaderless natives."[6] But in truth the most widespread mass protest of annexation by Hawaiians was yet to come.

IN THE REGULAR SESSION OF THE U.S. CONGRESS OF 1897, the anticipated vote on annexation had given way to yet another debate over the status of Hawaiian sugar. The American sugar growers had given the oligarchy a fright, but reciprocity had survived and, along with it, the base from which annexationists in both America and Hawai'i could resume their pursuit. During the break between the first congressional session and the second, which was held in late 1897, Senator John Morgan of Alabama arrived in Honolulu with his wife and four U.S. House members to promote annexation. It is tempting to ask whether this was not the first congressional junket to Hawai'i, particularly since Morgan stayed more than a month. But to say this was merely a junket would not do justice to the seriousness of Morgan's purpose and the unique light it shed on American attitudes, and also the attitude of the Hawaiians.

After Cleveland had declared America's role to be an act of war on a small and defenseless nation, and after the U.S. House had censured Minister John L. Stevens, John Morgan had gotten the pro-expansionist forces back on their feet by chairing a series of hearings of the Senate Foreign Relations Committee. These hearings were designed to justify America's actions in Hawai'i. They resulted in a report named for Morgan. On the dark plain of unexamined propaganda, the Morgan Report tended to neutralize the Blount Report. Thereafter John Morgan had fed Francis Hatch the plan to create an anti-Japanese record for the Republic. Hatch in turn had egged Cooper into his role of point man for such a plan, which led to the Republic turning back the four ships of Japanese immigrants.

Two weeks after his arrival in Honolulu, on September 30, 1897, Morgan met in Honolulu with Henry Cooper, now foreign minister, and Ambassador Francis M. Hatch, who had returned to Honolulu for the congressional break. The meeting was about Hawai'i's relationship with Japan. Cooper's presentation began with the Treaty of Peace and Friendship of 1871 between Hawai'i and Japan, as well as its subsequent amendments, which had to do with the rights of Japanese in Hawai'i and the question of whether Japan enjoyed a most-favored-nation status as typically defined in international law. His presentation moved on to the Republic's turning back the ships, as well as the dollar-a-gallon tax on Japanese *sake*.

Cooper gave a long recitation on refusing entry to the Japanese immigrants without either himself, Hatch, or Morgan acknowledging —at least in the fifteen pages of notes—that the impetus for such an act had come from Morgan himself by way of Francis Hatch. Cooper even got down to his ferreting out illegal immigrants by determining that their required fifty dollars was in fresh packets of crisp new yen. He confided that while many of the illegals were forced to return to Japan, some were issued legal labor contracts by the Hawai'i Board of Immigration to fill the continuing need for plantation labor.

For most of the meeting, Morgan remained silent. Perhaps it occurred to him that the sugar planters were habituated to the importation of low-cost labor, and that Japan was their most ready source. Although he was to say subsequently that being in Hawai'i was just like being in some new part of America, Cooper's discussion of international treaties of long standing may have brought home to him something of Hawai'i's status as an independent nation. Morgan asked only a few simple questions aimed at clarifying what kind of international baggage America might be acquiring. Was there only one treaty with Japan? Yes. Was there only one (no-longer-used) labor agreement with Japan? Yes. Was it mutually acknowledged between Japan and Hawai'i that these agreements could be dissolved? No.

Morgan asked one last question that curiously pried open the status of Japanese immigrants in America's future. Did Japan allow expatriation, meaning the renunciation of Japanese citizenship? Cooper said he knew of one person of Japanese ancestry who was a citizen of Hawai'i (an answer that did not quite get to the point of Morgan's question, since the person Cooper described more than likely held dual citizenships). As far as Morgan knew, Japan had not objected. Then, Morgan asked, did Japan claim jurisdiction over the Japanese immigrants in Hawai'i? Cooper said, "I think it has been generally understood that it did claim such jurisdiction."

Morgan replied, "This is a very interesting question as to what becomes of the Japanese after his term of service expires and he fails to go home."

It was a calm, mostly factual conversation that was most notable for what was *not* discussed. There was no mention of a plot by Japan, no mention of a peaceful invasion by the Japanese, and no mention of a threat to the future of Western civilization. In other words, the original perpetrators of the Yellow Peril idea gave no indication in the fifteen pages of notes on the meeting that they actually believed such a peril existed. Such thoughts were also for the consumption of others, such as the president of the United States. Morgan also was to try them out on the Hawaiians the next day.

	PALAPALA HOOPII KUE HOOHUIAINA.		PETITION AGAINST ANNEXATION.

PALAPALA HOOPII KUE HOOHUIAINA.

I ka Mea Mahaloia WILLIAM McKINLEY, Peresidena, a me ka Aha Senate, o Amerika Huipuia.

ME KA MAHALO:—

No KA MEA, ua waihoia aku imua o ka Aha Senate o Amerika Huipuia he Kuikahi no ka Hoohui no ia Hawaii nei ia Amerika Huipuia i oleloia, no ka noonooia ma kona kau mau iloko o Dekemaba, M. H. 1897; nolaila,

O MAKOU, na poe no lakou na inoa malalo iho, na wahine Hawaii oiwi, he poe makaainana a poe noho hoi no ka Apana o _____, Mokupuni o _Molokai_, he poe lala no ka AHAHUI ALOHA AINA HAWAII O NA WAHINE O KO HAWAII PAEAINA, a me na wahine e ae i like ka manao makee me ko ka Ahahui i oleloia, ke kue aku nei me ka manao ikaika loa i ka hoohuiia aku o ko Hawaii Paeaina i oleloia ia Amerika Huipuia i oleloia ma kekahi ano a loina paha.

IKEA—ATTEST:

Mrs Lilia Aholo
Kakauolelo—Secretary.

PETITION AGAINST ANNEXATION.

To His Excellency WILLIAM McKINLEY, President, and the Senate, of the United States of America.

GREETING:—

WHEREAS, there has been submitted to the Senate of the United States of America a Treaty for the Annexation of the Hawaiian Islands to the said United States of America, for consideration at its regular session in December, A. D. 1897; therefore,

WE, the undersigned, native Hawaiian women, citizens and residents of the District of _____ Island of _____, who are members of the WOMEN'S HAWAIIAN PATRIOTIC LEAGUE OF THE HAWAIIAN ISLANDS, and other women who are in sympathy with the said League, earnestly protest against the annexation of the said Hawaiian Islands to the said United States of America in any form or shape.

Mrs Kuaihelani Camp
Peresidena—President.

	INOA—NAME.	AGE.		INOA—NAME.	A
330	Mrs. Kaiakonui Hutchison	59	356	Kaahapamewa	a
331	" Kinini	60	357	Makaoumi	5
332	" Kuo	57	358	Mekana	3
333	" Kanamu	54	359	Kalaina	5
334	" Pookela	54	360	Sarah Ulapai	2
336	" Kala Kahua	20	361	Kawahie	5
337	" Kipa	32	362	Hanaini	5
338	" Kewa Kapule	32	363	Mariana Wilikoki	2
339	" Maria Piirce	27	364	Paina Mahulua	3
340	Lilia Rice	21	365	Mrs Kamala	5
341	Kawae Hoopii	44	366	Kailiawu Kapiioho	1
342	Mrs Naralina Makuna	50	367	Bike Mole	3
343	Piikula	67	368	Lucy Robinson	2
344	Alapai	60	369	Maunahina	
345	Maria K. Pahau	21	370	Kahomokau	
346	Sapela	42	371	Lahapa Koboa	2
347	Ailau	67	371	Kalimawela	5
348	Lilia Likeke	40	382	Manoa	1
349	Maria Kupa	60	383	Mrs. Kalalina Krapf	
350	Mokihana	21	384	Sarah Kona	2
351	Kamala Isacha	82	385	Pepela Palau	5
352	Beeky Ah Kun Loy	33	386	Mareka Kikau	

CHAPTER NINETEEN

The Hawaiian Petition

In the weeks before Senator Morgan's arrival in Hawai'i, in response to the United States signing a new treaty of annexation with the oligarchy, the Hawaiians began a new round of protest. The newspaper *Ke Aloha 'Āina* cautioned *hui* members that there were several petitions circulating in Honolulu, but theirs was still being written. On September 6 the Hawaiian *hui* held a rally against annexation at Palace Square, across from 'Iolani Palace. James Keauiluna Kaulia, by then president of Hui Aloha 'Āina for nearly a year, said he had heard talk that annexation would enrich Hawai'i, "but I am saying, it is something that will destroy the people to whom the land belongs." He said the Hawaiians might as well agree to being buried alive as agree to annexation. He predicted that foreigners would "snatch away jobs and resources."

"Then where will we live?" Kaulia asked.

"In the mountains," the crowd replied.[1]

As with the queen and other prominent Hawaiians of the time, Kaulia was inclined to vent his anger on the oligarchy, but to be more temperate in his criticisms of the United States.

The government of the Republic, he said, "became a shelter in which their dirty deeds disappeared." He said that annexationist newspapers had threatened people who attended the rally, but that they must not be afraid. "Be steadfast in aloha for the 'āina, and be united in thought," Kaulia said. "Protest forever the annexation of Hawai'i to America, until the very last aloha 'āina." If Hawaiians stood up against annexation, they would succeed: "If the nation remains steadfast in its protest of annexation, the Senate can continue to strive until the rock walls of 'Iolani Palace crumble, and never will Hawai'i be annexed to America!"

David Kalauokalani, the president of Hui Kālai'āina, talked about the content of the treaty. He said the oligarchy was proposing to give away, and America to take, the land and water of the Hawaiians, as well as their bays, harbors, and government buildings.

The idea of a great mass petition was in motion. The heading of the petition said, in Hawaiian only, "Petition of the Nation Protesting Annexation." It went on to say that all the signers protested annexation to the United States "in any form or shape." The organizers of the rally warned against Morgan's impending arrival and said another rally would be held while he was in Hawai'i. One of the newspapers said, "Eia iho ka haole la he mea hoomakaulii aina." Here comes the *haole*, the one who covets land.[2]

IN THE COURSE OF HIS TRIP, JOHN MORGAN demonstrated a curious preoccupation with selling Hawaiians on America. His main public appearance was at Kawaiaha'o Church, the missionary church that sits within sight of 'Iolani Palace. One of the annexationist newspapers said the original idea was for Morgan to speak only to Hawaiians, but so many white people wanted to come that the doors were opened to Americans, Portuguese, and "a solitary Chinaman," about whose people various abusive things would be said. The church filled, and people spilled over into the gallery and onto the front steps. The newspaper estimated the crowd at seven hundred. Two hundred seventy-five were said to be Hawaiian, among them James Kaulia, who had come to listen and plan what he might say in response. Morgan spoke for an hour and a half, counting the time it took for a translator to repeat his speech in Hawaiian.

The theme of Morgan's speech was that America had come to help the Hawaiians and open its arms to Hawai'i. He cited Kamehameha's attempt to cede Hawai'i to the British, through the explorer George Vancouver. Now Britain, France, and Germany had taken over almost all the islands of the South Pacific and "the only salvation for the Hawaiian Islands is in annexation to the United States." Within a week he would be predicting immediate statehood for Hawai'i, but his remarks at Kawaiaha'o Church centered on the idea of America as an association of sovereign states. "Every state is an independent Republic," he said. "Now, whether you come as a Territory or as a State, you come as a separate Republic; you take no oaths, with this exception, you agree to become American citizens." He said that in his opinion, no man is as proud of his citizenship as an American.

Stories had been circulating in the Hawaiian press about the American treatment of black people and native Indians, an issue that Morgan now addressed. A product of Selma, Alabama, which in 1967 would become a battleground for the right of black people to vote, Morgan said that his fellow Negro citizens "vote just as I do, and they enjoy the same opportunities as I, and are respected by the people amongst whom they live according to their merits." He said America had about 108 different kinds of Indians, "ranging from the utter savage to the civilized man, able and educated," and Indians were active in politics as well as blacks. As to the Island natives, "There is no power in the Constitution of the United States to prevent a Hawaiian from becoming President of the United States; it rests entirely upon his merit."

Morgan next got around to what he, Hatch, and Cooper had not bothered to talk about—the perils of the Asian immigration. The Hawaiians knew about law and Christianity, he said, and were therefore not like the Chinese or Japanese, "bowing his knee before their potentates." Being smothered by Asiatics, he said, would be like being smothered by a landslide. "You understand just as well as I do what is going on in Hawai'i," Morgan said. If Hawaiians refused the opportunity to become part of America, he said, they would "be going to ruin." To this, later in his visit, he would add a prediction that when "Japan has filled these islands with her people," the Hawaiians would sink, "as the rains sink into the thirsty soil."

Kaulia responded with an open letter making the essential point he had made at the previous rally—that the United States was obligated to hold a referendum on annexation. He challenged Morgan to use his influence to let Hawaiians vote.

Morgan replied that he was not disposed to interfere in Hawaiian affairs. However, he said he did not think it necessary "or fair" to submit annexation to a popular vote. "Your Constitution provides for annexation without such a vote," he said, ignoring the fact that Hawaiians had been shut out of writing the constitution. He said if Hawai'i lapsed back into monarchy, it could not become part of the United States. "I would prefer to save the liberties of the people, through annexation, to a tawdry show of royalty by a few persons set in authority over them, who would be compelled to do the bidding of some supreme monarch."

Was confusion loose? Is there a basis in history for people's confusion today over the history of Hawai'i, and the history of America's expansion into the Pacific? Morgan was working to force the Hawaiians into America against their will, while simultaneously agitating to free the Cubans from Spain. Was America embarking on an anticolonial crusade, or a highly calculated colonization movement? Morgan's Library of Congress biography did not address this particular question, but rather said that although "he was a dedicated Southerner, Morgan developed a world vision and supported an aggressive national foreign policy."[3] He was receiving mail from young men who were looking for a way to go fight the Spanish in Cuba. "May God guide your efforts for Cuba Libre," one wrote, adding that as a citizen of Tennessee, the Volunteer State, he knew that every mother's son was ready to defend "our rights and those of our Cuban brothers."[4]

In addition to support for annexation, and support for a war in Cuba, Morgan was widely known for promoting construction of the canal that was to connect the Atlantic with the Pacific. It is this third item on his agenda that resolves any seeming contradiction between the first two. The common denominator of Morgan's causes was the same as Roosevelt's, namely, global power and a big, two-ocean navy.

Shortly after Morgan's visit, a senator from South Dakota, R.F. Pettigrew, appeared in Hawai'i and held his own meetings. He said he had been told that many Hawaiians favored annexation, but "I have failed to find a Native Hawaiian who was not opposed to annexation."[5] Pettigrew returned home with a strengthened determination to do battle against the takeover of Hawai'i, and he would emerge from the trenches of the Senate as the most desperate, determined opponent of annexation.

THE HAWAIIAN ANSWER to the new annexation drive evolved in the course of Morgan's visit. An account, developed by the Hawaiian scholar Noenoe Silva, traces a process in which the three societies—Hui Aloha 'Āina, Hui Kālai'āina, and the Women's Patriotic League—undertook a coordinated protest drive aimed at Washington, D.C. It was what James Kaulia had proposed at the rally in September—a massive display of Hawaiian resistance to annexation. *Ke Aloha 'Āina*[6] described the leaders of the *hui* traveling throughout the Islands to drop off petitions, meet with district captains to secure signatures, and then return to pick up the petitions. *Hui* leaders went to Maui, Kaua'i, Hawai'i, and Moloka'i. There was a branch of the *hui* at the leprosy settlement at Kalaupapa, on Moloka'i, and dozens of the disease victims carefully signed their names.

Two of the key women leaders went to Hilo, on Hawai'i Island, to meet with chapters of the Patriotic League and to collect their petitions. One was Joseph Nāwahī's widow, Emma, now publisher of *Ke Aloha 'Āina*. The other was Kuaihelani Campbell, the unwavering royalist who had served as president of the Women's League from its inception. They were welcomed at Hilo Bay, where the people insisted they ride ashore on a beautiful double-hulled canoe decorated with leis. They were invited to drop by one of the women's groups for a snack. There they were given roast pig, fish, rare ferns, fruits, and other delicacies. Two young Hawaiian women wore dresses made from Hawaiian flags, with sashes that said, "*Aloha ku'u mō'ī wahine,*" meaning "My queen is beloved."

On October 8, there was a rally against annexation in Honolulu. The crowd was somewhere between the "eight hundred to two thousand" described by the annexationist *Pacific Commercial Advertiser* or the four to five thousand of *Ke Aloha 'Āina*. The latter said, "*Lulu ka makani i ka nui o na kanaka.*" The wind shakes because of so many people. Silva's readings of the Hawaiian newspapers suggest that Hawaiians could still laugh. James Kaulia was introduced as a combatant who would "swoop down on the battlefield, swirling the steel point of his sword (his pen) in the face of the enemy. The weapons of war will crackle and snap, and the bright light of the opening of fire will shine when the armaments clash. It will be brains against brains, and Morgan's treaty will fall into the fire pit of Hell."[7]

James Kaulia appears to have become the most popular orator among the Hawaiians, in keeping with his position as president of the largest patriotic organization. He felt pressed to justify why he had attended Morgan's speech at Kawaiaha'o Church because, it appeared, most Hawaiians were so offended by Morgan that for one of their leaders to be in his presence required explanation.[8] "I wanted to get his positions for myself," Kaulia said, "... in order to stand and fight with Morgan, who is the War General of the annexationist circle."

Kaulia's cleverest jabs appeared in an open letter to Morgan on the front page of one of the royalist newspapers. Kaulia quoted at length from Morgan's pious description of God's ultimate praise: "Well done thou good and faithful servant." Since Morgan was so steeped in goodness, Kaulia said, it followed that he would not want to be involved in the theft of anything, let alone the theft of another people's country. Kaulia outlined the political tradition through which America had confined itself to the North American continent and practiced a philosophy of, "Friendship with all nations and entangling alliances with none." Inevitably, Kaulia said, if America acquired Pacific possessions it also would acquire entangling alliances. Prophetically, he went on: "The shore lines of American policy, once crossed, are crossed forever, and one acquisition leads but to another."[9]

Kaulia addressed his conclusion to Morgan: "Ask for the voice of Hawai'i on this subject, Mr. Senator, and you will hear it with no uncertain tones rising out from Niihau to Hawaii—'Independence now and forever.'"

A well-known Caucasian attorney, J.O. Carter, spoke as an American descendant. While having entrée into annexationist circles, Carter had been a consistent voice against annexation and in support of restoring the queen to her throne. "I come," Carter said, "believing that if I have a talent I shall let you know it and not put it in a napkin and bury it." What he said next might have gone unnoticed in the outpouring of words at a large rally, but it resonates with the passing of a hundred years:

"I want to say to you as a Hawaiian, I am indignant at the action which took place here on the 17th of January, 1893. As an offspring of American parents, I am ashamed of that action. I believe that all that has followed that fatal day—all that has been laid upon us during the last four years—was because of a false step... all that has been undertaken by the present Government has been because the men in power took counsel of their fears and not their good judgment."

J.O. Carter knew intimately of whom he spoke. He was the son of H.A.P. Carter, who had served as the ambassador of the Hawaiian Kingdom to America. He had written for the newspapers, served in the Legislature, served in the cabinet, and also been the chief executive of C. Brewer, which would become one of the Big Five corporate lords of Hawai'i. Charitably he said that on the day of the overthrow, the acquaintances of his boyhood had taken a "false step" and then had been guided, above all, by their fears.

THE RALLY AND THE PETITION drive together were a resounding denunciation of annexation and a direct rebuff to Morgan's appeal for the Hawaiians to accept America as their new country. Thirteen hundred and fifty dollars was raised to send a delegation to Washington with the petitions. The heads of the two male organizations, James Kaulia of Aloha 'Āina and David Kalauokalani of Kālai'āina, along with two other noted royalists, William Auld and John Richardson, departed on November 20, 1897.

The queen was still in Washington, and the arriving delegates immediately met with her. They held a strategy session in which John Richardson was chosen chief spokesman for key conversations with members of Congress. They then met with Richard Pettigrew, the South Dakota Democrat who had visited them in Hawai'i. Pettigrew took them to the Senate, where they turned over the Hui Aloha 'Āina petition, with its nearly twenty-one thousand signatures. Based on an agreement among themselves, the Hawaiian delegates held back the presentation of the Hui Kālai'āina petition, which was said to have seventeen thousand additional signatures. Their concern was for how the Kālai'āina petition's explicit appeal to restore the monarchy would be received, as opposed to the Aloha 'Āina petition's more generalized statement protesting annexation.[10]

The difference in phrasing reflected the differing origins of the two organizations. Hui Kālai'āina had been formed to support the monarchy during the time of the Bayonet Constitution, while Hui

Aloha 'Āina was formed in 1893 as a mass protest organization. While Aloha 'Āina supported the queen throughout the prolonged crisis, many of its most prominent members—Joseph Nāwahī foremost—had previously questioned the institution of the monarchy.

The petitions were described extensively in both the Hawaiian and English language presses of the day. There also is a reference to a "monster petition" in the Congressional Record. For anyone who is looking, a researcher, an historian perhaps, references to the petitions are plainly visible in newspaper accounts, but the mass petitions were overlooked and then forgotten.

Apparently to suggest the diversity of material to be found in the National Archives of the United States, the Archives used a page of the petition as a graphic element in a brochure published in the mid-1990s. Noenoe Silva read the brochure, was struck by the extraordinary content of the petition, then traced it to where it is filed, under the Senate Committee on Foreign Affairs. A few of the ends of the five thick folders of paper are tattered, partly from age, partly from the paper being a little long to fit comfortably in the archives. Each of the 556 pages is numbered by hand. The statement of opposition to annexation is printed in Hawaiian on the left and English on the right. All the pages are signed by two of the key leaders of the men's or women's organizations. A space was left blank—then filled in by hand—for the district and island from which the petitions came, such as Hālawa, Moloka'i, Hāna, Maui, and Kona, Hawai'i.

Within the file, the petitions are preceded by a long memorandum from Lorrin Thurston. Other petitions in the file are marked "Thurston" or "Thurston Table," giving credence to the oligarchy's boasts that as time passed Thurston practically sat on the Foreign Relations Committee. The petition had been given to Thurston, and he obviously devoted an enormous amount of time and energy to analyzing it. He attacked it much as he attacked the character of his opponents. He questioned "both the genuineness and good faith of the petition." He said it contained "what purport to be" a collection of male and female signatures. He made a great point of saying that just under five thousand of the twenty-one thousand signatures were purported to be people between the ages of fourteen and twenty.

The implication was that the reader should discount the opinions of minors who were not voters, which was a curious line of attack because it ignored the fact that adult Hawaiians had been effectively disenfranchised. This was not a petition from voters. Actually, Thurston went on, the petition was even worse than that. He found the names of seven boys and six girls under the age of two. Some of the names were in the same hand, such as the hand of a royalist named Edward Lilikalani, with whom he had served in the Legislature. Thurston said he knew that signature well. Finally, the Ks in many instances were similar.

The vast majority of the signatures are original and distinctive. Women's names from Moloka'i, for example, include Mrs. Kaiakonui Hutchinson, Mrs. Kanamu, Pookela, Pii Kula, Lilia Likeke, Ana Kahuna, and Mareka Kekau. Men's names from Moloka'i include C.N. Kalakai, George Keolunui, Aumai, D. Kaaoao, Joanne Haake, George A. Rice, and Solomon Keliiokalani.

A census had been taken by the Hawaiian Kingdom in 1890 and a second by the Republic in 1896, with nearly identical results—that approximately forty thousand people of Hawaiian ancestry were left in the Hawaiian Islands. However much a person quibbled over details, the size of the petitions was what James Kaulia had envisioned—the most thoroughgoing evidence that Native Hawaiians actively and continuously opposed annexation, and that they had not become any more friendly to the idea the longer they had lived with it. The petitions also served as a powerful reminder of what different members of the oligarchy—Thurston, Hatch, Cooper, Smith—acknowledged over and over in their conversations with high-level people in Washington. If Hawai'i were to be annexed, the question could never be put to the potential voting population of Hawai'i, because they would vote a thunderous no.

The research is unfinished. The Hawaiian newspaper claim of twenty-one thousand Aloha 'Āina signatures was substantiated by the existence of this petition in the National Archives. While the claim of an additional seventeen thousand Kālai'āina signatures was not similarly substantiated, the existence of the first twenty-one thousand signatures gives credibility to the total claim of thirty-eight thousand signatures, as does the extensive record of close cooperation between the two *hui*. This means that not only a majority of Hawaiians, but virtually all Hawaiians remaining in the Hawaiian Islands, petitioned against annexation in late 1897, just a few months before the U.S. Congress moved into its final stages of deliberation.

The historian Merze Tate, in a rare reference to Hawaiian protest after 1895, briefly described the signatures of 21,269 people "remonstrating against annexation." William Russ described seven signatures on a petition in late 1897, presumably those on the transmittal sheet, but did not go on to describe the other thousands.

Other than the newspapers and the petitions, the records of the political *hui* could not be found for the purposes of this story. The newspapers recorded that the delegates met with Cushman Davis, the Republican chairman of the Senate Foreign Relations Committee. The *Pacific Commercial Advertiser* quoted Davis as saying he had been working for annexation for five years and in that time there had not been a single Hawaiian in Washington "to tell how the native people considered the matter."[11]

The influential senator from Vermont, George Hoar, was a particular object of lobbying by the Hawaiian delegation. The delegates described tramping through the snow and freezing cold at night to meet with him in his home. Hoar was known to have deep reservations about annexing Hawai'i, and he received them courteously. After their conversation, the Hawaiians went away reinforced in their belief that Hoar would stand by them.

In late February, after two months in Washington, the Hawaiian delegates left their second petition with friends in the Senate. They returned home believing that the annexation campaign had been stalled, perhaps indefinitely. Since it had been widely thought that annexation would sail through the Senate after the sugar tariff was resolved, the Hawaiian delegates believed with reason that they had had a hand in blocking the two-thirds vote that would have ratified the treaty.[12]

BY THE END OF 1897, and perhaps by the end of the first week in December, the campaign to ratify the treaty of annexation had been shelved for a lack of votes. Francis Hatch wrote from Washington, "The latest outlook is a long fight ahead of us." It was as if the dark impulses of the entire scheme had descended to plague them. Hatch inquired about reports of dissension in Honolulu among the annexationists. He asked whether they had come so far only to break ranks and scatter. The Japanese immigrants kept moving in, and the government of the Republic could not stop them, because the government's only real constituents, the planters, didn't want them stopped. The *Pacific Commercial Advertiser*, which so often was a propaganda arm of the annexation movement, castigated the government for drifting "along the stream of prosperity even if it carries us into the Asiatic sea."[13] The *Advertiser* said the government had let more Asian males into Hawai'i during the first few months of 1898 than the total number of males in the combined American, German, and British populations. The racial remedy of expanding white immigration was "idle talk," it said, lacking in both practicality and commitment.

Dryly, the scholar Hilary Conroy wrote, "The basic weakness of the Hawaiian Republic is easy to identify but it's roots ran very deep. The government had no substantial population behind it."[14] The members of the oligarchy had given themselves six-year terms of office in the repressive constitution of 1894, which meant the end of their self-assigned tenure was in sight. Various members of the oligarchy's Executive Council began to argue over what they would do if they did not achieve annexation.

Samuel Damon, the treasurer, had always tried to maintain a courtly relationship with the queen in particular and Hawaiians in general. He said that Hawai'i could survive as an independent nation only if there was a new sharing of power with Hawaiians. The *Pacific Commercial Advertiser* implored white people to stand by the government they had created. "There are hardly 2,000 of us 'able bodied' men who are trying to hold the fort of white civilization here against 80,000 or more who oppose us."[15] Not all of white society was ready to stand up with the *Advertiser*. The British sugar tycoon, Theophilus Davies, distributed ten thousand copies of a letter in the Hawaiian language proposing that Hawaiians disassemble the existing government and lead the way in creating a true Republic. It was a revival of the idea advanced by the Hawaiian writer John Bush and the Hawaiian rebel Robert Wilcox in the turbulent period between 1889 and 1892.

To Francis Hatch's apparent chagrin, a group of the white elite held a hurried session in Sanford Dole's office in 'Iolani Palace, now called the Executive Building, and decided that Dole should go to Washington. Ambassadors often live in fear of their presidents taking a direct hand in foreign affairs, and Dole's trip was to demonstrate why. In response to a reporter's asking what would happen without annexation, Dole was quoted as saying that if necessary Hawai'i would persevere. He went on to say—in an amazing slip—that the Japanese were not a serious menace after all. Although he subsequently denied the statement, Dole had disavowed the most essential feature of the annexationists' propaganda campaign during the preceding eighteen months. Additionally, while Japan's "peaceful invasion" of Hawai'i was designed to obscure the issue of justice for the native people, the indigenous people of Hawai'i kept appearing in Washington in full color. When Dole arrived in the capital, Kaulia and Kalauokalani were still on the scene, and Lili'uokalani gave an especially ambitious reception for her American friends. Hatch complained that it was intended to upstage Dole.

An irreverent New York newspaper said of Dole, "He is not the president of the Hawaiians, but the representative of the descendants of missionaries, gentlemen who have captured alive the souls which their pious fathers intended to control only after death."[16] Hatch and the others struggled to have Dole treated as a head of state, rather than a lobbyist. McKinley responded by throwing a lavish dinner at the White House for Mr. and Mrs. Dole. In their meetings, McKinley told Dole that the two-thirds vote that was needed in the Senate for passage of the annexation treaty was probably lacking.

McKinley attempted to bolster Dole by saying they could go to their fallback plan—a joint resolution by both houses of Congress, requiring a simple majority vote. The problem was that the House of Representatives was governed by a powerful speaker, Thomas Reed (also of Maine), who was bitterly opposed to America becoming a colonial overlord. Speaker Reed had said, "Empire can wait." Part of Reed's objection was that Hawai'i might become a state, sooner rather than later, and that it would then have representation in Congress. Reed's comment catalyzed a possible solution—to make Hawai'i a county of the state of California, with the right to send a delegate to the California assembly.[17]

As the proponents of annexation shifted to their strategy of a joint congressional resolution, their opponents seized more firmly on the point made by the Hawaiian petitions—that the vast majority of the people of Hawai'i opposed annexation. Senator Augustus Bacon of Georgia proposed that a plebiscite of Hawai'i's citizens be held, and that the outcome determine the fate of annexation.

When one senator said the only way to save the treaty was to include a clause providing for a plebiscite, Hatch declined. He asked his correspondent, Cooper, "What sort of position would we be in if we took an unrestricted vote and it was against us?"

In Honolulu, the response of the *Pacific Commercial Advertiser* was an intellectual mixture of Senator Morgan and Professor Burgess. It said a few intelligent natives saw that rule by the "stronger race" was their only security against being destroyed by Asians. However, the newspaper went on, it was obvious that annexation could not be brought to a vote because most Hawaiians would simply follow their leaders, as the Irish and Germans had followed their leaders in maintaining the scandal-ridden Tammany Hall machine in New York.

ALMOST SIMULTANEOUSLY, AN ODD VARIATION of Social Darwinism emerged in Honolulu with the organization of a Young Men's Research Club, where young white males made solemn remarks about the other ethnic groups. The Portuguese were described as being upstanding, frugal, and eager to acquire property. The Chinese were deemed likely "to hold their own in the struggle." A study paper on Hawaiians asked what would happen if annexation failed. "White government," the speaker said, "could be maintained only by the sword, and our Anglo-Saxon Island Republic would be a military occupation."[18]

A young man who spoke about the Japanese must have surprised everyone. He announced that "instead of the Japanese or the other Orientals being the invaders, the real immigrants were the Anglo-Saxons." His proof was that the Japanese had proved to be much better suited to the environment and "every physical feature favored their advancement towards the goal of triumph." By contrast, the Anglo-Saxon body was "but a speck," incapable of engaging in hard work in Hawai'i's warm climate. As pioneers of higher civilization the Anglo-Saxons had turned out to be "merely money-makers."

Errant members of the Legislature of the Republic began to raise their voices. A.B. Loebenstein of Hilo aroused the wrath of the oligarchy by proposing that the oath of opposition to the monarchy be discarded from the loyalty oath of the constitution of the Republic. In effect he was proposing to remove the main barrier to Hawaiians voting. Loebenstein argued that since the constitution had been adopted by the creators of the Provisional Government and by delegates who had been elected by such a small minority of the population, it deserved amendment. Adding insult to injury, he questioned the expenses of Dole's trip to Washington.

The week of Loebenstein's irreverent outbursts, Lili'uokalani published her book, *Hawaii's Story*. Her most biting words were aimed at the sons of the Christian mission. The Hawaiian people, she wrote, had nourished in their bosom those who now sought to destroy the nation. "If we did not by force resist their final outrage," she said, "it was because we could not do so without striking at the military force of the United States." The native people of Hawai'i, she said, had been "overawed by the power of the United States" and were now in danger of being relegated to the status of the American Indian.

"Is the American Republic of States to degenerate, and become a colonizer and a land-grabber?" she asked. "And is this prospect satisfactory to a people who rely upon self-government for their liberties? There is little question but that the United States could become a successful rival of the European nations in the race for conquest, and could create a vast military and naval power, if such is its ambition, but is such an ambition laudable? Is such a departure from its established principles patriotic or politic?"

In her most penetrating voice, she remained the studious *ali'i* child who had been tutored by the American missionaries. "Oh, honest Americans," she wrote, "as Christians hear me for my down-trodden people! Their form of government is as dear to them as yours is precious to you. Quite as warmly as you love your country, so they love theirs." The god of the missionaries, she said, was a judgmental god, and the sins of a father would be visited on his sons.

Father Damien of Moloka'i had once greeted Lorrin Thurston as a son of Belial, who appears in the Bible in the Book of Kings spreading lies about Naboth. The purpose of the lies is to enable King Ahab to steal Naboth's vineyard. Naboth refuses on the ground that his vineyard is from God, and his tie to his vineyard is inalienable. Lili'uokalani advised Americans to "not covet the little vineyard of Naboth's, so far from your shores, lest the punishment of Ahab fall upon you, if not in your day, in that of your children." She alluded to God's temporarily forgiving Ahab but telling Ahab that his sins would survive him. Thereafter when Ahab falls in battle, dogs drink his blood, and it is said that his children are doomed to a similar fate.

The Hawaiian people, the queen said, were children of this same God, and they were crying aloud to Him in their time of trouble, and He would keep His promise to them. Of the American people and their Congress, she said, "As they deal with me and my people, kindly, generously, and justly, so may the Great Ruler of all nations deal with the grand and glorious nation of the United States of America."

Theodore Roosevelt and the Rough Riders

Cuba and the Philippines

A navy officer's wife wrote that anchoring the battleship *Maine* in Havana Harbor was like waving a lighted candle over an open barrel of gun powder. In her figure of speech the flame was the Cuban rebellion against the Spanish, which had begun in 1896. In a revival of anticolonial feeling, Americans had reacted with sympathy for the Cubans. The Cuban nationalist forces struggled on while McKinley won the election, took office, and tried to establish his priorities, including the annexation of Hawai'i. Cuba was a distraction, but it was more and more difficult for McKinley to ignore. Cuba posed an issue of proximity, unlike the Philippines, where a rebellion against the Spanish was also underway. The government of Spain was eager to avoid conflict with America, but the Cuban rebels pressed their cause. Sympathy for the Cuban nationals rose on the strength of inflammatory publicity, and Spain vacillated between repression and appeasement.

While American expansionists worked for the annexation of Hawai'i, they also hovered ever closer to the Cuban problem. To drive tottering Spain out of the Caribbean Sea fit perfectly into their essentially three-part plan to control the Caribbean, to build a canal between the Atlantic and the Pacific, and to gain control of the north-central Pacific. The plight of the Cuban people made the Cuban end of the grand plan relatively simple. The Cubans were victims of colonialism. Perhaps America could help.

As Roosevelt developed his base of power in the navy, he seems to have alternately disturbed the lumbering McKinley and attracted his favorable attention. While the U.S. Senate debated the treaty to annex Hawai'i, McKinley took his pushy young appointee for a carriage ride around the White House grounds. To Roosevelt's surprise, McKinley told him that he had been correct in his outspoken denunciation of Japan's opposition to the annexation of Hawai'i. Whether America took over Hawai'i was none of Japan's business. Encouraged, Roosevelt said something must be done about Cuba.

In fact, Roosevelt was at that moment having naval staff officers devise a war plan for dealing with Japan in Hawai'i and the problem of Spain's faltering empire as well. It was the two-ocean war that kept the really committed expansionists awake at night—the ultimate challenge that was to justify the most ambitious military plans. Three days after the carriage ride, McKinley invited Roosevelt to dinner at the White House to talk further. After another three days, they were back in the carriage.

Historians have variously suggested that Theodore had to prove his warlike nature because of his asthma, and because his father had dodged the Civil War. The biographer Nathan Miller wryly remarks that many other leading figures in the imperial era were likewise warlike, with or without asthma, including Henry Cabot Lodge, John Hay, and Albert J. Beveridge. "Roosevelt differed from them only in being less circumspect in his remarks," Miller said.[1] In his autobiography Roosevelt portrayed himself as an idealistic warrior in an age of business barons. He wrote, "In the reaction after the colossal struggle of the Civil War our strongest and most capable men had thrown their whole energy into business, into money-making, into the development, and above all the exploitation and exhaustion at the most rapid rate possible, of our natural resources— mines, forests, soil, and rivers."[2] He said while many of these men had good qualities, "including the fighting virtues," others were hucksters and pawnbrokers.

While Roosevelt said he abhorred the strong bullying the weak, the truth was he was interested in a fight. He told a friend, "I should welcome any war, for I think this country needs one."[3] He told the Naval War College, "All the great masterful races have been fighting races, and the minute that a race loses the hard fighting virtues, then no matter what else it may retain, no matter how skilled in commerce and finance, in science or in art, it has lost its proud right to stand as an equal of its greatness." In *The Winning of the West*, he said the most righteous of all wars "is war with savages, though it is apt to be also the most terrible and most inhuman." Specifically he saluted the wars of Americans against Indians, Boers against Zulus, and New Zealanders against the Māori, the Polynesian cousins of the Hawaiians. "The rude fierce settler who drives the savage from the land lays all civilized mankind under his debt," wrote Roosevelt. As among white people, he particularly favored those who spoke English. The spread of English over the course of three centuries, he said, "has been not only the most striking feature in the world's history but also the event of all other most far-reaching in its effects and its importance."[4]

For a person of such mind, taking over Hawai'i seems to have been assumed. Although heavily involved in the annexation drive, he makes no mention of it in his autobiography. It was as he had revealed himself in his first long letter to Mahan—Hawai'i should be taken over immediately. He was after something bigger—a master stroke of which Hawai'i would be only a part.

On the many days that Secretary John Long rested or vacationed, Roosevelt continued to execute decisions and write orders that advanced his global strategy. "The secretary is away," he boasted, "and I am having immense fun running the Navy." One newspaper said he practically had the navy on a war footing. He became fixated on finding the right commander of the U.S. naval forces in the Far East. He chose a man who had sat at the table of the cabal, a man who had a reputation for combativeness, Admiral George Dewey. "I knew that in the event of war," Roosevelt wrote, "Dewey could be slipped like a wolfhound from a leash." Roosevelt dedicated himself to giving Dewey "that half-chance" he needed to strike. He had laid plans and issued orders that were now to take on lives of their own.

All the while he successfully juggled his relationships with John Long and President McKinley. Long's diary described a particular day in which Roosevelt sensibly reviewed several items of navy business, then went on and on in a way that apparently wore Long down. "He bores me with his plans of naval and military movements," Long wrote, "and the necessity of having some scheme of attack arranged for instant execution in case of an emergency."[5] He said

Roosevelt in the course of the next twenty-four hours would have drawn a half-dozen reporters together to talk about his ideas, spoiled twenty pages of good writing paper, then laid awake half the night.

While Roosevelt was one of the most energetic American figures, Long was—at least by this stage of his life—one of the least energetic. In a series of letters written in June, July, August, and September 1897, Roosevelt encouraged Long to forget work. Although Roosevelt was thinking about war with Japan, and although the Cuban situation was deteriorating, he wrote to the vacationing Long: "There isn't the slightest necessity of your returning. Nothing of importance has arisen." By late August he was sending snapshots of his children and passing along low-level political gossip. By then Long was at a family homestead in Maine, and Roosevelt was saying, "Yes indeed I wish I could be with you for just a little while and see the lovely hill farm to which your grandfather came over ninety years ago." Roosevelt said that thanks to Long, he saw the place "with my mind's eye." He blathered on shamelessly: "Now, stay there just exactly as long as you want to. There isn't any reason you should be here before the first of October, unless something unexpected turns up." Roosevelt bragged to Lodge that he had run the navy for seven straight weeks. With brief and widely spaced interruptions by Long, his nearly exclusive tenure probably ran to months. Roosevelt used this time to strengthen the navy, against a backdrop of increasing tension in Cuba.

Cubans rioted in Havana in early January 1898, and the U.S. *Maine* pulled into Havana Harbor on January 24 to assert an American presence. In early February a letter written by the Spanish ambassador to Washington leaked out. It described McKinley as "a bidder for the admiration of the crowd," a politician who kept open as many options as possible while staying in overall close touch with "jingoistic sentiment in America." The Spanish diplomat's description was close to what Roosevelt himself would soon say about McKinley, but it nonetheless set Roosevelt off that night at a reception. Senator Marcus Hanna was there listening to Roosevelt in the company of a French woman. Nathan Miller describes Roosevelt waving his arm ever closer to the bodice of the woman's gown as he pursued his harangue. "Finally," Miller wrote, "his elbow ripped off a silk rose and some gauze from her shoulder, and she uttered a shocked 'Mon Dieu!' Roosevelt immediately showered her with apologies in French." After the woman's dress was pinned back together, Roosevelt vowed he would live to see the flags of Spain and Britain removed from North America. Hanna inquired what Roosevelt found wrong with Britain's presence in Canada. As Hanna was driving the woman home he remarked that if McKinley had put Roosevelt in the State Department, "We'd be fighting half the world."

THE *MAINE* blew up on the night of February 15. Two hundred sixty-six of the 354 officers and men were killed. As McKinley pondered how the explosion had occurred—including the possibility that it was an accident—Roosevelt told friends that McKinley had "no more backbone than a chocolate éclair." Roosevelt was certain that the deadly explosion was an act of Spanish sabotage. He wanted war.

National attention fixed on Cuba, and attention paid to the possible annexation of Hawai'i waned. Francis Hatch descended further into his gloom.

Ten days after the explosion of the *Maine*, Long took an afternoon off. Roosevelt was in a particularly agitated state. With Long away, Roosevelt took it upon himself to redeploy ships, order ammunition, requisition coal, and reassign the most promising fighting men to ships most likely to be in battle. Most importantly, he sent Admiral Dewey orders in the western Pacific to keep his ships full of coal and otherwise get ready to fight. In the presence of Senator Henry Cabot Lodge, who had dropped by his office, Roosevelt wrote Dewey that in the event of war, "your duty will be to see that the Spanish squadron will not leave the Asiatic coast and then offensive operation in Philippine Islands." All Dewey needed, Roosevelt said, was a chance to do his work without the interference of "those not on the ground."

When Long returned to the Navy Department the next day, he was upset. "The very devil seemed to possess him yesterday afternoon," Long said. Roosevelt's wife was in extremely ill health, and Long concluded that the illness had aggravated Roosevelt's already high-strung temperament. Nonetheless, Roosevelt's orders stood, including the order to Dewey.

Varied though the performance of government may be, this was not how we think of government functioning. The president's policies were the object of constant guessing, the State Department was run by the under secretary (William Day), and all significant moves within the navy emanated from the assistant secretary. The man at the top of this government professed to love peace, but followed the advocates of war. He wanted only peaceful expansion of American trade, but took the imperialists into his carriage.

In the obfuscation of Hawai'i's story, the McKinley Administration is an essential source of confusion. Who *was* McKinley, and what was his Administration about? McKinley represented a Republican coalition of two elements. One was made up of business interests that nursed vaguely expansionist ideas. The second was a small elite of aggressive imperialists whose goal was to transform America into a great power. McKinley had known war and did not want it. Roosevelt knew nothing about war firsthand, but was entranced by it. McKinley was most at home with the National Association of Manufacturers— a venue that seemed to transform him into a political master. Roosevelt was at home addressing the Naval War College. Where McKinley was a broker of business interests, Roosevelt scorned the hum-drum of business and looked for a higher calling in the code of the warrior.

WHILE THE CAUSE OF THE ANNEXATIONISTS SEEMED BLEAK, Lorrin Thurston saw a situation in which much could change in a short period of time. He dropped by Roosevelt's office and proposed that the U.S. navy stockpile coal in Honolulu to support its operations between the West Coast of America and the Western Pacific. It was the idea of the map that he and Roosevelt had drawn to illustrate the strategic value of Hawai'i, except now the idea was to be put into action. Roosevelt said that Thurston had just the right idea, and the American consul would go to work on it right away.

The United States consul general asked the Republic's Executive Council for more space to store coal. The Republic set aside four vacant lots, which eventually were piled eight feet high with coal. Hatch wrote home stressing the need for confidentiality on the coal storage project, to avoid a sudden rise in coal prices. Mum was the word. "There seems to be a drift of sentiment our way," Hatch wrote.

Should the Republic be neutral, fearing an attack by the Spanish? Or should it go all out to score points with America? The issue was actively debated in Honolulu. Harold Sewall, the American minister, said the oligarchy hoped the United States would provide protection for defenseless Hawai'i, and Hatch reported that McKinley was appreciative. The partnership with the U.S. was maintained.

McKinley agonized a long while over whether to go to war. On March 20, nearly five weeks after the *Maine* disaster, a naval board of inquiry said the explosion probably was caused by an underwater mine, but could cite no evidence. The clock was ticking, and the mood of the public was becoming more belligerent. In 1976, Admiral Hyman Rickover was to review the *Maine* tragedy and say the explosion likely resulted from internal combustion in the boiler room. It was the most logical conclusion, not only from the physical evidence (the hull bowed out, not in) but also because Spain did not want to provoke America. Logic notwithstanding, public opinion increasingly demanded a war.

The most powerful newspaper publishers of the day, William Hearst foremost, clamored for war. Hearst sent the artist Frederic Remington to Cuba to illustrate the conflict between Spanish overlords and Cuban insurgents. Remington wired Hearst that he did not think there would be a war. Could he come home? Hearst's reply survived in journalism schools: "You furnish the pictures and I'll furnish the war." Hearst's *New York Journal* ran what it purported to be a scientific study proving the blast was the "WORK OF THE ENEMY."

Roosevelt was furious with the president's continued indecision. McKinley, he said privately, was a white-faced cur. At the annual Gridiron Dinner of the National Press Club, the club president noted the presence of both Senator Marcus Hanna and Theodore Roosevelt. He asked Hanna if there would be a war. Hanna responded with a brief antiwar speech. The emcee then turned to Roosevelt. Normally in such a situation, an assistant secretary would have deferred to a U.S. senator, particularly one who had managed the president's campaign, but Roosevelt was full of his cause. He glared at Hanna and said, "We will have this war for the freedom of Cuba, Senator Hanna, in spite of the timidity of the commercial interests."

President McKinley presents Dewey as a hero.

Admiral George Dewey

The Battle of Manila, which lasted a morning, made Hawai'i a coaling station.

American troops arrived by the thousands in Honolulu en route to the Philippines.

American troops were entertained with a lūʻau in Honolulu.

The Dole government seemed, at last, secure.

Americans fought a brief war in Cuba and a prolonged war in the Philippines.

McKinley finally could forestall the seduction of war no longer. He apparently became convinced that the United States was going to war, with or without him, and "he preferred to retain his credibility as a leader."[6] His particular definition of honesty would not allow him to say the Spanish had sunk the *Maine*, but rather that its sinking reflected a lack of security "that is intolerable."

On April 11, McKinley asked Congress to pass a declaration of war. On April 19, at three o'clock in the morning, the declaration passed. Northerners and Southerners joined together in singing the "Battle Hymn of the Republic," which the white militia had sung in Honolulu in 1893, on the first night it had occupied Ali'iolani Hale. In some large and shadowy way, all of this had to do with returning to America's course of expansionism before it was disrupted by the Civil War, and now the war was a mere ghost.

ONE OF THE ODDITIES of the Spanish-American War was that most Americans thought it was about Cuba, but the fighting began in the Philippines. Between the two, it was the Philippine theater of the war that redirected the history of Hawai'i, to say nothing of American and world history. As John Dobson describes in his foreign policy study, *Reticent Expansionism*, the only effective military plan for the army and navy in both the Pacific Ocean and the Caribbean Sea was the navy's plan to attack the Spanish fleet in Manila Bay. Authorship of the plan is credited to a Lieutenant William Kimball. It was embraced and given life by Theodore Roosevelt, who maneuvered Dewey's assignment to the Far East and wrote his orders. Dobson, it should be noted, argues that Roosevelt's influence on events is generally overrated. He points out that Long and McKinley wrote confirming orders to attack the Spanish before Dewey was forced out of Hong Kong Harbor by the British overlords, who were concerned with maintaining neutrality.

It is a short way from Hong Kong to Manila. On May 1, 1898, Dewey maneuvered the Asiatic fleet past Corregidor and into Manila Bay. At dawn the American sailors shouted "Remember the *Maine!*" They fired. Where once Spain had been the greatest naval force in the Pacific, by noon eleven of its twelve ships had gone down. The twelfth surrendered.

Dewey sent an encoded message to Washington, but a reporter for the *New York Herald* scooped Dewey's report by wiring his story into his city room at three a.m. The *Herald* nonetheless failed to rob Roosevelt of his final moment of drama as assistant secretary of the navy. He emerged from the navy decoding room with the official word, surrounded by reporters. Not one American had died in the battle. Everyone cheered.

When he had ridden in McKinley's carriage, Roosevelt had announced that if the war came, he would resign his desk job, go to the field, and fight with the men. McKinley asked how his wife would feel, perhaps alluding to the fact that Mrs. Roosevelt recently had undergone surgery and nearly died. Roosevelt said this was a case where neither she nor Henry Cabot Lodge would be consulted. She was recovering and faithfully supported his plan to leave her with their six children. Both President McKinley and John Long asked him to stay in Washington, but Roosevelt had made up his mind. Another of his acquaintances said, "I really think he is going mad."[7] Long said Roosevelt was acting like a fool, but then had his second thoughts. "How absurd all this will sound," he wrote, "if, by some turn of fortune, he should accomplish some great thing and strike a very high mark."

In the chain of command in his new army unit, Roosevelt deferred to the Indian-fighting experience of the White House doctor, Leonard Wood. He served as the second in command in one of the twenty-six regiments mobilized to fight the Spanish in Cuba, but it nonetheless became known as Roosevelt's regiment—a mixture of Ivy League blue-bloods, cowboys and gunslingers, many of whom Roosevelt knew personally. They were men, he was to write, with whom he had ridden the long circle. They were indeed to become known as Rough Riders, and Roosevelt was to fight his way with them up San Juan Hill.

THE UNITED STATES HAD NO SPECIFIC PLAN for what to do in the wake of Dewey's attack. Had America liberated, or had it captured, the Philippine Islands? Reasoning that Dewey would need support, the War Department on May 4 issued a call for troops to organize on the West Coast. The army's commander asked McKinley whether he wanted the U.S. army to take over Manila, or should it take over all of the Philippines? McKinley said he didn't know. Later McKinley reflected, "If old Dewey had just sailed away when he smashed that Spanish fleet, what a lot of trouble he would have saved us."

A brief clip of moving film[8] shot by a crew of Thomas Edison survives, showing American troops loading into their ships in San Francisco. From bow to stern, the eager soldiers crowd the deck, gaily waving as they depart the shore. Ladies in gowns, in the company of gentlemen wearing three-piece suits and bowler hats, line the dock. All cheer in great excitement. At this point, the men on the ship, the citizens ashore, and those who had organized and dispatched the army, could all ponder what Lorrin Thurston and Theodore Roosevelt repeatedly had been saying. The Hawaiian Islands lay directly on the route from North America to the Philippine Islands. With its supplies of food, water, and coal, Hawai'i was the only place to replenish a troop ship within several thousand miles.

"Millions of Americans, for the first time, study the maps of the Pacific Ocean, and know something about its geography," the *Advertiser* said. The *New York Herald* reported that as a result of the need to support Dewey and his men in the Philippines, "the question of annexing Hawai'i forced itself to the front."[9]

Roosevelt's closest friend, Henry Cabot Lodge of Massachusetts, along with Senator William Frye of Maine, went to the Navy Department the day after the battle of Manila to press for annexation of Hawai'i. "We never needed it as much as we need it today," Lodge said. He dwelled on the image of "our gallant Asiatic squadron" fighting in a distant sea, without a ready line of supply and communication, possibly lacking coal for its ships, and with "all foreign ports" closed to it. What it needed, Lodge said, was logistical support from an American Hawai'i. Lodge said reasonable people all could agree on immediately accepting "the generous and thoroughly business-like proposition of the Hawaiian government." John Long, who had been writing assurances to his niece, Julia Castle, in Honolulu, said he regretted the country's failure to annex Hawai'i several years earlier.[10]

On May 3, a year to the day after Roosevelt wrote Mahan his outline of the imperial plan, Francis Hatch huddled with the former secretary of state, John Foster, in Foster's home to discuss a mobilization of the annexation forces. The weather was stormy, but Foster rode off to the Senate, where he met with some of the key backers of the annexation scheme. With Senator John T. Morgan in tow, Foster next went to see McKinley "and went over the whole situation with him."[11]

Hatch's letter to Henry Cooper gives important details of the inner workings of this final drive, illustrating the degree of coordination and cohesion that went into the effort. Hatch says that Foster was "right in the front rank," then generalizes that the friends of annexation had set in motion the machinery of a joint resolution originating in the House of Representatives. The day after Hatch's meeting with Foster, Representative Francis Newlands of Nevada, chair of the House Foreign Relations Committee, introduced the joint resolution of annexation.

William Day, McKinley's man from Ohio who first had served as assistant secretary of state, then displaced John Sherman as secretary, also was heavily involved. "He (Day) is fully alive to the fact that this is the moment for a supreme effort," Hatch wrote. "It will be made … " News arrived in Washington on May 7 of Dewey's victory in Manila, and Hatch met with Day on May 10. Regarding the influence of Day, which essentially equated with the influence of the president, Hatch wrote, "The action of the Committee on Foreign Affairs in the House follows so closely upon his [Day's] assurance to me, that there can be no doubt about the influence which set the committee in motion." Hatch is explicit about the catalyzing impact of the United States' involvement in the Philippines. It was "bringing home to the minds of many, who have hitherto been doubtful, the necessity of closing up the annexation business at once."

In a period of several days, the president, his new secretary of state (Day), James Blaine's successor as secretary of state (Foster), John Morgan, and various annexationist senators, as well as Hatch, were all involved in coalescing behind the strategy of the joint resolution. In the process, the tradition of a Senate treaty, requiring a two-thirds vote of the upper house, was being discarded, and with it the fiction of an independent nation of Hawai'i turning itself over to the American nation by means of an international treaty. Through Newlands, the American government was moving to acquire Hawai'i by a majority vote of both houses of Congress. In their meeting at

Canton, Ohio, before the inauguration, McKinley had asked Henry Cooper, if a two-thirds vote in the Senate were not forthcoming, would a joint resolution do? Yes, Cooper had said.

Francis Newlands said he believed that annexation of the Hawaiian archipelago would define the "scientific boundaries" of the United States. On May 10, the day of Hatch's meeting with Day, Newlands convened a remarkable hearing to elicit the opinion of John Schofield, who had toured the Islands in civilian clothes twenty-six years earlier, studying the coastlines, waterways, bays, and harbors of Hawai'i. Pearl Harbor, Schofield said, was perhaps the best natural harbor in the world for the purposes of a modern navy.[12] It was large enough to anchor a fleet of ships out of the range of an enemy ship's gunfire. The mouth of the harbor was small and easily defended, and it lent itself to being developed for coaling, maintenance, and repairs.

Schofield embraced the expedition to the Philippines as a good example of Pearl Harbor's utility. The fleet logically should stop in Hawai'i and take on coal and supplies. Otherwise the navy would have to fill the ships with fuel and cargo and leave troops sitting on the dock.

Schofield said other world powers would jump at the chance to acquire Pearl Harbor, but they recognized "our pre-emption." His next sentence should be preserved as a study in the interrelationship of missionary and military interests in the process of colonization: "We got our pre-emption title to those islands through the volunteer action of our American missionaries, who went there and civilized and Christianized those people and established a Government that has no parallel in the history of the world considering its age, and we made a pre-emption which nobody in the world thinks of disputing provided we perfect our title."

Schofield contended that if Spain were stronger, it would take Hawai'i and use it as a base for attacking the United States, while Japan was an ever-present menace. Schofield resurrected the contention that the Japanese field workers were really soldiers, a point that no one in the hearing questioned. "In a very few years," Schofield said, "Japan can get physical and political control of the islands."

Representative Champ Clark of Missouri announced, "I think it is proper for us to take anything we want anywhere on the face of the earth." However, he wanted to know why America now had to have Hawai'i after getting along without it for over a hundred years.

"We have gotten into a foreign war," Schofield replied.

"We have been in foreign wars before," Clark said.

"Not to amount to anything," Schofield said.

Newlands asked whether America would be better off to annex Hawai'i or create a military protectorate through control of Pearl Harbor. Schofield said annexation was essential because much of the population surrounding Pearl Harbor was Japanese. The people of Hawai'i needed to be brought into the American system and made "part of the reserve militia," so troops would not have to be sent from California to defend Hawai'i.

John Williams of Mississippi wanted to know if Hawai'i could be taken without giving it congressional representation. "Yes," Schofield replied, displaying a fearless disregard for the purely political nature of the question. "Don't you do that here in the District of Columbia now?" The time had come for America to be a great power, he said, and to do so required control of Hawai'i.

Schofield's testimony was echoed by a prestigious navy witness, the Admiral John J. Walker, who had walked the grounds of 'Iolani Palace in his fatigue uniform on the day the Republic of Hawaii was proclaimed. Walker said that so far as he knew, people in Hawai'i were not concerned with being represented in the government, but were willing to be governed by the United States.

The cheapest way to protect the West Coast, Walker said, was to fortify Hawai'i, which would cost less money than a single battleship. It was a day of certitude. Opinions arose to meet almost every contingency, and there were precious few questions left, but John Williams of Mississippi did manage to ask whether, the saving of money notwithstanding, "If we owned Hawai'i would not we bring ourselves nearer the point of attack instead of removing ourselves farther from one?"

IN MARCH, THE ANNEXATIONISTS in Hawai'i were still debating whether Sanford Dole had done the right thing by telling a newspaper reporter that if annexation failed, the Republic would continue on its way. The idea of the nation of Hawai'i being reduced to a county of the state of

California came back around. The *Pacific Commercial Advertiser* reported from Washington that to quiet the issue of representation, advocates of Hawai'i were urging just such a solution to "disarm the objections of those who foresee statehood in a short time."[13]

For the oligarchy, news of the Spanish-American War arrived like the tinkling of a distant wind chime, then transformed quickly into the mad ringing of every available bell. The government struggled seriously, if briefly, with the question of what the Spanish navy might do when Spain discovered that Hawai'i was less than properly neutral. News of the battle of Manila Harbor turned the discussion toward the delicious thought that if America used Hawai'i to support Dewey, it would be violating international laws of neutrality unless it annexed Hawai'i.

The *Advertiser* asked, how much beer and how many bananas would ten thousand troops require in a day? How much would they spend on curios? When news came that three ships would arrive shortly for coal and supplies, the Fourth of July committee moved its agenda forward to organize a welcome for the troops. The *Advertiser* printed on its front page the names of American businesses so patriotic as to decorate in red, white, and blue.

A rally was held at the local militia's drill shed that turned into a communal bath of American jingoism. The evils of Spain and the wrongs done the Cubans were recited. Harold Sewall said Dewey's fleet had saved Hawai'i from the Spanish, who otherwise would have ravaged the Islands and then attacked the West Coast. America had been infinitely patient, but now was engaged "in this holy war." It was apparent, Sewall said, that all present "entertained thoughts of the grand fatherland beyond the sea."

W.O. Smith, who had managed the legal details of the Republic, described the big picture. "War has marked the great steps of human progress," he said. "It seems that this contest will establish and fix higher principles." W.A. Kinney, who had prosecuted the queen for misprision of treason, said that Native Hawaiians had failed to understand that Americans wanted them to be Americans. "There should be Hawaiians in the American navy," Kinney said, "where they will give a good account of themselves." The only argument was over how many could serve efficiently on the welcoming committee. To answer the clamor, Smith agreed to not sleep until he had appointed a "Committee of 100."

The forms and words of Hawaiian culture were adopted. The American women decided on a "hookupu," which is gift-giving, often with profoundly social and spiritual connotations. What the troops should be given, they decided, was a Hawaiian lei, as well as a Hawaiian lūʻau. On May 19, the British-born A.S. Cleghorn, father of Liliʻuokalani's heir apparent, Princess Kaʻiulani, said that he and the princess would open their estate in Waikīkī to the American troops.

From Washington, Ambassador Francis Hatch wrote,[14] "Let there be no halfway measures in the welcome offered." He said neutrality should not be discussed because events had progressed far beyond that point. "The reports of the tender of the Islands for war purposes have made a great impression on the public mind and have done great good," Hatch wrote.

At four p.m. on the first day of June 1898, the American fleet was sighted off the eastern shore of Oʻahu. The Committee of 100, the band, and representatives of the militia, raced in a steamer toward Diamond Head to give a warm greeting of aloha. When the three American ships docked in Honolulu Harbor, a photographer for the *White Anglo-Saxon Protestant Quarterly* of San Francisco recorded the scene. Hundreds of troops—twenty-five hundred in all—dangled from the decks, smiling and gawking at the well-dressed crowd below. The *Advertiser* put out a "Boys in Blue" edition, and the leis and lūʻau, beer and bananas, rolled out.

The American troops marched in review before Sanford Dole at ʻIolani Palace. Dole was photographed surrounded on every side by dozens of American soldiers. It was as if the white-bearded symbol of the Provisional Government was at last secure. The islands first settled by the Polynesian voyagers, where Kamehameha had fought with the forces of Kahekili, and where his widow Kaʻahumanu had kidnapped Kaumualiʻi—had become a coaling station.

In what was to become the most obscure of all U.S. wars, even more obscure than the Spanish-American War, four thousand American troops were to die in the Philippines. Armed with the new guns that the Republic of Hawaii had researched, the American troops were to kill over seventy thousand Filipino nationalists, who initially believed the Americans had come to aid them in their struggle for liberation.

BY THE TIME OF THE FINAL DEBATE over annexation, much of the opposition had been beaten down. Faceless businessmen and editors and ministers had swung behind annexation—people whose names we no longer recognize, such as Albert Beveridge of Indiana, who announced, "We are a conquering race." The American flag, along with American law, order, and civilization, would be planted "on shores hitherto bloody and benighted, but by those agencies of God henceforth to be made beautiful and bright."[15]

In opposition, certain congressmen tried to remind annexationists that they were in the grip of war fever. A congressman from Louisiana said that in response to Spanish brutality in Cuba, America had set out on a "chivalric war of humanity," but had been infected with "the jingo bacillus." A representative from Arkansas said the annexationists had gotten war into their blood, "and they are about to do a foolish thing." He said America might easily annex Hawai'i and take other islands as well, but, like the Republic of Rome, it would destroy the American Republic in the process.

In an extraordinary flight of rhetoric for such a quiet man, McKinley said, "We need Hawai'i just as much and a good deal more than we did California. It is manifest destiny." In private conversation with the prominent Senator Hoar of Vermont, McKinley ran out his line that America had to act quickly to prevent a Japanese takeover. "We cannot let the islands go to Japan," McKinley told Hoar. "Japan has her eye on them. Her people are crowding in there." To this he added an explicit endorsement of the conspiracy theory: "I am satisfied they do not go there voluntarily, as ordinary immigrants, but that Japan is pressing them in there, in order to get possession before anybody can interfere."[16] Hoar, who had welcomed the Hawaiian delegation into his home on a snowy night the previous February, believed his commander in chief. He changed his position from no to aye. The chairman of the Senate Committee of Foreign Affairs said of the Japanese in Hawai'i, "If they voted, (Hawai'i) would be converted into a Japanese Commonwealth immediately."

The debate reflected the distortion of fact that occurs when people commit themselves to obvious contradictions. It was only from the viewpoint of the grand strategy of the deceased James G. Blaine, and the strategy of America's future and most youthful president, Theodore Roosevelt, that the seemingly disconnected pieces made sense. America was in the final throws of debating the annexation of Hawai'i, and American troops were fighting the Spanish in Cuba. The navy was expanding rapidly, and war games had been developed for America to fight in both the Atlantic and Pacific simultaneously. Only the Panama Canal remained to be located, funded, and built.

Yet the perception of the inevitability of annexation is hindsight. In the House, Speaker Thomas Reed remained a highly formidable obstacle. Unless a way was found to defeat Reed, then the entire business of the Republic of Hawaii was in danger of coming undone. In his May 13 letter, Francis Hatch said that while things were suddenly starting to move, annexation was anything but a foregone conclusion. He said up to that time the votes simply had been lacking, and the opposition was still immensely powerful.

Hatch said reports in the Honolulu press of a sure thing were merely "pleasant reading," and that a correspondent from Guam probably could do better for accuracy. By June 9, Hatch wrote that the session was drawing to a close, and it was impossible to say what would happen. "Mr. Reed's opposition to us becomes more and more pronounced, more bitter, more aggressive, and more determined," Hatch wrote.[17] All their work was in danger. "The Sugar Trust people are moving heaven and earth to get an adjournment." March of 1899 would be a short session, and the war would be over. "There will be," Hatch wrote, "the slimest [sic] chance to be heard. Thus the situation we feared ... is almost upon us ... "

From the oligarchy's point of view, then, its entire strategy was about to come unraveled, just at the point when Speaker Reed capitulated. Powerful though he was, Reed could not withstand the pressure. On June 12, three days after his bleak assessment, Hatch wrote, "The Speaker has been routed." In the process of abandoning their opposition, longtime skeptics said that to vote against the annexation of Hawai'i had become like voting against a war resolution while America was under attack.

During this time, Hatch and the Republic, the U.S. State Department, and the government of Japan continued to negotiate Japan's demand for an indemnity to acknowledge the suffering caused to the Japanese immigrants who had been held in Honolulu, then returned to Japan. A representative of the State Department told Hatch to settle the claim, that the Japanese government was trying to accommodate the desires of the United States while avoiding an appearance that would inflame the Japanese public. Hatch squirmed. He was the architect of "the record," and he was determined to not let go of the illusion of conflict with Japan until it was of no conceivable use. While awaiting the Senate vote, he told Cooper to stall the issue in Honolulu, which still was nominally the scene of the exchange between Japan and Hawai'i. At the same time, Cooper was to avoid the appearance of avoiding a reasonable settlement. "We certainly do not want to give the impression that we are simply trying to unload our troubles on the U.S.," Hatch said.

Briefly, the victory in the House inflated Henry Cabot Lodge's hope to round up a genuine two-thirds vote in the Senate for the Treaty of Annexation, reflecting a concern for both the dignity and constitutionality of the method of annexation. After Lodge and the others assessed the opposition, the treaty, which had been awaiting a vote for five and a half years, was discarded for good.

When the Senate proponents moved for passage of the House resolution, the opposition responded with a filibuster. The session was supposed to be over soon, and they hoped to talk the resolution to its death. Opponents were driven by a wide range of reasons, but foremost was their perception that the rights of the native citizens were being trampled upon, and that an entire nation of people was to be placed under the American system of governance without their consent. Senators also complained that their traditional responsibility under the constitution for confirming treaties had been disregarded. The fury of the opposition kept Congress in session long after it was to have adjourned. The determination of the proponents also kept the session going, since the opposition gladly would have agreed to adjourn without voting—all of this in the midst of the Spanish-American War.

The filibuster went on for seventeen days. The length of the filibuster, the profound division in the Senate, and the expansionists' giving up on gaining a two-thirds majority—all reflected the American nation faltering as it approached the moment of acquiring empire abroad.

The last day of the filibuster was July 6, 1898. Augustus O. Bacon of Georgia again offered his proposal that annexation be approved provided a majority of voters in Hawai'i agreed. His proposed amendment was voted down by twenty to forty-two, with twenty-seven senators abstaining. Richard F. Pettigrew of South Dakota, who had failed to find a single Hawaiian in Hawai'i who favored annexation, proposed an amendment providing that all males born or naturalized in Hawai'i be given the right to vote. His proposal got only sixteen aye votes. The Senate now was on record as opposing any form of referendum involving the traditional citizenry of Hawai'i, affirming in a circuitous way Albert Willis's description of the Republic as "a country without a citizenship."

After the proposed amendments were defeated, the vote at last came up on the main motion. Lorrin Thurston sat in the gallery watching. Forty-two senators voted aye and twenty-one voted nay. Twenty-six did not vote. Of those who voted, exactly two-thirds voted yes, but nearly a third of the entire Senate ducked out of voting. As a result, America's annexation of the previously sovereign nation of Hawai'i rested on the votes of fewer than half the members of the United States Senate. The next day William McKinley, in bold script, wrote "Approved," along with his signature. The date was July 7, 1898.

WHEN MCKINLEY FIRST HEARD of Dewey's victory, he turned to his globe, searching for the vast archipelago of the Philippine Islands. He said he could not have guessed their location within two thousand miles. It was the type of statement that caused the American journalist Stanley Karnow to write, "Unable to lead, he was fated to follow." Ernest May of Harvard wrote that so far as he could tell, McKinley never wanted the war.

McKinley was inclined to say little for the sake of history, while Theodore Roosevelt was inclined to tell all. The two men—one so drab, one so colorful—left future generations wondering whether America had ever really wanted to become a colonial power, or whether Roosevelt and his cohorts had merely manipulated the development of an obscure, imperial war. The storied Theodore is useful because he is the only person whose name is widely recognized from the period. But the questions remains, was Hawai'i's fate sealed by a conscious American design, or did the door of history blow shut on the nation of Hawai'i as the result of a passing storm?

Howard Beale, in his analysis of America's rise to world power, said Roosevelt had used John Long's absences "to insure our grabbing the Philippines without a decision to do so by either Congress or the President, or at least of all the people." In this view, history resulted not from economic forces or democratic decisions but from "the grasping of chance authority by a man with daring and a program."[18] Nathan Miller quoted this passage approvingly. Stanley Karnow, on the other hand, quotes a note unearthed after McKinley's death in which McKinley wrote, "We must keep all we can get."

While the stories of Hawai'i and the Philippines are related by expansionism and imperialism, the conclusion about Hawai'i must be that a majority of Americans supported annexation, even while ignoring the less attractive details. Roosevelt—supported by such enormously influential figures as Lodge and Mahan—unswervingly contended that annexation could never happen soon enough. In contrast, McKinley trundled along methodically, but his communication with the oligarchy reflects that he moved in only one direction—toward annexation.

McKinley, no less than Roosevelt, was a creature of America's drive to expand. This drive had gone on in one form or another from the beginning of the century. It had been stopped by the Civil War, then picked up again in the last quarter of the century in the context of global imperialism.

The day annexation passed Congress, Senator John Morgan wrote a note to Francis Hatch, addressing him as "My dear young American." He said as an American expatriate transplanted to Hawai'i, Hatch had answered the question "that so puzzled the learned Jews. 'Can a man a second time enter his mother's womb and be born again' ... A citizen by birth and by adoption you enjoy a double right to our affectionate welcome, which I extend to you ... not without a sigh that Hawaii ceases to be an autonomous government."[19]

Word of annexation arrived in Hawai'i on July 13, 1898. The annexationists all congratulated one another, and the American minister, Harold Sewall, became a special focus of attention. In certain circles there was a brief but unsuccessful boom for him to be named governor. "Remember Maine," his backers said. Behind the scenes, at the instruction of the American government, Sewall pressured the oligarchy into settling Japan's claim for an indemnity. To resolve the issue arising from the Republic of Hawaii turning back its citizens, Japan agreed to a payment of $75,000. The oligarchy regarded the settlement as a bitter pill, but as a feature of the annexation agreement it turned its debts over to the U.S. government. Surely someone of W.O. Smith's mind must have paused to laugh.

THE QUEEN RETURNED to Hawai'i on August 1. Hundreds of Hawaiians poured down to the waterfront to greet her returning steamer, even though it was past midnight. Prince Kūhiō escorted her down the gangplank as the queen looked out onto the wharf teeming with Hawaiian faces. "Aloha," she said. A woman in the crowd began to chant. At Washington Place, her subjects brought her presents and bowed before her in a stream that ran through the following day and night. The Ke Aloha 'Āina newspaper, now published by Emma Nāwahī, said, "We are your aloha 'āina subjects (maka'āinana). From the time you left until today, we have kept an unshakable resolve, and sealed inside each of our hearts is aloha for the land and for our kupuna whose flesh has been wounded."[20] Photographs were taken that day in which she is perfectly flanked on all sides by admirers. While her subjects stand, she is seated, as if on a throne, and she is forever the queen.

On the day of the annexation ceremony, the palace was ringed with American troops.

CHAPTER TWENTY-ONE

Raising Old Glory

The ceremony in which the government of the Republic turned the Hawaiian Islands over to the United States was arranged to occur on August 12. The organizers of the ceremony had no way of knowing that on the same day the preliminary peace treaty would be signed by Spain and America, putting an end to the event that had provided the final rationale for annexation. As to the ceremony itself, the familiar photographic view of the scene is a relative closeup of the dais in front of 'Iolani Palace. The bunting and flags are visible, and Sanford Dole is taking an oath.

In a file in the National Archives of America, placed there by a military family, is a wider view. It shows the crowd surrounded on all sides by United States troops, standing shoulder to shoulder and several rows deep. The American troops stretch down the driveway of the palace nearly to the adjoining street.

Minister Sewall had suggested that Lili'uokalani, Kapi'olani, Ka'iulani, David Kawananakoa, and Jonah Kūhiō all be invited. He referred to each by their titles except Lili'uokalani, whom he referred to as the "Ex Queen." Prior to the ceremony, the patriotic societies published directives urging Hawaiians to boycott the ceremony. None of the Hawaiian leadership attended, nor did any but a few of the Hawaiian people. Dole, in his capacity as president of the Republic, yielded the sovereignty and property of the government of the Hawaiian Islands to Sewall, as the representative of the United States. Dole said he did so "in the interest of the Hawaiian body politic." Dole and Sewall stood face to face as Sewall administered the oath of office. If there was a division between those who had emanated from Maine, it was between these two—Dole, whose origins were upriver on the Kennebec, and Sewall, who was from downriver. Dole was passing from president to territorial governor, while Sewall unleashed an oration designed to position himself for Dole's job at a future date.

Sewall said the leaders of Hawai'i could not rest, but rather had to maintain freedom in the spirit they had sought it, "the spirit of fraternity and equality." He ran on, recalling at length the contribution of Hawai'i to the war in the Philippines. He also exhorted the *haole* to walk forward "hand in hand" with those who without faltering had loved their nation. While U.S. House Speaker Thomas Reed had said, "Empire can wait," Sewall now said, "Empire may wait indeed, but no hand save His who holds in the hollow of His hand the fate of nations can stay that destiny." In his convoluted way, Sewall had announced that Hawai'i was America's first step into an overseas empire, although a campaign of denial on that score was to begin immediately.

Other than Sewall's attempt at conciliatory words, it was a day for getting back. Sanford Dole gave the white soldiers of the Republic of Hawaii the American flag that five years earlier had been carried ashore by troops from the S.S. *Boston*. When the Hawaiian flag was lowered, the band played "Hawai'i Pono'ī," the national anthem composed by Kalākaua. It was said that the Hawaiian national anthem was played "for the last time."

The ceremony was timed for the American flag to be raised over 'Iolani Palace at high noon. The sailor chosen to hoist the Stars and Stripes was thought to be named Winters. Normally the chief quartermaster of the ship, the man in charge of flags and signals, would have done the honors, but his name was Czarnicke, and Czarnicke had been passed over in favor of someone with a truly American-sounding name. The American flag hoisted by Winters hit the top of the pole close to perfectly, at fifteen seconds past high noon. Only much later did Winters confide that his real name was not American, but Irish—Murphy. As a young man he had enlisted, gotten into some trouble, deserted, and enlisted a second time under an assumed name.

IN THE AFTERMATH OF 1898, America's overseas possessions reached across the Pacific to include not only Hawai'i, but American Sāmoa, Guam, the Marianas Islands, and the Philippines, as well as Puerto Rico and Guantanamo, Cuba, in the Caribbean. The Pearl River lagoon naturally came to be the headquarters of the United States navy in the Pacific, which it is to this day.

When Theodore Roosevelt returned from the Spanish-American War, he was elected governor of New York in the 1898 election. In 1900, he was elected vice president on the Republican ticket, succeeding to the presidency when McKinley was assassinated in 1901. Sounding the theme for a vast literature of denial, Roosevelt said, "The simple truth is that there is nothing even remotely resembling 'imperialism' or 'militarism' involved in the present development of that policy of expansion which has been part of the history of America from the day when she became a nation."

After a national debate over the Philippines, the phrase "American imperialism" ceased to be used as matter-of-fact description and became, instead, the property of academicians and devotees of the political left. Similarly, the tenets of Social Darwinism faded from conscious understanding. Although Honolulu came to have both a McKinley and a Roosevelt high school, and the U.S. army had its Schofield Barracks, the historical significance of the names was essentially lost.

Nonetheless the agenda of Blaine and Roosevelt moved forward unerringly. Following on the military successes of 1898, legislation was introduced in Congress in 1902 to build a canal across Panama between the Atlantic and Pacific. It was completed in 1914.

In 1903, Roosevelt apportioned five minutes of his presidential schedule to meeting Lili'uokalani of Hawai'i for the first and only time. She asked for the return of the Crown Lands of Hawai'i, which had been taken over by the American government. He declined.

In the course of Roosevelt's career, he developed second thoughts about America's hold on the Philippines, wondering if it might help embroil America in a war with Japan.

UNDER THE GOVERNMENT of the Territory of Hawaii, the elite represented by the Dole government took up where it had left off in

In the widely publicized view, Dole takes the oath of office from Harold Sewall.

In the Philippine-American War, Hawai'i became a staging area for the American army.

Harold Sewall   *Theodore Roosevelt*

When the queen returned, Ke Aloha 'Āina said, "...we have kept an unshakable resolve, and sealed inside each of our hearts is aloha for the land and for the kupuna whose flesh has been wounded."

the Republic. A small oligarchy held the political framework of the Territory in place through its relationships with the United States navy and the federal government (which appointed the Territory's governors), while running the sugar-based economy of Hawai'i through interlocking, plantation-based corporations. These are the corporations that became known as the Big Five.

Lorrin Thurston set the tone for Hawai'i's written history through his massive *Memoir of the Hawaiian Revolution.* In an interpretation that is still widely repeated today, he argued that the queen brought her troubles on herself. As a result, "she was forced to the wall; and the Monarchy went down to irretrievable ruin." He said if she had been as pliable as her brother, the monarchy might have survived. Thurston bought the *Pacific Commercial Advertiser,* which had quoted him so faithfully, and renamed it *The Honolulu Advertiser.* He died in 1931 at age seventy-three.

By 1925, the profession of Sanford Dole was identified in a Who's Who publication as "The Grand Old Man of Hawaii." Dole nurtured his relationship with the family of his adoptive *hānai* Hawaiian daughter, Lizzie Low, to whom he had retreated in the autumn of the year of the overthrow. In the fragility of old age, he was cared for by Hawaiians. He died in 1926 at eighty-two.

Harold Sewall, as the last minister to Hawai'i, filed an inventory of American acquisitions that included 200,000 rounds of ammunition from the arsenal of the Republic, in addition to nearly half the land. His ambition to succeed Dole as territorial governor was thwarted, and he returned to Bath, Maine. An understanding of the role of the Kennebec River community was lost in Hawai'i, even in its simplest, most essential features. James Blaine died a few days after the overthrow, without ever knowing what had happened. John Stevens died two years later.

ON THE DAY THAT NEWS of annexation reached Hawai'i, the Executive Council of the Republic approved the importation of 3,800 Japanese workers, and another 1,875 the next day. Their action—and the obvious pent-up demand for workers that it entailed—proved the utter phoniness of the oligarchy's claim that the migration was driven by a Japanese plot to mount a peaceful invasion.

OF THE TERRITORIES acquired in 1898, Hawai'i started out as the most "Americanized." For most people, the fiction of the Republic of Hawaii successfully obscured the nature of the conquest, as it does to this day. The act of annexation became something that just happened.

Paradoxically, Hawai'i had the strongest surviving indigenous tradition. Among America's new colonies, only the native nation of Hawai'i had established itself as a Western-style nation of long standing. On August 3, nine days before the annexation ceremony, the leaders of the political societies of the Hawaiian nation protested yet again. Already they had protested the overthrow, the first annexation treaty, the formation of the Republic, the martial-law trials, the second annexation treaty, its adoption in Hawai'i, and the adoption of the joint resolution in Washington, D.C. Now they protested the act of annexation, and in particular they protested the fact that it was occurring against their will. Following their usual form, their protest was written in Hawaiian and then in English.

After a recitation of some of the more unsavory aspects of the preceding five years, the petition said: "No ka mea: Ua hoike maopopo ae ke Kuahaua o ke Kuokoa Amerika ua loaa i na Aupuni ko lakou mau mana pono mai ka ae aku o na poe e hoomaluia ana ... " It was a "whereas" clause, citing the belief expressed in the American Declaration of Independence that governments "derive their just powers from the consent of the governed." Therefore, they went on, they protested annexation occurring without the consent of the people of Hawai'i. The protest was signed by James K. Kaulia, president of Hui Aloha 'Āina; Mrs. Kuaihelani Campbell, *peresidena* as even the English version said, of Hui Aloha 'Āina o Nā Wāhine, the women; David Kalauokalani, Hui Kālai'āina; Enoch Johnson, Aloha 'Āina; and Lydia K. Aholo, adopted daughter of Queen Lili'uokalani, and also a leader of Aloha 'Āina. The day after the ceremony, *Ke Aloha 'Āina* said, "*He o ia mau no kakou*—We indeed continue."

Within the limiting governmental framework of the Territory of Hawaii, the re-enfranchised Hawaiian voters reasserted themselves. Robert Wilcox served one term as Hawai'i's first delegate to Congress. He was followed by Jonah Kūhiō, Lili'uokalani's heir apparent, who served ten two-year terms. The queen herself was a political power behind the scenes. She was much sought after, even venerated, so long as she stayed within her prescribed bounds. She lived on at Washington Place in Honolulu until her death, at seventy-nine, in 1917.

ALTHOUGH THE EARLY POLITICAL SUCCESSES of Hawaiians under the territorial government belied the stereotype of a thoroughly dispirited people, the themes of loss and tragedy have followed Hawaiians throughout the twentieth century. Starting with World War I, events imposed by the outside world seemed to further marginalize the unique identity of Hawaiians. Their distinguishing characteristics seemed fated to disappear inside the powerful legend of America, inside the attack on Pearl Harbor, inside the Hawaiian Islands becoming—after sixty-one years—the fiftieth and most exotic of the American states. This seemed so until the early 1970s, when the Hawaiian Renaissance welled up like an underground stream that had suddenly found its way to the surface. In the late 1980s, serious discussion began of restoring a sovereign Hawaiian nation, and sovereignty today is the most engaging and perplexing issue on the agenda of the state of Hawai'i.

During the 1993 observance of the overthrow, the status of Hawai'i briefly intruded onto the American agenda. The United States Congress passed a resolution, signed by President Clinton, apologizing for the role of the United States in the overthrow. Its meaning has yet to be delineated. Nor has America seriously taken up the claims resulting from the extinction of Hawai'i as an independent nation, claims that arise from the unilateral actions of America as expressed in the joint resolution of annexation.

Why was Hawai'i taken over? The reasons were essentially military and geopolitical. With a ruthless assist from the missionary descendants, the takeover occurred at the time of America's choosing and according to its terms. From an American viewpoint, the surprise of history is the persistence of the Hawaiians.

The Hawaiian understanding of a hundred generations of history is enlightening. Only four to five generations ago, Hawai'i was a nation. Since that time the Hawaiian people have constituted a submerged nation. And it is in that context of generational time that Hawaiians today are redefining themselves and re-emerging into the wider world.

Notes and Acknowledgments

In the introduction, I referred to the Hawaiian writer John Dominis Holt and the importance he placed on exploring the theme of change over time. He molded many of the questions, perceptions, and aspirations that were my starting point for this book. Likewise the artist and writer Herb Kawainui Kane, designer of the canoe and father of the replicated voyage, helped me in many ways— particularly with the subject of contact between Hawaiian society and the West. I have valued traveling around the islands with Walter Ritte, Jr., visiting Hawaiian places and occasionally speaking with persons whose memories or sense of history stretched back into the nineteenth century. Likewise my long friendship with Bob and Pua Van Dorpe has given me a sense of the never-ending process involved in the renewal of Hawaiian culture.

With such introductions to the subject of the Hawaiian relationship to America, I nonetheless attempted to stay centered in my experience as an American and to write about annexation as an American event, believing that America will soon be dealing with the rising demand by Hawaiians for a renewal of national sovereignty.

My focus on the years 1893 to 1898 led to Noenoe Silva, a scholar and writer who combines a knowledge of the Hawaiian language with a study of history and political science. It was as a result of her influence that I was able to describe, to some extent, the functioning of the Hawaiian *hui* and newspapers up to the point of annexation. She contributed in many other ways, from abstract concepts to print photographs. I also read with interest the Hawaiian nationalist writings of Dr. Lilikalā Kameʻelehiwa and Dr. Jon Osorio. If I had found Dr. Osorio's excellent dissertation on the nineteenth century sooner, I would have written a somewhat different book.

PART OF JOHN HOLT'S IDEA was to examine Hawaiʻi as part of a wider Pacific story. I thought of this when I visited the tiny museum at Pago Pago, American Sāmoa, as I stared at the xs of the Samoan chiefs and the signatures of the American naval officers on the document of cession. I thought of it again on a trip to the Philippines, where I finally grasped that the elemental connector among different places I had been in the Pacific was American expansionism and colonialism. When I returned to Hawaiʻi, I found that Dr. Belinda Aquino, director of Philippine Studies, was one of the few people who had an understanding of America's imperial past. Dr. Aquino reinforced my interest and guided me to such important sources as William Appleman Williams (see, particularly, *The Roots of the Modern American Empire*).

Thereafter I set out to write only about the moment of imperial expansion, the Spanish-American War, as it impacted Hawaiʻi. Nathan Miller's refreshingly straightforward *Theodore Roosevelt, A Life* anchored many of the main characters for me, as did Stanley Karnow's *In Our Image*, which is about America and the Philippines. Both kindly gave interviews for the companion documentary *Nation Within*.

Discovery of the Japanese aspect of the story raised many questions about which I knew nothing. In a general way I should thank the Japanese Cultural Center of Hawaiʻi, because if I had not worked on the historical story line of the center I probably would simply have fled the question. After spending a long time with primary sources in the Archives of Hawaiʻi, I found several secondary sources helpful, including Hilary Conroy's *Japanese Frontier in Hawaiʻi*, Dr. Edward Beechert's *Working in Hawaii*, and Dr. Alan Murayama's *Imingaisha*. Dr. George Akita, professor emeritus of the University of Hawaiʻi, provided clues to Meiji Japan. Dr. Akira Iriye's *Pacific Estrangement* spoke directly to the inherent questions of Hawaiʻi in context of the nearly simultaneous development of imperialism in Japan and America. Further, his execution of multiarchival research was a revelation.

Even though the framework of the story grew, I promised myself I would recount only briefly the already much-discussed overthrow. Nonetheless, as I worked on the American end of the story, I was compelled to write about new interpretations of the overthrow, because I found that American scholars, in their study of the imperial era, are increasingly examining the story of Hawai'i. Dr. Edward Crapol of the College of William and Mary, who is now writing a biography of James Blaine, generously summarized American sources on the relationship of Blaine to Hawai'i. Dr. Paul Burlin, University of New England, gave me leads into Maine and the specifics on Harold Sewall. Anthony Douin of the Maine Historical Society, and Sumner A. Webber, Sr., an historian of Hallowell, provided many of the pieces to complete the Maine connection. The filmmaker and writer, Sam Low, roamed New England with me looking for scraps of ancestral heritage.

Among the people I interviewed for the documentary, Dr. Pauline King, professor of history at the University of Hawai'i, had the surest grasp of the interaction between the nation of Hawai'i (both as Kingdom and Republic) and the wider world. In her understanding of Hawai'i's functioning as a nation among nations, she was ahead of her time.

Regarding the essential but illusive point that the takeover of Hawai'i was America's first step into overseas imperialism, Julius Pratt's *Expansionists of 1898* and Sylvester Stevens's *American Expansion in Hawaii 1842-1898* are important.

Ralph Kuykendall's influence on the written history of Hawai'i is so far-reaching that I wondered whether the 1893-1898 period was a "black hole" simply because Kuykendall died before he got to it. It was not easy for him to labor under the shadow of the oligarchy's control of the Territory of Hawaii, so I must acknowledge his almost encyclopedic pursuit of the narrative, even if my interpretation differs.

The research and writing of Linda K. Delaney and Melodie Mackenzie formed the basis of the minority report of the federal government's Native Hawaiian Study Commission, in which otherwise the Republican Party of the 1980s attempted to gloss over truth almost as blatantly as did the Republican Party of the 1890s. The minority report was made possible by the courageous stand taken by the chair, Kīna'u Kamali'i, and was essential to retrieving an understanding that annexation was indeed an American event. Rich Budnick's book, *Stolen Kingdom*, provided a concise focus of the minority report, and his constant support and second opinion were extremely helpful.

The concern of Robert C. Oshiro, Kenneth F. Brown, and the trustees of the Queen Emma Foundation for a chronology of the Hawaiian settlement led to a grant for the documentary "O Hawai'i, From Settlement to Kingdom." Work done on that project was indispensable to *Nation Within*, and I am grateful for their vision.

While I had known of the existence of the "F.O. & Ex" (Foreign Office and Executive) file at the Archives of Hawai'i, it was only through *Nation Within* that I learned how much unpublished material of historical importance it contains. Thanks go to the hard work of its keepers, the staff of the Archives. Thanks also go to the librarians and archivists in the Library of Congress, the National Archives (particularly the personal interest of archivist Ed Schamel), and the Maine Historical Society.

KENNETH F. BROWN, LORIN T. GILL, Herb Kane, Lois Lee, Noenoe Silva, and Dr. Leialoha Apo Perkins read and commented on drafts of the manuscript. Noenoe Silva prompted me to work at getting the diacritical markings right. Ann Katherine Reimers edited and assisted with the indexing of the book. Eric Woo and Mardee Domingo designed it from cover to cover.

For such errors as survived, my apologies, and my apologies as well for running on here, but I think it is important to share a little of how we learn, since we in Hawai'i have the opportunity to break out of past molds and reach for a new, more nearly accurate understanding of Pacific history. To do so we must pursue multilingual and more nearly multicultural processes that are appropriate to the challenge.

Obviously we in Hawai'i today are in transition. We are variously living inside of—or in proximity to—an indigenous nation that has been submerged by the American nation. To see and sense the revival of this Hawaiian *lāhui*, to feel it thumping on the interior of the womb, is a thing of awe. Yet if destiny is not manifest, then outcomes are not inevitable. Our relative success in developing a more real and honest history will have something to do with determining the future—not only of Hawai'i, but perhaps of America as well.

Endnotes

CHAPTER ONE

[1] Research, personal communication, Noenoe K. Silva.

[2] Silva, Noenoe K., "Kanaka Maoli Resistance to Annexation," in *Kū'ē: The 1897 Petitions Protesting Annexation*, to be published by 'Ai Pōhaku Press, Honolulu, 1998.

CHAPTER TWO

[1] The migration story in the Pacific typically embraces three thousand or so years. The development of DNA research seems to be doubling the time frame as this book is being written.

CHAPTER THREE

[1] There are also interesting hints that one or more Japanese shipwrecks had floated ashore in Hawai'i before Cook's arrival, and that a Dutch shipwreck likewise made it to Hawai'i.

[2] S.M. Kamakau, newspaper columns eventually translated and published as *Ruling Chiefs of Hawaii*, Revised Edition, 1961, p. 175.

[3] Lilikalā Kame'eleihiwa, *Native Land and Foreign Desires, Pehea Lā E Pono Ai?*, Honolulu: Bishop Museum Press, 1992, p. 52.

[4] Lili'uokalani, *Hawai'i's Story*, p. 1.

[5] Kamakau, 1961, p. 162.

[6] Kamakau, 1961, p. 180.

[7] Actually for the second time.

[8] More accurately, she was given in a *hānai* relationship, for which there is no real cultural equivalent in Western adoption.

CHAPTER FOUR

[1] Miller, Nathan, *Theodore Roosevelt, A Life*, 1992, New York: Quill/William Morrow, p. 99.

[2] *Theodore Roosevelt, An Autobiography*, New York: DaCapo Press, originally published 1913, new edition 1985, p. 94.

[3] Miller, 1992, p. 200, quoting Frederick Jackson Turner.

[4]Turner, Frederick Jackson, *The Significance of the Frontier*, 1893. Turner wrote, "The frontier is the line of the most rapid and effective Americanization. The wilderness masters the colonist."

[5]Turner, *The Frontier in American History*, Holt, Rhinehart and Winston, 1962, p. 37.

[6]Roosevelt, Theodore, *The Winning of the West*, Vol. 4, Bison Book Edition/University of Nebraska Press, originally published 1889, new edition 1995, p. 3.

CHAPTER FIVE

[1]More subtly translated of late as "possessed of heaven."

[2]Budnick, Rich, *Stolen Kingdom*, Honolulu: Aloha Press, 1992, pp.113-114.

[3]Judd, Walter F., *Palaces and Forts of the Hawaiian Kingdom*, Palo Alto: Pacific Books, 1975.

CHAPTER SIX

[1]Miller, 1992, from Roosevelt's *Naval War of 1812*, p. 117.

[2]Judd, 1975, p. 55.

[3]Budnick, 1992, quoting W.D. Alexander.

[4]Budnick, 1992, quoting Robert Wyllie to Gerritt Judd, 1849.

[5]Luther Severance to Secretary of State Daniel Webster. January 14, 1851. Diplomatic Dispatches, American National Archives II.

[6]Budnick, 1992, p. 19.

[7]Budnick, p. 19.

[8]Budnick, p. 28, referring to U.S. Senator William Fessaden, R - Maine.

[9]Thurston, Lorrin A., 1936, *Memoirs of the Hawaiian Revolution*, The Honolulu Advertiser Publishing Company, p. 20.

[10]Schmitt, Robert C., 1968, *Demographic Statistics of Hawaii: 1778-1965*, University of Hawai'i Press, p. 74.

[11]Tyler, Alive F., *The Foreign Policy of James G. Blaine*, 1922.

CHAPTER SEVEN

[1]Damon, Ethel M., *Sanford Dole and His Hawaii*, published for the Hawaiian Historical Society by Pacific Books, Palo Alto, CA, 1957; pp. 5, 6.

[2]Thurston, Introduction to Sanford Dole's *Memoirs of the Hawaiian Revolution*, by Sanford B. Dole, *The Honolulu Advertiser* Publishing Company, 1936, p. xiii.

[3]Quoted by Damon, 1957, p. 181.

[4]Letter, May 31, quoted by Damon, p. 197.

[5]Thurston, 1936, p. 608, referring to a note the editor found in the pocket of Thurston's notebook, containing the names of the members of the Hawaiian League.

[6]From a message to the Legislature purported by Thurston to have been written, but not signed by, Kalākaua; *Memoirs of the Hawaiian Revolution*, p. 40.

[7]Thurston, 1936, p. 6. Described by him as the C. Brewer building at the base of Nu'uanu Avenue, around 1873.

[8]Thurston, 1936, quoting a letter from Kalākaua to Lili'uokalani, *Memoirs*, p. 162.

[9] Kuykendall, Ralph S., *The Hawaiian Kingdom, Vol. III, 1874-1893*, Honolulu: University of Hawai'i Press, 1967, p. 363.

[10] Thurston subsequently appears as secretary of the Kilauea Volcano House Company, an early tourist development.

[11] Pratt, Julius W., *The Expansionists of 1898*, p. 5, quoting John Fiske, "Manifest Destiny," *Harper's New Monthly Magazine*, LXX.

CHAPTER EIGHT

[1] Interview, Dr. Edward Crapol.

[2] Crapol, Edward P., *America for Americans: Economic Nationalism and Anglophobia in the Late Nineteenth Century*, Westport, CT: Greenwood Press, Inc., 1973, p. 155.

[3] Then called a "bounty," not a subsidy.

[4] Thompson, Carole, master's thesis on John Stevens.

[5] *Chicago Tribune*, undated clipping, Blaine file, Maine Historical Society.

[6] Conversation, Sumner A. Webbers, Sr., Collections Chair, Hubbard Free Library, Hallowell, Maine.

[7] Stevens papers, Maine Historical Society.

[8] *The Age*, May 24, 1855, and July 12, 1855, Maine State Library, Augusta.

[9] Stevens papers, letter from Frye, January 18, 1889.

[10] Stevens, Sylvester K., *American Expansion in Hawaii, 1842-1898*, Archives Publishing Company of Pennsylvania, Inc., 1945, p. 194.

[11] Stevens papers.

[12] Information on the history of Hallowell and Augusta, and their citizens, was kindly supplied by Sumner A. Webber, Sr. from the Hubbard Free Library, Hallowell.

[13] A good explanation can be found in Sylvester Stevens, p. 200.

CHAPTER NINE

[1] Campbell, Charles S., *The Transformation of American Foreign Relations, 1865-1900*, New York: Harper and Row, 1976, pp. 180-181. Cited in correspondence from Dr. Edward Crapol.

[2] Blaine also said Cuba and Puerto Rico were worth taking over.

[3] Quoted by Volwiler, Alfred T., *Correspondence Between Harrison and Blaine*, p. 206, from Harrison to Blaine, October 14, 1891.

[4] Kuykendall, 1967, p. 529.

[5] Stevens, 1946, p. 210.

[6] Kuykendall, 1967, pp. 533, 538.

[7] Thurston, 1936, p. 232.

[8] Sylvester, 1946, p. 208.

[9] Thurston said the overthrow had occurred "before I could get a reply from Mr. Hopkins." The editor of Thurston's memoir speculated that Thurston never read the letter until considerably after the overthrow.

[10] Stevens, John L., and W.B. Oleson, *Picturesque Hawai'i*, Hubbard Publishing Company, 1894.

[11] Kuykendall, 1967, p. 561.

¹²Ibid.

¹³Thurston, 1936, p. 240.

¹⁴Ibid, p. 254.

CHAPTER TEN

¹Minister Albert Willis.

²Loomis, Albertine, *For Whom Are the Stars?*, Honolulu: University of Hawai'i Press, 1976, p. 109.

³Silva, Noenoe K., *Women in Hawai'i: Sites, Identities and Voices. Social Process in Hawaii, Volume 38-1997, Kū 'ē! Hawaiian Women's Resistance to the Annexation*, p. 4.

⁴Morris, Dr. Nancy Jane, *Ka Loea Kalaiaina, 1898*; a master's thesis in Pacific Island studies.

⁵Sheldon, J.G.M., *The Biography of Joseph K. Nāwahī*, Honolulu Bulletin Publishing Co. Ltd., 1908, written in Hawaiian and translated to English by Marvin Puakea Nogelmeier.

⁶Sheldon, 1908, p. 167, translated by Nogelmeier.

⁷Morris, Nancy, quoting the Blount report, p. 1737.

⁸Kaulili, the Rev. Solomon Kamaha, *A Palace Servant Remembers the End of the Monarchy*, a diary written in Hawaiian and translated by Rubellite Kawena Johnson, in *Kukini 'Aha'i Lono* (Carry on the News), published by Topgallant Publishing Co., 1976.

CHAPTER ELEVEN

¹Cleveland went the extra step of contending that the queen's forces could have controlled Hawai'i militarily if Stevens had not intervened. Sanford Dole took exception by arguing, "The revolution was carried through by the representatives, now largely reinforced, of the same public sentiment which forced the monarchy to its knees in 1887, (and) which suppressed the insurrection of 1889..." (in other words, the white militia and the comparatively few Hawaiians who sided with them). While the so-called Reform Cabinet had lost its grip on the government, and while they were militarily unprepared in the narrow sense, the well-armed and well-drilled white forces seem to have remained essentially intact as a vigilante force. On this point I therefore am inclined to agree with Dole.

²Damon, 1957, pp. 151-152, also 265 and 267.

³Allen, Helena G., *Sanford Ballard Dole, Hawaii's Only President*, Honolulu: Mutual Publishing, p. 158.

⁴Damon, 1957, quoting a letter to relatives by Sanford Dole, p. 168.

CHAPTER TWELVE

¹Smith to Thurston, February 18, 1894, M&E file, Archives of Hawai'i (AH).

²Thurston to Hatch, March 9, 1894, AH.

³Thurston to Hatch, March 27, 1894, AH. Thurston said he did not take "much stock" in their views.

⁴*New York World*, March 26, 1894.

⁵Stevens to Thurston, March 31, 1894.

⁶Hatch to Dole, December 16, 1896, purportedly quoting a conversation involving himself, Henry Cooper, and Lodge.

⁷Thurston to Dole, March 10, 1894.

[8] Victor Forge, consul general of Hawai'i in Belgium, to Thurston, February, 18, 1894.

[9] W.O. Smith to Lorrin Thurston, March 3, 1894.

[10] Diary of Lili'uokalani, multiple mentions.

[11] He suggested John Bush, Joseph Nāwahī, William White, Wilson Colburn, Samuel Parker, T. H. Davies, J.O. Carter, Arthur Peterson, Paul Neumann, Cornwall, Cleghorn, and MacFarlane, but not "small fry."

[12] Russ, William Adams, Jr., *The Hawaiian Republic*, republished 1992, Selinsgrove: Susquehanna University Press, 1961, p. 19.

[13] From *The Inflation Calculator* Web site, citing pre-1975 data from *Historical Statistics of the United States*, and post-1975 data from *Statistical Abstracts of the United States*, as maintained by S. Morgan Friedman.

[14] Castle, Alfred L. "Advice for Hawaii: The Dole-Burgess Letters," Vol. 15, *The Hawaiian Journal of History*, pp. 24-30.

[15] Noenoe Silva, translations and original research.

[16] See the documentary film *Act of War*, a collaboration of the Hawaiian Studies Department, University of Hawai'i, and Nā Maka o ka 'Āina, Joan Landers and Puhipau.

[17] Williams, William Appleman, *The Tragedy of American Diplomacy*, p. 31.

[18] Williams, *The Roots of the Modern American Empire*," p. 366.

[19] Ibid, p. 366.

[20] Ibid, p. 356.

[21] Called the Wilson-Gorman Act.

CHAPTER THIRTEEN

[1] N.B. Emerson.

[2] Loomis, 1976, p. 89.

[3] Ibid, p. 187.

[4] Sheldon, 1908.

[5] Stevens, John L. and W.B. Oleson, *Picturesque Hawaii*, Elgood Publishing Co., Philadelphia, 1900 (five years after Stevens's death).

CHAPTER FOURTEEN

[1] Stephan, John J., *Hawaii Under the Rising Sun*, Honolulu: University of Hawai'i Press, 1984, p. 18.

[2] Beechert, Edward W., *Working in Hawaii, a Labor History*, Honolulu: University of Hawai'i Press, 1985, p. 41.

[3] Conroy, Hilary, Berkeley Press, *The Japanese Frontier in Hawaii, 1868-1898*, 1953, p. 106.

[4] Conroy, quoting Dole to Thurston, December 14, 1893, private letter book of the minister of Foreign Affairs, pp. 90-91.

[5] Conroy, 1953, p. 115.

[6] Hatch, apparently directly to Sanford Dole ("Dear Judge"), February 17, 1896.

[7] In earlier correspondence, W.O. Smith used this slur with a period at the end, as if it were an abbreviation: "Japs." Hatch's 1896 letter is the first time I saw "Japs" used unadorned. Routinely the word was as used in the post-World War II environment—Japanese.

[8] Hatch to "Dear Judge," Minister Correspondence of AH, February 19, 1896.

CHAPTER FIFTEEN

[1] The transcript actually quotes McKinley as saying, "How do the Hawaiians feel themselves?" which, if accurate, presumably came out differently when spoken than when written.

[2] Smith's memorandum for file, March 25, 1897, Hatch papers, AH.

[3] Cooper to Hatch, March 29, 1897, Hatch papers. Accounts of numbers conflict, but all reflect that well over one thousand persons were penned up in the immigration station, then returned to Japan.

[4] *Pacific Commercial Advertiser*, April 17, 1897.

[5] Cooper to Dole April 13, 1897, Hatch papers, AH.

[6] Smith to Hatch, April 22, 1897, Hatch papers.

[7] *Pacific Commerical Advertiser*, April 9, 1897.

[8] *Pacific Commercial Advertiser*, April 23, 1897.

[9] Miller, 1992, p. 251. Miller's Ch. 12, "The Supreme Triumphs of War," provides good insight into the evolution of American imperialism.

[10] Theodore Roosevelt correspondence, Library of Congress (LOC).

[11] Morgan, William M., "The Anti-Japanese Origins of the Hawaiian Annexation Treaty of 1897," quoting Robert Seager II and Doris Maguire, *Letters and Papers of Alfred Thayer Mahan*.

[12] Eldridge to Cooper, April 12, 1897, Hatch papers, AH.

[13] Miller, 1992, p. 253.

[14] Five persons with Japanese surnames, as well as Akiyama, are listed as guests at the May 15 press party. All descriptions of the event are from the *Pacific Commercial Advertiser*.

[15] George Akita, professor emeritus of history, University of Hawai'i, stresses the essential conservatism and caution of the Japanese government during this period. Edwin O. Reischauer and others have described the *samurai* tradition of the Japanese press.

[16] Lorin Gill, a lifelong resident of Honolulu and a keen student of history, heard the story as a boy from his father after meeting Mr. Hapai.

[17] Sewall to Sherman, June 29, 1897. From Diplomatic Despatches, Honolulu to Washington, in State Department Archives at National Archives II. The number of the despatch is blank.

[18] Cooper to Hatch, June 18, 1897, Hatch papers, AH.

[19] Russ, 1961, quoting Hatch to Day, May 22, 1897, Notes from Hawaii (State Department Despatches).

[20] Hatch to Cooper, April 24, 1897.

[21] Burlin, Dr.Paul, Summer/Fall 1995, *Maine History*.

[22] *Commercial Pacific Advertiser*, April 1897, "That Interview."

[23] American National Archives, Senate Committee on Foreign Relations, petition file, 55th Congress.

[24] Russ, 1961, p. 188.

[25] National Archives, 55th Congress, Committee on Foreign Relations, (Petitions A-K).

[26] Russ, 1961, p. 195, quoting Kinney to Dole, June 17, 1897, Dole papers.

CHAPTER SIXTEEN

[1] I am indebted for the entire account to not only the translation but the scholarship of Noenoe Silva.

[2]Stillman, Amy K., *History Reinterpreted in Song: The Case of the Hawaiian Counterrevolution*, Vol. 23, Hawaiian Historical Society, 1989.

[3] The newspaper was dated December 3, 1896. It had the same name as the *hui*, in the style of the time.

[4] All accounts are from *Ke Aloha 'Āina* newspaper, researched and translated by Noenoe Silva.

[5] Stillman, 1989, p. 15-16.

[6] The generalization is Ms. Silva's, based on her extensive reading of *Ke Aloha 'Aina* and *Ka Loea*.

[7] Lili'uokalani, 1898, p. 303.

[8] Ibid, p. 305.

[9] Kuykendall, 1961, p. 115.

CHAPTER SEVENTEEN

[1] *Pacific Commercial Advertiser*, March 1897.

[2] Thurston, 1936, pp. 573-574.

[3] Ibid, p. 573.

[4] Roosevelt to Mahan, June 9, 1897, LOC.

[5] The importance of the June 7 dispatches from Hawai'i to Washington and the impact of the Ōkuma letter are derived from William M. Morgan's "The Anti-Japanese Origins of the Hawaiian Annexation Treaty of 1897."

[6] Dobson, John, *Reticent Expansionism, the Foreign Policy of William McKinley*, Pittsbugh: Duquesne University Press, 1988, p. 38.

[7] Thurston, 1936, pp. 566-567.

[8] Cooper to Hatch, January 7, 1897, Hatch papers, AH.

[9] George R. Ariyoshi, an American of Japanese ancestry, became the first American governor of nonwhite, minority ancestry. He was first elected in 1974 and served three terms, until 1986.

[10] Cooper to Hatch, July 1, 1897, Hatch papers.

[11] Smith to Hatch, June 30, 1897, Hatch papers.

[12] At the outset of this project, I was unaware of the issue of Japan. I had worked with the history committee of the Japanese Cultural Center of Hawaii at length, formulating an exhibit on the Japanese experience in Hawaii. The scare relating to annexation was never discussed. Likewise, a leading scholar on the ethnic experience of the Japanese was unaware of it, as was a prominent scholar on Meiji Japan.

[13] Iriye, Dr. Akira, *Pacific Estrangement, Japanese and American Expansion, 1897-1911*, Cambridge: Harvard University Press, 1972, p. 32.

[14] Ibid, p. 45.

[15] Stephan, 1984.

[16] Ibid, pp. 18-19.

[17] Iriye, 1972, p. 53.

[18] Ibid, p. 19.

[19] Conroy, 1953, pp. 137-138.

[20] Treat, Payson J., 1938, *Diplomatic Relations between the United States and Japan 1895-1905*, Palo Alto. Stanford University Press, quoting Buck to Sherman, Despatches from Japan to Secretary of State, Library of Congress, No. 54, November 5, 1897.

[21] *Pacific Commercial Advertiser*, July 1, 1897.

[22] Iriye, 1972, pp. 49-50.

[23] Roosevelt autobiography, 1913, pp. 212-213.

[24] Russ, 1961, p. 155, quoting Roosevelt to Long.

[25] Burton, *Confident Imperialist*, University of Pennsylvania Press, p. 36, quoting letter to James Bryce, September 10, 1897, Roosevelt Letters.

CHAPTER EIGHTEEN

[1] Lili'uokalani, 1898, p. 337.

[2] Hatch to Cooper, February 7, 1897, AH.

[3] Lili'uokalani, 1898, p. 331.

[4] Miscellaneous references, diary of Lili'uokalani, early 1898.

[5] Lili'uokalani, 1898, p. 353.

[6] Russ, 1961, p. 198.

CHAPTER NINETEEN

[1] Focus and intepretation by Noenoe Silva.

[2] Focus and intepretation by Noenoe Silva.

[3] Scope and Content Note, Morgan Papers, LOC.

[4] Morgan Papers, LOC.

[5] Pettigrew is quoted extensively in the Congressional Record, 55th Congress, as a leader of the filibuster.

[6] Silva, Noenoe, "Kanaka Maoli Resistance to Annexation," the introduction to *Kū'ē: The 1897 Petitions Protesting Annexation*, soon to be published by 'Ai Pōhaku Press, Honolulu, 1998, referring to *Ke Aloha 'Āina*, October 7, 1897.

[7] Ibid, observation of Silva based on her reading of *Ke Aloha 'Āina*, October 16, 1897.

[8] Ibid.

[9] *The Independent*, October 11, 1897.

[10] The account is drawn mainly from the work of Noenoe Silva from *Ke Aloha 'Āina*. The observation regarding the difference in the organizations' petitions is Ms. Silva's.

[11] *Pacific Commercial Advertiser*, March 29, 1898, from a story on the report of Kaulia to a rally, made on the delegates' return to Honolulu.

[12] From the work of Silva, drawn from *Ke Aloha 'Āina*.

[13] *Pacific Commercial Advertiser*, March 13, 1898.

[14] Conroy, 1953, p. 131.

[15] *Pacific Commercial Advertiser*, March 10, 1898.

[16] Russ, 1961, p. 232, quoting *New York Evening Journal*, January 2, 1898.

[17] *Pacific Commercial Advertiser*, datelined from Washington, February 23, 1898, printed March 4, 1898.

[18] *Pacific Commercial Advertiser*, March 12, 1898.

CHAPTER TWENTY

[1] Miller, 1992, p. 255.

[2] Roosevelt 1913, p. 210.

[3] Karnow, Stanley, 1989, *In Our Image: America's Empire in the Philippines*, New York: Random House, Philippines reprint, p. 89.

[4] Roosevelt, Theodore, *The Winning of the West, Vol.1*, p. 1.

[5] Miller, 1992, p. 262.

[6] Dobson, 1988, p. 65.

[7] Miller, 1992, p. 273.

[8] Thomas Edison paper film collection, LOC.

[9] *Pacific Commercial Advertiser*, printed May 12, 1898 from a May 2 dispatch.

[10] Ibid.

[11] Hatch to Cooper, May 13, 1898.

[12] Transcript of hearing held May 10, 1898, House Committee on Foreign Affairs, National Archives.

[13] *Pacific Commercial Advertiser*, March 4, 1898.

[14] Hatch to Cooper, May 13, 1898.

[15] Karnow, 1989, p. 109.

[16] Quoted by the *Native Hawaiian Study Commission report*, 1983, Vol. I.

[17] Hatch to Cooper, June 9, 1898. The late date of his alarmist letter is interesting.

[18] Beale, Howard, *Theodore Roosevelt and the Rise of America to World Power*, Baltimore: Johns Hopkins University, p. 63.

[19] Morgan to Hatch, Hatch papers, July 6, 1898.

[20] Translation by Noenoe Silva, *Ke Aloha 'Āina*, August 6, 1898.

Index

Civil War 15, 34, 71–72, 81, 87, 111,
126, 207, 212, 217, 246, 290, 300, 312
Cleghorn, A.S. 307
Cleveland, Grover 2–3, 87, 95–96, 127,
141–147, 149, 151–152, 163–169,
177, 179, 180, 197, 200–201, 209,
220, 226, 228, 241–242, 250,
263–264, 267–268, 270
colonialism 2, 62, 67, 98, 289, 326
Columbia University 34, 72, 89, 161,
261
Committee of 100 307
Committee of Annexation 2, 120–122,
124–126, 143, 181, 198, 200, 243, 251
Committee of Safety 121, 125
Conroy, Hilary 190–191, 256, 259, 283, 326
Constitution of 1840 89
Constitution of 1887 86, 103, 106,
115, 181
Constitution of 1894 170, 172, 181,
198, 214, 225, 283
Cook, Captain James 11, 13, 23–28,
30, 40, 45–46
Cooper, Henry 115, 121, 125, 198,
200, 204, 206, 220–221, 223, 225,
231, 236, 243–244, 248–249, 251,
254, 257, 264, 270, 303–304
Crapol, Edward 92, 327
Cuba 5, 247, 261, 276, 289, 290–293,
295, 300–301, 308–309, 317

D

Damien, Father 74, 286
Damon, Ethel 69, 70, 71
Damon, Samuel C. 71
Damon, Samuel M. 71
Darwin, Charles 89
Darwinism, Social 34, 89, 158, 206,
261, 285, 317
Davis, Isaac 40, 43, 46
Day, William 225, 248–249, 257, 294, 303
Democratic Party 142, 164–165, 210, 226
denizen, denizenship 36, 198
Denmark 88
Dewey, Admiral George 291
Diamond Head 30, 170, 307
Dimond, W.H. 150
Dole, Daniel 69, 70, 97, 100

Dole, Sanford 69–73, 79, 81–82, 87,
89–90, 100–101, 121, 126, 142,
145, 152, 155, 158, 190, 192, 199,
204–205, 214, 224, 228, 232, 234,
238–239, 242, 248, 251, 253, 258,
263, 284, 305, 307, 315–316, 321
Dun, Edwin 256

E

Emma, Queen 61, 67, 72, 136, 328
England 10, 23–24, 102, 108, 138,
185. See also Great Britain
Europe 8, 13, 20, 66, 90, 226, 239, 246
European population
immigration 283
expansionism 69, 92, 98, 101, 164,
203, 206, 211, 221, 254–255,
258–259, 300, 312, 326
extraterritoriality 187, 188

F

Fiske, John 89
Ford Island 87
Fornander, Abraham 13–14
Fort Elizabeth 45
Fort of Honolulu 47, 56, 60, 80
Foster, John W. 118–119, 127, 143, 252, 302
France 52–58, 63, 65, 67, 102, 138,
183, 215, 230, 236, 274
Frye, William P. 92, 99, 114, 226, 228, 302

G

Gannen Mono 186
Garfield, James 66, 95
George, King of England 29, 43
Germany 65, 88, 215, 226, 274
Gibson, Walter Murray 68, 75, 81–82, 200
Grant, President Ulysses S. 62, 95, 99
Great Britain 10, 27–29, 55–56,
59–60, 65–66, 68, 87, 123, 126,
146, 151, 161, 163, 183, 196, 200,
206, 215, 230, 236, 245, 261, 267,
293. See also England
Gresham, Walter Q. 150–151, 167–168,
178, 180–181, 203, 229, 250
Guam 309, 317

H

Hale Nauā 66, 86
Hanalei River 45
Hanna, Marcus 210, 212, 217, 292, 295
Harrison, Benjamin 92, 96, 99, 110–113,
    117, 119, 122–124, 127, 135, 141,
    143, 165, 181
Hastings, Frank 151–152, 198, 230
Hatch, Francis M. 87, 146, 151–152,
    179–181, 197, 199–207, 212–214,
    216, 220, 223, 225–226, 230–232,
    234, 239, 242, 245, 248–251, 253,
    256, 264, 267, 270, 275, 281–282,
    284–285, 293–295, 302–304, 307,
    309, 310, 312
Hawaiian Bureau of Information 242
Hawaiian League 80–83, 122
Hawaiian nation xiv, 2, 10, 27, 67, 115,
    139, 235, 240, 243, 252, 322–323
Hawaiian population 8, 39, 55, 86
Hawaiian Renaissance (Hawaiian
    Movement) xii, 109, 323
Hawai'i
    island of (Hawai'i Island) xi, 20, 21,
        25, 27, 40, 50, 138, 140, 145, 237;
    Kingdom of Hawai'i 1, 4, 8, 9, 39,
        43, 55, 73;
    Republic of Hawaii ix, 2, 155,
        162–164, 168, 180, 190, 203, 207,
        214, 216, 221, 233, 248–251, 258,
        260, 263, 267, 305, 309, 313, 316,
        322;
    Territory of Hawaii 317, 323, 327
"Hawai'i Pono'i" (Hawaiian national
    anthem) 316
Hayes, Rutherford 95
Hearst, William 295
Heleluhe, Joseph 171, 239, 265–269
Hilo 20, 138, 179, 237, 277, 286
Holomua 136, 161–162, 169
Holt, John Dominis xiii, 109, 325
homesteading 242, 252
Honolulu 5, 7–8, 39, 43–51, 53–54,
    57, 59, 69, 72, 80, 82, 87–88, 101,
    107, 113–114, 118–120, 123–126,
    142–143, 146, 152–154, 170,
    177–179, 184, 196, 199–201, 203,
    207, 213–215, 217, 221–223, 225,
    227, 231, 235–236, 240, 247–248,
    255–258, 265, 267, 270, 273, 277,
    283, 285, 294–295, 300, 302,
    309–310, 317, 323
Honolulu Advertiser, The (newspaper)
    xii, 321
Honolulu Harbor 30, 45–47, 51, 59,
    123, 142, 170, 224, 307
Honolulu Rifles 81, 83, 103, 106,
    122–123
Hopkins, Archibald 118–119
Hoshi, Tōru 250, 255, 260
Hui Aloha 'Āina (Hawaiian Patriotic
    League) 3, 139, 178, 236, 240, 263,
    269, 273, 277, 279, 322
Hui Kālai'āina 103, 105, 120, 137, 178,
    236, 240, 263, 269, 274, 277, 279

I

'Ī ao Valley, Battle of 73
Iaukea, Curtis Piehu 88, 188
Imperialism, American 165, 221, 249, 317
Imperialism, Japanese 326
'Iolani Palace 7, 39, 54, 62
Iriye, Dr. Akira 254–255, 259, 326
Irwin, R.G. 190–192, 199, 256

J

Japan 5, 64–67, 86, 102, 146, 156,
    159, 183–192, 196–208, 213–217,
    220–231, 243, 245, 247–249,
    253–260, 267, 270–271, 290,
    304, 308, 310, 317, 326
Japanese population
    immigration 187–191, 197, 199–201,
        204–205, 207, 213–215, 221, 223,
        229, 243, 245, 253, 256, 275
Joesting, Edward 42, 46
Joint Resolution (of Annexation) 213,
    284, 303–304, 322–323
Jones, P.C. 150
Judd, Albert Francis 138, 172

K

Kaha'i 19
Kahekili 25, 28–29, 41, 307

About the Author

Tom Coffman is an independent researcher, writer, and producer. He graduated from the William Allen White School, Kansas University, with a Bachelor in Journalism, and became a reporter for United Press International in New Mexico in 1965. Within a year, the managing editor of the *Honolulu Advertiser* loaned Coffman plane fare to come to Hawai'i, where he became state government reporter for the *Advertiser*. He moved to the *Honolulu Star-Bulletin* two years later and became political reporter and bureau chief. In 1972, he wrote *Catch a Wave*, a widely read chronicle of the 1970 gubernatorial campaign and the social and political turmoil of that period. A year later, he left newspaper reporting to work as an independent writer and media producer.

Expanding on research for *Catch a Wave*, his productions increasingly incorporated historic themes. Under the guidance of the legendary Hawaiian writer John Dominis Holt, he began to integrate a chronology of the development of Hawai'i, which led to the television documentaries *O Hawai'i: From Settlement to Kingdom and Nation Within*.

Tom Coffman's work has won national awards for production of video, film, interactive media, and multi-image. *Ganbare*, about the early wartime experiences of Japanese Americans, was selected Best Film by a Hawai'i Filmmaker at the 1995 Hawai'i International Film Festival. Two of his books—the first edition of *Nation Within* and *The Island Edge of America: A Political History of America*—received Ka Palapala Po'okela Awards for Excellence in Nonfiction from the Hawai'i Book Publishers Association. After publication of *Nation Within*, Coffman also received the Hawai'i Award for Literature, the highest recognition given by the state of Hawai'i for outstanding literary achievement. He is currently working on a film about the assassination of Benigno Aquino, Jr., in the Philippines.